Theory and Practice
in the Teaching of Composition

Theory and Practice in the Teaching of Composition

Processing, Distancing, and Modeling

Edited by

Miles Myers
University of California, Berkeley

James Gray
University of California, Berkeley

National Council of Teachers of English
1111 Kenyon Road, Urbana, Illinois 61801

To Walter Loban, who for over thirty years has been crossing the boundary between research and practice, letting the other side know what was happening "over there"

NCTE Editorial Board: Paul T. Bryant, Thomas L. Clark, C. Kermeen Fristrom, Jane Hornburger, Robert F. Hogan, *ex officio*, Paul O'Dea, *ex officio*

Book Design: Tom Kovacs for TGK Design

NCTE Stock Number 53992

Library of Congress Cataloging in Publication Data

Main entry under title:

Theory and practice in the teaching of composition.

    Bibliography: p.
    1. English language—Composition and exercises.
I. Myers, Miles.   II. Gray, James, 1927–   .
LB1576.T485   1983   808'.042'07   83-2288
ISBN 0-8141-5399-2

Contents

Preface

This book resulted from a need to show teachers how their approaches to the teaching of writing reflect a particular area of research and to show researchers how the intuitions of teachers reflect research findings. Since 1974 the Bay Area Writing Project has brought teachers and researchers together to discuss their common understandings about how to teach writing, from kindergarten through high school.

Patterned after the Bay Area Writing Project is a network of similar writing institutes and workshops, the National Writing Project. One of the main assumptions of the project is that the best teacher of teachers is another teacher. Each summer, in hundreds of institutions throughout the country, teachers are describing an approach to writing that works for them. Their colleagues are experiencing the approach by doing what the students do, are assessing the workability of the approach in various classroom settings, and are exploring the theoretical basis for the approach. They are combining research findings with successful classroom practices.

Such a combination of research and practice is the aim of this book. It is not intended for researchers who want an in-depth review of what is known about the teaching of writing. Neither is it intended for teachers who only want a good idea for Monday. It is our belief that successful teachers know why they do what they do and that this book will contribute to an understanding of the relationship between the what of teaching and the why. Our biggest problem was deciding what to include and what to leave out, a perennial problem in the institutes and workshops of the National Writing Project.

We hope we have included enough to suggest the range of the field. The gaps we leave for later. Our thanks for support go to the National Endowment for the Humanities, the Carnegie Corporation of New York, the National Institute of Education, and the University of California, Berkeley.

James Gray and Miles Myers
University of California, Berkeley

Part One: Introduction

1 Approaches to the Teaching of Composition

Miles Myers

The teaching of writing is often characterized these days as a hodge-podge of gimmicks without a foundation in theory and research and without systematic methods of evaluating student writing. A close examination of practice and theory suggests, however, that there are at least three approaches to teaching writing, each with a different set of researchable assumptions and each with useful suggestions for teaching writing to different types of students. Furthermore, each approach has a different way of diagnosing problems in student papers. Because good teachers usually use aspects of each approach, no one approach can claim to be the only way to teach writing—or the only way to diagnose problems in students' writing.

The three approaches to writing explored in this book are *processing*, *distancing*, and *modeling*. In *processing*, attention focuses on the sequence of steps or stages in the writer's mind. Research has concentrated on the speed, storage limits, and organizing principles of the mind. In *distancing*, the focus is on the relationships between the speaker and the subject and between the speaker and the audience. Research has looked at the social context for writing as a communication act, giving some attention to the developmental stages in a learner's social awareness and identifying the social rules or participant roles in an act of communication. In *modeling*, the focus is on the imitation of written texts. Research has examined language patterns, either as sequences of stimulus-response or as patterns of text and sentence production. The three areas of focus—mental processes, social context, and language patterns—have many overlapping interests, but nevertheless they are distinctly different ways of doing research and asking questions about writing.

What follows is a description of research findings and teachers' reports on the theory and practice of *processing*, *distancing*, and *modeling*. *Modeling*, stemming from behavioral theories, is discussed first.

3

Modeling: Writing as the Approximation of Texts

Research on *modeling* has been based on two schools of thought—one that says writing is small bits of imitated behavior reinforced by the responses of others, and another that says writing is an innate capability triggered by the presence of language in the environment. The latter school has been led by Noam Chomsky and the former by researchers focusing on sequences of stimulus-response or stimulus-response-reinforcement. Both schools assume that the learner imitates or approximates the language present in the environment.

In the first school, stimulus-response theorists believe that association by contiguity is the main principle of learning. W. J. Brogden (1939) exposed a dog to a sound followed by a light, and after several repetitions, the animal learned to associate the two events. Brogden then conditioned the animal so that it attempted to run away when the light went on. Finally, to test whether the animal had learned to associate the sound and the light, Brogden simply turned on the sound. The result: the animal that attempted to run away when the light went on also attempted to run away when it heard the sound. Brogden observed that this behavior could be interpreted as evidence of sensory conditioning. D. O. Hebb, W. E. Lambert, and G. R. Tucker (1973) argue that Brogden's result may also be described as latent learning, which includes "perceptual learning and learning that we would call an association of ideas" (p. 57).

What Brogden calls "sensory conditioning" E. R. Guthrie (1942) labels "association by contiguity." Says Guthrie, "A stimulus pattern that is acting at the time of a response will, if it recurs, tend to produce that response" (p. 23). Guthrie adds, "what is associated is some stimulation of sense organs and a corresponding muscular contraction or glandular secretion. By calling them associated we mean that the stimulation has become the occasion for the response because of the past association of the two" (p. 43).

Guthrie's view, like that of Pavlov, focuses on classical conditioning—because the food was repeatedly presented after the bell, the salivary response to the bell was strengthened. The attention of B. F. Skinner (1938) was on the acts of the animal rather than the glands. In a 1953 study he describes how the hungry rat in the Skinner box would accidentally push the bar down, find food dropping into the tray, and ultimately "learn" that pushing the bar down was a way to get food. Skinner's conditioning of what some considered a voluntary act is called *operant* or *instrumental* conditioning, and the sequence in learning is stimulus-response-reinforcement.

Skinner (1967) sees language as one of many pieces of human behavior, all capable of analysis as a sequence of stimulus-response-reinforcement, without consideration of intention and meaning:

> We could no doubt define ideas, meanings, and so on, so that they would be scientifically acceptable and even useful in describing verbal behavior. But such an effort to retain traditional terms would be costly. It is the general formulation which is wrong. We seek "causes" of behavior which have an acceptable scientific status and which, with luck, will be susceptible to measurement and manipulation. To say that these are "all that is meant by" ideas or meanings is to misrepresent the traditional practice. We must find the functional relations which govern the verbal behavior to be explained; to call such relations "expression" or "communication" is to run the danger of introducing extraneous and misleading properties and events. The only solution is to reject the traditional formulation of verbal behavior in terms of meaning. (P. 323)

The behavioral theorists, then, answer the question "What do students do when they write?" by saying, "The student imitates what he hears or sees by developing a bond or association between visual and auditory stimuli." Skinner responds somewhat differently: "The student repeats reinforced behavior." In several studies that examined the assumptions of behavioral theory, Roger Brown, Courtney Cazden, and Ursula Bellugi (1969) found no evidence that parental approval or disapproval were contingent on the syntactic correctness of the utterances of children. Susan Ervin-Tripp (1964) found that children imitated only those structures that had already begun to appear in their spontaneous speech. For example, when a child at the two-word stage tried to imitate longer utterances, the child typically produced only two-word sentences:

Adult: I'll make a cup for her to drink.
Child: Cup drink.

Adult: Mr. Miller will try.
Child: Miller try.

Brown and Bellugi (1964) found that the child made highly systematic reductions of his mother's sentences, but that the processes of imitation and expansion "are not sufficient to account for the linguistic competence that children regularly acquire" (p. 144). They conclude their study of the child's acquisition of syntax by suggesting that learning a language is innate and possibly not within the province of any learning theory current at the time:

> We have described three processes involved in the child's acqui-
> sition of syntax. It is clear that the last of these, the induction of
> latent structure, is by far the most complex. It looks as if this last
> process will put a serious strain on any learning theory thus far
> conceived by psychology. The very intricate simultaneous differen-
> tiation and integration that constitutes the evolution of the noun
> phrase is more reminiscent of the biological development of any
> embryo than it is of the acquisition of the conditioned reflex.
> (P. 151)

Noam Chomsky (1959), in the most famous attack on Skinner's
position, also argues that careful arrangements of contingencies of
reinforcement were not the basis for language and some learning (see
Miller and Dollard, 1941, for a discussion of "meticulous training").
Chomsky pointed first to latent learning, showing that learning takes
place without reward or reduction of, for example, the hunger drive
(Blodgett, 1929). Next Chomsky pointed to the phenomenon of imprinting in animals, which he called the "most striking evidence for
the innate disposition of the animal to learn in a certain direction"
(p. 334). Two examples of research on imprinting in animals are
Konrad Lorenz (1966) and W. E. Jaynes (1956). The fact that children
acquire a good deal of their verbal and nonverbal behavior by casual
observation, even learning rapidly a second language in the streets, and
the fact that people both understand and speak sentences they have
never heard before indicate, says Chomsky, that "there must be
processes at work quite independently of 'feedback' from the environment" (p. 334).

For some teachers, the attack on Skinner's work has implied that
such useful notions as reinforcement should be abandoned in all
circumstances. Such is obviously not the case. Reinforcement schedules
can play a useful role in the classroom. However, the research evidence
suggests that teachers need at times to turn to other assumptions for
useful models of language learning. One additional assumption, made
by Chomsky, is that language learning is innate and that the student
needs a releaser to trigger the language capacity that is inside.

These two sets of assumptions—language behavior is an imitation
of others and language behavior is triggered by the language of
others—have given considerable support to the *modeling* approach to
teaching writing. Three methods of applying this approach—using
drills, sentence combining, and imitation—will illustrate the influence
of the two sets of assumptions.

Drills

First, the work of B. F. Skinner and other stimulus-response-reinforcement theorists gave theoretical support to the use of drills as a way to

teach writing. The drill, focusing on the imitation of a single "habit" or language convention, has had many different classroom applications:

1. *Students learn the parts of speech and identify sentence patterns.* Rationale: Skinner warns that teachers must avoid the seduction of thinking about ideas that are in the child's head. Thus, children must be taught explicitly the parts of speech and sentence patterns. Teachers cannot assume children know them well enough to use them. Critics argue that students may not need to use such information.

2. *Students learn word lists by reading them and saying them aloud.* Rationale: Discrimination learning can establish a referential relation between visual input and vocalization. The conditioned response of associating a visual word with a sound results in what some people call meaning. To make certain that students know what response is being reinforced, the teacher must introduce language practice in small bits, preferably single words, and in a well-planned sequence. Critics argue the part is not the whole.

3. *The writing program becomes a series of learning packages addressed to a long list of discrete skills and accompanied by a classroom management schedule.* W. W. Cooley and Robert Glaser (1969) describe the basic model as individually prescribed instruction. Rationale: Because students require different schedules of reinforcement, instruction must be individualized. Critics argue that large classes make this impossible.

For a time, individualized learning meant computer-assisted instruction, but limited school budgets have dimmed the vision of terminals at every desk. Most of the computer programs marketed as writing programs were simply multiple-choice questions about grammar, punctuation, usage, and so forth. One of the most ingenious attempts at a learning package was the method used by Skinner and Sue Ann Krakower (1968) to teach handwriting to primary-grade pupils. The various letters were printed on chemically treated paper, and the child traced over them with a special pen. When the letter was traced accurately, the pen produced a gray line. If the pen strayed off the letter, a yellow line was produced.

Drills can be a helpful way of teaching conventions to some students. Mina Shaughnessy (1977) reminds us that we often mark papers as if we were journal editors reading the manuscripts of experienced writers, not teachers attempting to understand the logic of what the beginning student was doing. Her introductory lesson (chapter four) on subject-verb agreement illustrates the necessity for expanded coverage, using drills, to help a student with a seemingly simple point. She suggests that grammatical concepts should be taught in a language clear to the student and within the context of a particular editing problem.

Shaughnessy's emphasis on context reminds us that a series of drills alone cannot be considered a writing program. It cannot be a substitute for the process of actually writing an essay. The sum of all the parts of the drills still does not equal the total act of writing.

Thus, the conception of writing as bits of verbal behavior is not an entirely adequate description of what the writer does. A sentence such as "I like her cooking" is ambiguous (it could mean I like *her* when she cooks, I like the *cooking* she does, or I like *her* when she is full of energy) without an understanding of what is going on in the heads of writer and reader. Just teaching writing by imitation of small bits of behavior is a pedagogical mistake because, as Michael Polanyi (1958) points out, the particulars of writing as rule-governed behavior become meaningless if the student loses sight of purpose:

> Subsidiary awareness and focal awareness are mutually exclusive. If a pianist shifts his attention from the piece he is playing to the observation of what he is doing with his fingers while playing, he gets confused and may have to stop. This happens if we switch our focal attention to particulars of which we had previously been aware only in their subsidiary role. . . . All particulars become meaningless if we lose sight of the pattern which they jointly constitute. When we use words in speech or writing we are aware of them only in a subsidiary manner. This fact is usually described as the transparency of language. (Pp. 56–57)

Trying to teach writing with only a sequence of drills is obviously a dubious activity. One of the most interesting studies on the use of drills was a New Zealand study of the results of three programs—one teaching transformational grammar, one teaching traditional grammar in a series of exercises, and one teaching writing in the context of a literature course. The question was whether or not traditional grammar instruction, as taught in the third-form through the fifth-form years, contributed to better instruction in how to write. From February 1970 until November 1972, the students in the three programs were regularly observed and assessed. At the end of this period, the researchers reported, "The results presented show that the effects of such grammar study are negligible. . . . It is difficult to escape the conclusion that English grammar, whether traditional or transformational, has virtually no influence on the language growth of typical secondary school students" (Elley, Barham, Lamb, and Wylie, 1976, pp. 17–18). Because the literature course placed less emphasis on drill and memorization of "facts," one might argue that the study suggests the limited value of drill in language learning.

Sentence Combining

Sentence combining, a second method within the *modeling* approach, is a way of giving grammar a functional role in writing. This method uses very few terms or none at all, yet it sharpens the student's grammatical insights and intuitions. Sentence combining argues that giving the beginning writer an essay assignment is equivalent to assigning all of the problems of composition at once. Like drills, sentence combining focuses the lesson on a small bit, in this case the sentence. Attention to only the sentence provides some discrete boundaries within which teachers and students together can examine the basic principles of composition. But unlike many drills, some sentence-combining activities allow different responses from students.

Sentence combining has its roots in the work of Noam Chomsky. Before Chomsky, linguistics was a classificatory science, a sort of "verbal botany" (Searle, 1972, p. 16), producing in the schools what were called structural grammars. These grammars provided a list of sentence types, and many teachers, as part of their writing programs, prepared assignments in which students either identified the patterns of given sentences or wrote examples of various types of sentences—subject-verb-modifier, subject-linking verb-modifier, subject-verb-object, subject-verb-indirect object-object, and so forth.

Chomsky (1957) found that structural linguistics did not account for the differences in such sentences as "John is easy to please" and "John is eager to please." The structural grammars in most schools classified both sentences as subject-linking verb-modifier (or predicate adjective), but the first sentence means *someone* is trying to please John and the second means that *John* is trying to please someone. If the two sentences have the same structure, as structural grammar tells us, then the words in the two sentences should *not* have different relationships.

Chomsky argues that structural linguistics could not account for the different meanings of these two sentences and others like them because the differences in meaning pointed to differences in the deep structure of the two sentences, differences not evident on the surface. The fact that native speakers can paraphrase the different meanings of the two sentences shows that some kind of deep structure exists. Chomsky thought linguistics should abandon its goal of classifying the *surface* structure of sentences and examine the *deep* structure and the rules that govern the changes from deep to surface structure—that is, how the speaker puts the sentence together to make the surface structure we see and hear. Although in both sample sentences *John* appears on the surface to the be subject, deep structure shows that *John* is the object of *easy to please* and the subject of *eager to please*.

Chomsky argues that "the notion 'grammatical' cannot be identified with 'meaningful' in any semantic sense" (p. 15). He used as his evidence the two sentences "Colorless green ideas sleep furiously" and "Furiously sleep ideas green colorless." Both are equally nonsensical, but any speaker of English recognizes that only the first is grammatical. Structure, therefore, must be considered separate from meaning. But this assumption sometimes proved impossible to maintain, and the central problem now facing linguistic study is how to account for the relationship between meaning and structure.

Charles Fillmore's case grammar (1968) is one attempt to describe patterns of meaning and their relationship to structure. For instance, all of the italicized words are the subject of the sentence:

1. The *door* opened.

2. *Chuck* opened the door.

3. The *key* opened the door.

But of these three syntactic subjects, only one has the semantic or meaningful role of *agent*. Fillmore identifies six semantic categories in case grammar: agent, instrument, dative, objective, factitive, and locative. *Door* is in the objective case, *Chuck* in the agent case, and *key* in the instrument case. All, of course, are in the syntactive position of subject.

What Chomsky, Fillmore, and others did for the teaching of composition was to give the sentence a history—the story of the transformations taking place between deep structure and surface structure, or the traces between one surface structure and another. Kellogg Hunt (1966), using units of analysis from Chomsky and other transformational-generative grammarians, found that as children grow older, their sentences or surface structures have a more complicated history. For example, in the sentence "He was a rare white whale with a crooked jaw," the average eighth grader consolidates five clauses: (1) He was a whale, (2) The whale was white, (3) The whale was rare, (4) The whale had a jaw, and (5) The jaw was crooked.

Says Hunt: "Average fourth graders do not ordinarily write like that. In fact, in the five-thousand clauses written by fourth graders we found a single nominal that resulted from as many as five of these consolidations only three times. Five is simply too many for a fourth grader, but he often consolidates three" (p. 736). In another study (1977), Hunt found that the cumulative sentence (additive: He stood, wearing a hat, holding a cane, wondering what to do next) did not appear until late high school and adulthood.

In a recent study, Marlene Scardamalia (1981) used sentence combining as a measure of a child's cognitive capacity—the amount a child can process at a given time. Her work is testing some of the hypotheses of recent Neo-Piagetian models (Pascual Leone, Goodman, Ammon, and Subelman, 1978), but Scardamalia admits that her task analysis is a good deal looser than the analysis used by Pascual Leone et al. Scardamalia began by teaching children to write a paragraph that included all of the information in the matrix in Figure 1.

The purpose of the study was to examine how well students integrated the information in individual sentences. Level 1, the lowest integration, had four separate sentences. A level 3 integration read: "In Michigan the climate is cool so their fruit crop is apples. In California the climate is warm so that their fruit crop is oranges."

Unlike Scardamalia, Hunt does not place his work in the tradition of cognitive psychology. Nevertheless, Hunt's studies of changes in syntax of children as they grow older can be understood as a contribution to our understanding of information processing systems. Hunt's work raised the question of whether or not special lessons in adding, deleting, and embedding could accelerate the growth of students in their syntactic maturity. John Mellon (1969) found that this indeed could be done. But he also found that the students who had received direct instruction in sentence combining did not achieve higher essay scores than students who had not received the instruction. Frank O'Hare (1973), on the other hand, modified Mellon's exercises and found that both the essay scores and syntactic maturity improved as a result of direct instruction in sentence combining.

The exercises patterned after those by Mellon look something like this:

Directions: Combine the two statements in each problem into one sentence. Follow the instructions given in the parentheses after

	State	
At Harvest	Michigan	California
Climate	cool	warm
Fruit Crop	apples	oranges

Figure 1. Matrix of elements for student writing assignment.

the second statement. The word in parentheses indicates what type of transformation you should use.

The Fact That or *That* transformation:
A. Jim and Bill knew *something*.
   O. J. Simpson scored three touchdowns. (*That*)
   Answer: Jim and Bill knew that O. J. Simpson scored three touchdowns.
   Or: Jim and Bill knew O. J. Simpson scored three touchdowns.
B. *Something* influenced his grade.
   He was late. (*The Fact That*)
   Answer: The fact that he was late influenced his grade.

Who, What, Where, When, How, Why transformation:
A. The two people near the door wondered *something*.
   The music had stopped for some reason. (*Why*)
   Answer: The two people near the door wondered why the music had stopped.
B. *Something* concerned the deep sea divers.
   Something had happened to the boat. (*What*)
   Answer: What had happened to the boat concerned the deep sea divers.

These exercises increase in complexity until students are using several transformations in one sentence: *Although what happened to the boat concerned the man who was waiting at the dock, he calmly watched the duck waddling along the beach.*

Such exercises modeled on Mellon's have been criticized. Some teachers find them to be too much like rote drills, limiting the possible responses from students. Francis Christensen (1967) argues that Mellon's sentences are too heavily embedded with subordinate clauses and phrases and therefore not representative of the style of modern professional writers. These writers, Christensen claims, write "cumulative sentences," which feature a high proportion of free modifiers. For example, the sentence above could be rewritten as a cumulative sentence: *The man waited at the dock, concerned about the boat, calmly watching the duck waddling along the beach.* Frank O'Hare's exercises (1975) and those of William Strong (1973) modify Mellon's basic approach, providing more exercises with cumulative sentences.

In both O'Hare and Strong, the student is asked to recreate a surface sentence based on kernel sentences. The previous sentence would be presented as:

1. The man waited at the dock.

2. The man was concerned about the boat.

3. The man was watching the duck.
4. The duck was waddling along the beach.

In any class, students will produce a dozen or more variations for the sentence and then discuss the reasons for the difference.

Instead of giving students the kernels, James Gray (1969) gives them a photograph for subject matter and a Christensen sentence for form. He asks the students to model their own sentence after the Christensen example, using their own words and their own perceptions of the photograph. Teachers who use Gray's approach have different sequences of instruction, one of them being first the additions, then the direction of modification, and finally the subordinate and coordinate arrangements:

Additions:
Verbs–The surfer stood on his board, skimming across the waves, holding his arms high, smiling to himself.
Nouns–The woman entered the bus, her coat buttoned, a flower in her lapel, a newspaper under her arm.
Adjectives–He opened the gift, tired but happy, hopeful about the contents.

Direction of Modification:
A. Holding his arms high, the surfer, smiling to himself, stood on his board, skimming across the waves.
B. Her coat buttoned, a flower in her lapel, the woman entered the bus, a newspaper under her arm.
C. He, tired but happy, hopeful about the contents, opened the gift.

Arrangements:
A. The cattle rushed into the valley, bellowing, heads down, churning the dust. (1-2-2-2 coordination)
B. The house burned to the ground, its door still standing, the door knob glazed, hot to the touch. (1-2-3-4 subordination)
C. Two girls came out of the house and ran to the back, one carrying a small kitten, black with a white spot, the other swinging her Sunday hat, the ribbons twisting in the wind. (1-2-3-2-3 mixed)

The principles of the sentence, says Christensen, can be extended to the paragraph by *modeling* examples of coordinate and subordinate paragraphs. While writing, students hear what other students have written, then read their sentences aloud, making revisions where necessary. The fact that all students are writing from the same photograph means that each student is aware of the options available to the others. When students hear only essays from personal experience, they do not know how their linguistic choices might differ from what another writer has done.

Advocates of Christensen materials argue that most of the basic principles of composition can be taught in a Christensen sentence. For example, additions are practice in the development of an idea; coordination and subordination are ways of organizing whole essays; and varying direction of modification is an exercise of coherence and emphasis. The students learn what a sentence is at different levels—at the simple level of base clauses and at the complicated level of modification and coordination. They also learn the key words that make consolidations possible.

Teachers who use sentence combining report several problems. Most teachers find that when they move from the sentence to the paragraph, students will at first regress to simple sentences, momentarily forgetting the combinations they have learned. Later, consolidations begin to appear once again. Another problem is the perennial search for subject matter that students can share. Overheads and text materials have been supplemented by improvisations, demonstration films, and the scenes out the classroom windows.

A third problem with sentence combining is the pedagogical baggage in some of the published materials. Insert, output, T-Fact, 1-2-3-2—these and other examples of special language have had to be replaced in the classroom with "Try attaching this material to this sentence." Jackson Burgess (1963) simply has his students write a single sentence on the view out the window and then discuss together the ways the sentences differ and the reasons for those differences, skipping entirely the special model sentences and special language. The models become those sentences other students have written.

Most secondary teachers find that their students do not write the Christensen cumulative sentence unless models are introduced and the sentence assigned. Students almost always find this sentence a new experience in their own writing. Sentence combining in general may be teaching more about processing strategies than sentence types. Strong (1976) says that the "mental activities in sentence combining are what make it such a powerful approach." He argues, "If sentence combining works because it trains a kid to hold longer and longer discourse in his head—to imbed and subordinate at greater depth as a means of expressing thought . . . it is a means to intervene in cognitive development and, perhaps, to enhance it" (p. 60).

Imitation

But sentence combining limits its focus to sentence structure, and there are those who criticize the approach for that reason. A third method in the *modeling* approach focusing on large units is the imitation of given texts. This third method has three alternative forms of imitation: *genre models, dictation,* and *paraphrasing.* In genre models, the student is given an example of an argument or description and asked to "do one of your own like that." This time-honored approach features collections of essays arranged by genre—description, narration, argument, exposition, and so forth. The students are asked to write an introduction, then a body, and finally a conclusion, following the assigned model. One of the commonsense assumptions in the genre models lesson is that students learn to write by reading.

An extension of the genre method is Christensen's approach to paragraphing, asking students to model subordinate, coordinate, and mixed sequences. In a different approach, Josephine Miles (1979) emphasizes the importance of the cohesive ties—how sentences are connected. Her organizational classification includes the chronological and spatial (and-and/then-then), the conditional (if-then/because-therefore), the disjunctive (either-or/not this-but that), and the concessive (though-yet). She argues that predication of the thesis sentence often establishes a given type of organization. Teachers who use Miles's ideas often give students predications to select from, attempting to push students toward different types of organizational patterns.

Dictation is another useful form of imitation. Rollo W. Brown (1915) emphasizes the importance of dictation lessons in which the instructor reads to students from acknowledged master works and asks them to copy exactly what they hear. These lessons are supplemented by exercises in which students memorize materials for recitation to the class and in which the class collectively dictates a story to the teacher, using a prescribed opening, closing, and transition word. According to Brown, dictation helps students to concentrate on how good writers write, to internalize "good standards of speech," and to avoid "separating language and writing." The passages selected should always be a little more difficult than the average reading level of the class.

For early grade elementary teachers, dictation usually refers to the practice of the teacher writing down captions for student pictures according to what the children dictate. Some secondary teachers have found dictation very useful for teaching punctuation. Students record the passage as it is read. Then a copy of the original is distributed, and students compare their copy with the original.

Instead of copying words exactly, I. A. Richards (1938, 1943) recommends a paraphrase method, having students imitate ideas by trying to write paraphrases or translations of lines and passages while limiting themselves to a basic English vocabulary of 850 words. Richards felt that learning to write in the basic vocabulary was "an exploration of the most important devices of English syntax" (1938, p. 208). Some teachers have modified Richard's approach by progressively increasing the number of words on the list that can be used for translation or by simply asking students to "use your own words" to reduce long selections to a paragraph or a page. This, of course, results in the précis, which Richard Hood (1967) describes as an exercise of the highest value in vocabulary building, in sentence construction, and in clear, concise expression.

In his autobiography, Benjamin Franklin described how he learned to write by imitating the style of the *Spectator*, taking notes from his reading and then trying to put the notes back into the original form, turning some of the tales into verse and then, after a time, attempting to turn the verse into the original prose. Reported Franklin, "By comparing my work afterwards with the original, I discovered many faults and corrected them." The problems that Franklin set for himself are very much like the assignments described by Rollo Brown and by Richards, and one cannot read Franklin, Brown, or Richards without being aware that the learner is involved in interesting and useful activities. Sensitive teachers know from experience that the approach works.

Phyllis Brooks (1973) proposes a different approach to paraphrasing. She believes that the traditional paraphrase "tests the student's ability to read, and to write an acceptable form of standard English, but it does not *add* anything to his repertoire of skills" (p. 162). She suggests instead a *persona paraphrase,* which she believes adds to the student's awareness of the variety of expression and usable sentence structures. Her exercises ask the student to use the structural models in a given passage and to attempt to imitate the style of the author, but to use one's own subject matter. Thus, Rose Macaulay's "Once the capital of imperial Rome; later the greatest city in Christendom" becomes a student's description of Bodie, California: "First an assemblage of mining claims; later the largest gold camp in the north." Walker Gibson's *Tough, Sweet, and Stuffy* (1966) is an excellent resource for classifying and contrasting persona as used in Brooks's paraphrases.

The persona paraphrase can be as simple or as complex as one wants to make it. The selection must, however, always be at the upper edge of the student's reading ability. Elementary teachers have students imitate fairy tales: "Once upon a time, Susie and I were playing kickball at recess." A sixth grader did this paraphrase of the proverb "A bird in the hand is worth two in the bush": "A hamburger in your pocket is worth two in the McDonald's line." A tenth grader did an interesting paraphrase of James Baldwin's lines from "Stranger in the Village":

> I thought of whitemen arriving for the first time in an African village, strangers there, as I am a stranger here, and tried to imagine the astounded populace touching their hair and marveling at the color of their skin.

The tenth grader's paraphrase:

> I thought of seventh graders arriving for the first time at Roosevelt Junior High, strangers there, as I am a stranger in my own home, and tried to imagine the amused ninth graders watching those seventh graders trying to find their way to class.

And two teachers did an amusing paraphrase of Faulkner's opening lines from *The Unvanquished:*

> Behind the smokehouse that summer, Ringo and I had a living map. Although Vicksburg was just a handful of chips from the woodpile and the River a trench scraped into the packed earth with the point of a hoe, it (river, city, and terrain) lived, possessing even in miniature that ponderable though passive recalcitrance of topography which outweighs artillery, against which the most brilliant of victories and the most tragic of defeats are but the loud noises of a moment.

The two teachers' paraphrases:

> On top of the garage every spring, Vince and Bud had a flagpole. Although "Old Glory" was just a torn sheet from the mending basket, and the pole assembled from leftover beanpoles nailed together with Daddy's hammer, it (flag and pole) stood, providing even in its shabbiness that symbolic though limited means of communication which proclaims patriotism, by which the largest of nations and the most timid of peoples are still identified in a moment.

> In the schoolyard that fall, Cathy and he had a torrid affair. Although sex was but a dream on the horizon, and love a bargain struck between the enamoured pair with the delicacy of a detente, it (sex, love, and relationship) flowered, obeying even in quietude that forceful though nebulous passion of youth that withstands parents, against which the most stubborn of attacks and the most humble of pleas are but the inconsequential mutterings of a substitute teacher.

The various classroom applications of the *modeling* approach use the language models for exact duplications, as in most drills, for triggering ideas and language in the student, as in most persona assignments, and sometimes for both duplication and triggering, as in many of the Christensen sentence exercises. Sometimes a classroom method shows an evaluation from imitation and duplication to triggering. For example, the first sentence-combining activities (Mellon, 1969) were tightly structured and required exact duplication of a given sentence. Recent work of Strong (1973), however, uses the kernel sentences as a trigger allowing students to produce many different combinations of the same basic material. The exercise often triggers ideas from the students and does not require exact duplication of a given sentence.

The *modeling* approach, in addition to providing a theoretical framework for various classroom lessons, also provides a rationale for different ways of diagnosing student papers. The following writing sample is an example of the type of writing that would be improved by *modeling* activities:

> The very special thing in my life is my bike. I can go anywhere I like. I ride when I am angry. I just ride untill I get tired. Or util I have relived all my tensions. To feel the cool breeze on my face riding down slopes on hills is just wonderful. I drive a car. But a car cannot run on people power. It runs on gas. Gas takes money and on a bike there are no traffic jams, no one to get in front of you and no one to hit you, no one to tell you how fast to go. I like fixing on my bike taking it apart and putting it back together on my car I wouldn't know what the heck to do with it if it breaks down.

First, the sentence style is choppy, and sentence-combining activities should help the student become aware of the uses of adding and embedding. Second, the overall organizational structure is confused, and the experience of writing subordinate, coordinate, and mixed paragraphs (a la Christensen) should help the student to develop some judgment about sequencing material. In addition, close examination of the organization implicit in the thesis (a la Josephine Miles) and the reading of descriptive and narrative essays might also be helpful.

In summary, one purpose of writing is the making of texts, very much the way one might make a chair or a cake. One way to learn how to make anything is to have a model, either for duplication or for triggering one's own ideas. To be understood, a model must have parts—in the example of writing, letters, words, sentences, paragraphs, transitions, and so forth comprise the parts. But the whole is always greater than the sum of the parts. In *modeling* approaches, classroom lessons and diagnostic methods focus on these parts of the text one at a time. The result is clarity of focus but not the whole truth about writing.

Processing: Writing as a Sequence of Stages or Fluctuation of Strategies

Processing approaches shift the focus from the text, as in *modeling* approaches, to the strategies or stages in the writing process—the steps that writers go through, particularly the way writing can be used for both discovery and communication. The research in *processing* shifts the focus from the language behavior, either the words in oral language or the sentences and paragraphs in written text, to the processes in the writer's head. The studies of the mind's process have had two important directions: one a description of the mental map maker and the other a description of the steps or stages in the writing process. These two directions are complementary and often intertwined.

Researchers who study the writer's mental maps turn stimulus-response and stimulus-response-reinforcement into sign-significate sequences. That is, according to E. C. Tolman (1932), the organism learns not movements and responses but "sign-significate expectations" or what-leads-to-what relationships. Contiguity of stimuli, of course, will build up expectations, and practice certainly plays a role in confirming and strengthening expectations. But it is not response potentials or habits that increase in the developing organism; rather, what increase are the breadth and clarity of mental maps that help the organism make accurate predications. Tolman (1948) sees the brain as a map maker, not a switch watcher:

> [The brain] is far more like a map control room than it is like an old fashioned telephone exchange. The stimuli, which are allowed in, are not connected by one-to-one switches to the outgoing responses. Rather, incoming impulses are usually worked over and elaborated in the central control room into a tentative, cognitivelike map of the environment. And it is this tentative map, indicating routes and paths and environmental relationships, which finally determines what responses, if any, the animal will finally release. (P. 192)

Edmund Burke Huey (1968) made a similar claim forty years earlier in 1908 when he said that "meaning, indeed, dominates and unitizes the perception of words and phrases" (p. 116). Huey's point was that a reader reads for meaning, not a letter, syllable, or word at a time. Huey concluded, "The first factors of perception in reading are not usually total form, word length, etc., but certain striking 'dominant' parts, the apperception of word-form and word-length coming a little later" (p. 109). In other words, meaning is more than the sum of its parts.

Cognitive theorists use a wide range of terms for the map or internal hierarchies: schemata (Bartlett, 1932), images and plans (Miller, Galanter, and Pribam, 1960), strategy (Bruner, Goodnow, and Austin, 1956), subsumption (Ausubel, 1965), frames (Minsky, 1975), and problem solving (Gagne, 1970). But recent sign-significate theorists have started personifying the term: operator, executive, and executive organizer (Ammon, 1977). One reason for the theoretical shift in emphasis to the map maker is its active role as an agent that changes sensory inputs and is itself changed by sensory inputs.

In cognitive psychology, the brain is viewed as a system for processing and storing information (Simon, 1981), very much like a computer, and the program is the field or map. The value of the information-processing model is illustrated by an experiment in which an animal is presented with two choices. In the traditional learning laboratory, a monkey, like most other animals, has a difficult time making the right choice in a delayed reaction experiment. In this experiment, a light signals the correct choice, but the light goes out before the monkey is allowed to make a response. The monkey often has difficulty remembering which choice was correct. However, if a similar problem is carried out under field conditions, animals have no such difficulties. A chimpanzee was carried around in the company of an experimenter who hid pieces of fruit in eighteen different places. After some delay, the chimpanzee was released. Menzel (1973) describes the result:

> Usually the test animal ran unerringly and in a direct line to the exact clump of grass or leaves, tree stump, or hole in the ground where a hidden food lay, grabbed the food, stopped briefly to eat, and then ran directly to the next place, no matter how distant or obscured by visual barriers. (Pp. 943–44)

Obviously, the animal had an internal map, and the hidden fruit was more "meaningful" than the light signal. What are the qualities of these organizers or maps? How does meaningfulness help one remember? The maps must have qualities that make it possible to store them in memory. George Miller (1956) suggests that the working memory can at any moment only process about seven pieces of random information, plus or minus two. He reports, for example, on an experiment by I. Pollack (1953) testing the limits of listeners making absolute judgments of auditory pitch. The channel capacity (or limit) was 2.5 bits, and because a bit is the amount of information needed to make a decision between two equally likely alternatives, the actual number of pitches to be distinguished was about five or six. Simon and Chase (1976) think the limit for short-term memory is closer to four than seven.

Thus, working or short-term memory has an upper limit, be it four, seven, or nine and be the random items letters, numbers, or whatever. Obviously, people remember more than nine pieces of information. The limit is extended by what Miller calls chunking—the organization of the random material into "meaningful" units. For example, although one might have a limit of seven random letters, the limit of seven also applies to words, which could have thirty or more letters that one could recall by remembering the meaningful unit—the words.

To say that the word *school* is a familiar chunk is to say that there is already information stored in long-term memory that permits the letters of *school* to be recognized as a chunk. In other words, it is useful to conceive of more than one type of memory—a very brief sensory memory, a monitor of the passing scene; short-term, working memory, which has a limited capacity and where information gets organized for learning; and long-term memory, where maps are stored (Simon, 1976). Short-term memory is not a buffer between the senses and long-term memory, but it is temporary storage for pointers to long-term memory, pointers that have been produced by the recognition mechanism of this memory. Long-term memory has two components—the recognition memory or index for identifying the familiar, and the information storage itself, sometimes called semantic memory. According to Endel Tulving (1972), semantic memory contains episodic information (facts about everyday events that can be dated) and general knowledge (facts and generalizations that cannot be dated). The episodes may be stored in the form of a network of propositions—or chunks of meaning—or in the form of images.

Ulric Neisser (1976) describes an experiment in which the subjects had difficulty giving an answer because they had to look at two visual images at the same time—one real and the other the imagined mental map. In the experiment, the subjects were shown a large block F, were told to remember it, and later were asked to describe the succession of corner points as one moved around it. On the first task, the subjects were asked to answer yes for each point that was either on the extreme top or on the bottom of the F, and no for each point in between. On the second task, the subjects were asked to point to a printed series of yeses and noes. Pointing was more difficult. When the subjects had to point to a visual image, the visual perception interfered with their imagined image or map. Says Neisser, "Visual images are apparently produced by the same integrative processes that make ordinary perception possible."

Besides propositions or categories with words arranged in a hierarchy of meaning, long-term memory must store verbatim materials.

Furthermore, the tip-of-the-tongue experiment by Roger Brown and D. McNeill (1966) suggests syllable structure, stress patterns, and phonetic segments are also stored, perhaps independently. Brown and McNeill induced the tip-of-the-tongue experience by reading the following definition and asking people what it meant: "A navigational instrument used in measuring angular distances, especially the altitude of sun, moon, and stars at sea." Some people knew the word *sextant* immediately, others not at all. Some had a tip-of-the-tongue experience, and for those Brown and McNeill had four questions: (1) How many syllables does it have? (2) What letter does it start with? (3) What words does it sound like? (4) What words are similar in meaning? The subjects were right on the number of syllables 57 percent of the time (chance: 20 percent) and correct on initial letters 62 percent (chance: 8 percent). The importance of the first sound suggests that the index or retrieval system of long-term memory begins its work like a dictionary.

If the memory skill is an indication that a map is present, then the maps in long-term memory get clearer as young subjects get older. As a general rule, as children get older, their memory skills improve (Hagen, 1971). In fact, in most research situations preschoolers do not remember any better when told to do something than when no such instructions are given (Appel, Cooper, McCarrell, Sims-Knight, Yussen, and Flavell, 1972; Flavell, 1970). One exception to the increase of long-term memory skill with age is that three-year-olds do almost as well as adults on problems asking that they identify which set of objects or pictures they have seen before and which set is new, even when there is a delay of days or weeks (Berch and Evans, 1973; Permuter and N. A. Myers, 1974).

Saying that children remember better as they get older is another way of saying that children think in ways substantially different from adults. At one time, thinking and seeing were considered completely separate activities. That is, the traditional view has been that form perception can be reduced to the perception of contours and that contour perception in turn can be reduced to abrupt differences in light intensity that cause certain neural units in the retina and brain to fire. Irvin Rock (1974) concludes from a number of his experiments that the traditional view of perception is inadequate: "Although the work I have described does not deny the possible importance of contour detection as a basis of form perception, it does suggest that such an explanation is far from sufficient, and that the perception of form depends on certain mental processes such as description and correction" (p. 78).

Jean Piaget's conservation experiment is an example of how the mental processes shape what one perceives and how these processes change with age. Some researchers believe that these changes in mental processes result from developmental changes in limits of mental capacity (Ammon, 1977). In Piaget's conservation experiment, a child is presented with a situation in which water is poured from one of two identical beakers into a tall, thin beaker; water from the second beaker is poured into a short, squat beaker. When asked which has more, the child will maintain that the tall beaker has more water. In time, the child becomes capable of *decentration,* is able to evaluate several dimensions at once, and can reverse operations, aware that conditions can be returned to their original state. Later, around ages eleven or twelve, these concrete operations, reversing and conserving of concrete objects, begin to be applied to abstractions. In Piaget's terms, this development occurs because the child inherits two basic tendencies—organization and adaptation—which combine to produce cognitive structures or schemata that govern how a child handles such matters as the conservation problem.

Some researchers de-emphasize the developmental limits on mental capacity. For example, George Miller suggests that people can increase their mental capacity with bigger chunks: "Since memory span is a fixed number of chunks, we can increase the number of bits of information that it contains simply by building larger and larger chunks, each chunk containing more information than before" (1967, p. 37). Thus, the six or seven chunks can be six or seven letters or six or seven sentences or stories:

1. L B C G H D
2. Love/Boy/Cat/Girl/Head/Dog
3. The boy saw the house.
   The cat lives comfortably.
   The dog has a bone.
   The girl drives a car.
   The tree fell down.
   A man lost his hat.
   The sky is blue.
4. Once upon a time the little boy saw a house. In the house, the cat lived comfortably. And the dog had a bone. A girl lived in the house. She drove a car. The girl's father also lived in the house. He lost his hat. One day the man and the girl planted a tree. The next day it fell down.

I have experimented with my own children, asking them to listen to the seven items once and then repeat the items. They consistently had more trouble remembering the seven sentences than they did remembering the story. In fact, the recall on the story was almost perfect. One reason for this is probably the fact that the story is so cohesive it might be considered a single chunk. In addition, several times my children would start to paraphrase a sentence and then remember its exact wording, suggesting, I think, that many facts are represented in memory as propositional (see Rumelhart, 1975).

Researchers who examine the interaction between the mental map and the environment believe that the association-contiguity-modeling theory is not the only basis of language behavior, that mental maps or chunking mechanisms are more important than stimulus control, and that these mental maps are hierarchical as well as linear (Herriot, 1970). These researchers see their major task at the moment to be the study of executive processes—or, put another way, assembly and control mechanisms that organize the maps and integrate new information into the maps. These researchers start with the question "What are the advance organizers or executive processes that students use when they write?" To find the outlines of the executive processes, these researchers do task analysis, preparing protocols of what subjects do in the task (Simon and Chase, 1977), and controlled experiments on memory span and retrieval, describing what is remembered and for how long (Brown and McNeill, 1966). One issue, for instance, is how long it takes for a subject to move information from short-term memory to long-term memory. One estimate is fifteen seconds.

In summary, the writer's mental map maker has a short-term memory of four to nine pieces, a fifteen-second storage time from short-term memory to long-term memory, a chunking mechanism for reducing information to a single piece, and a reliance on visual imagery to map information. Every part of this general outline is questioned by some researchers, but the assumption that the learner is a map maker is widely accepted.

What, then, has the map-maker model of learning and memory done for the teaching of writing? One result is that it has encouraged teachers and researchers to shift their attention from words on the page and textual models to the steps and strategies used by students in the writing process. Janet Emig (1971) comments that of the five hundred pre-1963 studies cited in the bibliography of *Research in Written Composition*, only two deal even indirectly with the process of writing among adolescents: "Proposals for the Conduct of Written Composition Activities in the Secondary School Inherent in an Analysis of the Language Composition Act" by Lester Angene and "Factors Affecting Regularity of the Flow of Words during Written Composition" by John Van Bruggen. Angene looked at completed student themes, and Van Bruggen examined the physical rate at which eighty-four junior high students wrote. Other than these two studies, the process of writing had not been examined.

Emig selected for her study eight sixteen- and seventeen-year-old students. She found that "prewriting is a far longer process in self-sponsored writing" and that "in school-sponsored writing, there is often no time provided for this portion of the composing process" (p. 92). She also found that students do not voluntarily revise school-sponsored writing, that they do revise self-sponsored writing, that in school-sponsored writing works of literature are the most common stimuli, and that in self-sponsored writing "human relations" and "self" are the most frequent stimuli.

Like Emig, Donald Graves (1975) used the case study method to examine writing in the first grade. He selected a sample of eight seven-year-olds, two each from four different classes, and observed them writing in school from December 1972 to April 1973. He observed fifty-three writing episodes, interviewed children on their views of their own writing and their views of the "good" writer, presented general findings, and prepared specific background and observational details on one boy student. Graves found that formal environments for writing seem to be more favorable for girls and informal environments more favorable for boys. In either case, unassigned writing is longer than assigned writing. Graves recommended developmental studies of children's writing and has received an NIE grant to research this topic.

Incidentally, when Graves reviewed the literature in 1973, he found that only two previous studies had involved the actual observation of writers in the process of writing: Emig's 1971 study and an unpublished doctoral dissertation by Barbara Holstein (1970), "Use of Metaphor to Induce Innovative Thinking in Fourth Grade Children."

One of the problems in a process description of writing is how to distinguish between one stage and another. D. Gordon Rohman (1965), who coined the term *prewriting*, divides the writing process into three stages: "We divide the process at the point where the 'writing idea' is ready for words and the page: everything before that we call 'prewriting,' everything after that 'writing' and 'rewriting'" (p. 106). Graves and Emig use Rohman's stage theory in their examination of the writing process, but their writing samples do not clarify when a "writing idea is ready for words and the page" and when it is not. Sometimes the writing appears to be a process of discovery.

To account for this discovery process, Emig introduces a period of planning that follows prewriting and that begins with words on the page. She says that prewriting, on the other hand, "extends from the time a writer begins to perceive . . . to the time when he first puts words or phrases on paper elucidating that perception" (p. 39). The separation of perception in the prewriting stage from discovery in the planning stage can obscure the way language can be used as an instru-

ment of thought or perception. W. L. Chafe (1979), for instance, argues
that the linguistic output of verbalization is "not a replica of the input
to these processes." He continues: "Not all interpretations take place
during perception: there is much that takes place while we are talking
as well" (p. 220).

Many researchers believe that students are involved not in three or
four distinct stages of writing but in a tension between parallel levels of
concern—one level for discovery, another for organizational matters,
another for conventions (spelling, punctuation), and so forth. Linda
Flower (1979) divides the writing process into two stages, writer-based
prose and reader-based prose, the first for getting the material on paper
and the second for communicating information to a reader. She also
suggests a relationship between these two types of prose and Tulving's
two types of memory (1972), arguing that "one way to account for why
Writer-Based prose seems to 'come naturally' to most of us from time to
time is to recognize its ties to our episodic as opposed to semantic
memory" (p. 34).

Flower and John Hayes (1978) define writing as a problem-solving
cognitive process, and based on George Miller et al. (1960), they identify
the following types of strategies in the two-stage process: (1) making
plans; (2) operating, memory search, procedures that get things done;
and (3) testing, evaluating the results of the plans and operations.
These strategies were identified by means of comments made by writers
during the writing act.

Flower and Hayes identified three implications for teaching: (1) it is
possible to diagram the problems of weak writers in terms of their
procedures rather than their errors; (2) writers' images of the writing
process can help or hinder when encountering such situations as plans
that contradict one another (asking how student writers learn an image
of the process); and (3) writers without reader-plans are the weak
writers.

James Britton, Tony Burgess, Nancy Martin, Alex McLeod, and
Harold Rosen (1975), drawing from the work of Edward Sapir (1961),
distinguish between expressive writing and transactional writing, similar to the Flower/Hayes distinction between writer-based and reader-
based prose: Expressive language is "the ebb and flow of the speaker's
thought and feeling," and "the essentially expressive nature of all
speech . . . moves to a greater explicitness at the expense of its expressive features when the need to communicate increases" (p. 10). Britton
et al. cite the research of L. S. Vygotsky and George Kelly as evidence
that expressive writing can be used as an instrument of thought.

Vygotsky (1962) reports that when forced to stop and think, a child
"is likely to think aloud." He continues:

> We have seen that egocentric speech is not suspended in a void but is directly related to the child's practical dealings with the real world—it enters as a constituent part into the process of rational activity; . . . and that it increasingly services both problem solving and planning as the child's activities grow more complex. (P. 19)

To Vygotsky, inner speech is "condensed, abbreviated speech" and writing is "a separate linguistic function." "The change from maximally compact inner speech to maximally detailed written speech requires what might be called deliberate semantics—deliberate structuring of the web of meaning" (p. 100).

To Britton et al., expressive writing is the use of language to explain some matter to oneself. Transactional writing is the explanation of some matter to another person. For them, the use of language to explain something to oneself is an example of the finding by Kelly (1963) that learning is not a special kind of human behavior, but behavior at its most typical:

> Man looks at his world through transparent patterns or templates which he creates and then attempts to fit over the realities of which the world is composed. The fit is not always very good. Yet without such patterns the world appears to be such an undifferentiated homogeneity that man is unable to make any sense out of it. Even a poor fit is more helpful to him than nothing at all. (Pp. 8–9)

This recurrent theme of using language both for writer-based prose and reader-based prose appears, as Martin Nystrand (1977) suggests, in the work of a number of researchers—in addition to Britton, Vygotsky, and Flower and Hayes:

Researcher	Writer-Based Prose	Reader-Based Prose
Graves (1975)	reactive writer	reflective writer
Emig (1971)	reflexive	extensive
Sapir (1961)	expressive	referential
Polanyi (1958)	heuristic act	routine performance
Nystrand (1977)	heuristic act (accommodatory)	explicative investigation (assimilatory)
Flavell (1977)	private-cognitive	social-communicative
Krashen (1979)	subconscious language learning (acquired language)	conscious language learning (monitor language)
Olson (in press)	conversational utterance; interpersonal, ideational	prose text; rhetorical, logical
Bobrow and Norman (1975)	data driven process	concept driven process
Bereiter (1979)	associative writing	communicative and epistemic writing

The *processing* approach, then, has two research traditions—one describing the mental map maker—speed, storage limits, and organizing principles—and the other describing processing strategies for the writer, one set of strategies assuming a stage or developmental process and another set assuming that writing is recursive or a shifting back and forth among different areas of attention. In the classroom, *processing* has two main methods: one that emphasizes the *steps* in the writing process and another that emphasizes *visual and verbal maps* that students can use in their writing.

Steps Method

In the classroom, the steps method means that not all writing is graded as a final draft. Students are taught to use writing as an instrument for self-discovery, not just as a means of communicating something to someone else. Therefore, students are given extensive practice in prewriting, simply filling a page in order to learn how writing helps them discover what they know, what they do not know, and, in fact, what they want to write about. They are not expected to write a thesis and an outline *before* they have written something; writing is considered a means of discovering one's thesis and organization. The workshop approach of Ken Macrorie (1970, 1973) is a useful guide for getting the class organized and underway. Peter Elbow (1973) helps clarify the distinction between prewriting and garbage.

This prewriting, in journals or otherwise, is a regular assignment and can become the resource for more focused assignments, such as Notion papers of one or two pages on a single idea or event. The Notion papers become the resources for Submission papers of two or three pages on a single idea or event. Submission papers are read in writing groups, and students respond to the papers they hear, confirming strengths and offering suggestions for change. Semi-final papers are sometimes read by an outside adult whom the student must recruit as a reader, and Final papers are read by the writing group before being handed in to the teacher. The separation of the writing task into different steps is one way of overcoming the limits of working memory. Do not do everything at once. Do different things in different drafts.

Students have the option of doing as many drafts as they wish, but they must keep a portfolio of all of their work and must submit a minimum number of final drafts for each marking period. Class time, then, is spent writing papers, discussing papers, or organizing one's portfolio. All Final papers are posted in the room (unless it is a personal paper with a specific request for privacy) and later posted on bulletin boards in the school library, in the hallway, in the administrative offices, and sometimes outside the school.

Vincent Wixon and Patty Stone [Wixon] (1977), following Robert Zoellner's description of the talk-write approach (1969), pair students into teams of two, giving each team a felt-tip pen and a section of butcher paper, and assign each team a composition problem—memory writing, argument, exposition, whatever. One student may be assigned to be the writer and the other the editor, or both students may share responsibilities as they write the composition together. Students who cannot get started may get help by watching another team work. Students who finish early can help teams that are having difficulty. In all cases, students are talking out their ideas and then writing and revising. The butcher paper makes it possible for students to watch their compositions develop.

One of the most effective methods of developing revising skills is the writing group. Mary K. Healy (1980) tapes students in groups as they read and comment on student papers; then she plays the tapes in class for discussion. Daniel Fader (1976), in a writing class at the University of Michigan, puts students into groups of three, selecting for a range of interests and abilities. On each paper he gives a grade for the writer and the two editors. The result, says Fader, is that the members of the group become dependent on each other and are constantly sharpening each other's perceptions. How to select members of these groups, how to ease the group through early troubles, how to use the tapes to sharpen editing skills—these are problems that need more examination.

The postwriting step is also a very important feature of the steps method. Preparing class magazines, posting papers in the room and hallways, reading papers aloud, presenting certificates of merit for special recognition on a work of writing—any activity that gives the student writer a response to a final draft contributes to better writing. Another important feature in the steps method is the development of heuristics that help students learn to use language as an instrument for discovery. For example, Richard E. Young and Alton Becker (1975) believe that for anyone to know something, whether concrete or abstract, three questions are especially helpful: (1) How does the thing or event differ from everything else? (2) How much can it change and still be itself? (3) How does it fit into larger systems of which it is a part? One of the most common heuristics in writing is the "reporter's guide": who, what, when, where, how, and why. Richard Larson (1968) has developed an elaborate set of questions organized into such categories as "abstract concepts," "completed events," and "collection of items." Larson believes that questioning procedures help students state propositions because the questions "force students to become as familiar as possible with the facts, and possible relationships among the facts" (p. 128). A teacher cannot assume that young writers have propositions ready to be argued. Yet, says Larson, classical rhetoric did assume the proposition was ready and waiting only for the means of persuasion:

> If there is one critical difference between the treatment of "invention" by classical rhetoricians and by the authors of texts on "rhetoric" today, it is this: for the classical rhetoricians "invention" is one step in what Aristotle called "finding the available means of persuasion in a given case." (P. 126)

The aim of heuristics is to study the methods and rules of discovery and invention, especially heuristic reasoning, which is, says Michael Polanyi (1958), "provisional and plausible only, whose purpose is to discover the solution of the present problem." Janice Lauer (1970) reports that psychologists interested in problem solving have found that "creative people have developed an effective set of heuristic procedures" (p. 396). One cannot find in this literature, however, much that is directly useful for composition teachers. The application of heuristics in the teaching of writing means prewriting assignments, questioning procedure, and sometimes comparison and contrast (for a discussion of comparison and contrast, see Lee Odell, 1977).

One of the primary rhetorical and psychological issues is whether or not heuristics means think-write, or write-write, or even talk-write. Think-write sees mental reflection as a prerequisite to writing, while write-write and talk-write see the act of speaking or writing as the act of thinking. The last position is taken by Zoellner (1969), a view that Young (1976) calls "a provocative alternative, and a radical one since it repudiates mentalism itself" (p. 36).

Zoellner's assumption that talking and writing *are* thinking underlies most of the practices in the steps method: giving writing assignments that move students from journals to drafts to final assignments; organizing writing groups that discuss papers at various stages of completion; discussing writing topics in class or small groups prior to writing; providing a list of questions that can help the writer or group explore the possibilities of a topic; keeping folders of all student writing; and organizing postwriting activities such as publishing, posting, and displaying the writing, reading samples aloud to the class, and sending the writing to a selected audience.

Sometimes teachers identify some axioms for students to follow in their writing: "Do not worry about spelling and punctuation when you first start writing your paper," "Just start writing, beginning with a phrase like 'I am writing about,'" and "As you write, ask yourself 'Who, what, when, where, why.'" In class, students are asked to share the various devices they use when they write. The purpose of the axioms is not so much the general rules themselves as the development among students of metacognitive awareness, a recognition that there are two types of knowledge—knowledge about things and knowledge about how to know. The various steps methods attempt to teach students that one can learn how to remember and how to discover things with language.

The Map Method

The map method is a second example of the *processing* approach. Maps can take many forms. One form is the outlandish assignment, which students can reject if they find a topic of their own. Some students seem not to know what they want to write about until they are told what they must write. In a sense, some students do not see the truth until they are told something outlandish, and then they see the truth shining through the nonsense. The story lessons used at Circle Pre-School in Oakland, California, for example, often include the "Mix-Up Monster"—a familiar character in group presentations who confuses hello and goodbye, shakes feet instead of hands, calls children by the wrong names, and tells stories such as "The Big Green Rooster" (instead of "The Little Red Hen") or "Goldilocks and the Three Pigs." The children love to correct him, dictating back to the Mix-Up Monster the correct word, phrase, sentence, or story. The children's joy in the game comes from the shock of recognizing what they know—it is hands that shake, not feet, for example—when they hear obvious nonsense.

The verb can be a helpful map for students, one that they can either reject or accept. Miles (1979) argues that it is the predicate that shapes and moves the writing, not the noun. In other words, *My home town* is not a topic for an essay, but *My home town stinks* is. *Stinks* shapes the material into some organization, some movement of assertion. The bigness or smallness of an assertion is determined by the predicate, not the noun. Thus, Kansas is not inevitably a larger topic than Kansas City.

Teachers who write suggested topics on the board should consider including a predicate. Sometimes students are better able to find their own predicates if they are required to write the first paragraph without using *was, is, were, are,* or some other form of the verb *to be.* To be has a tendency to lead many students in circles, turning the writing into a list of characteristics without direction or any central tendency. Without *to be* as a crutch, students are forced to make assertions that begin to give the writing direction and shape. Like the children responding to the Mix-Up Monster, students sometimes discover predicates better if they have a predicate to reject, such as *Oakland High is the most beautiful place on earth.*

Many teachers believe that a student's ability to predicate or frame a world view depends on skills in mapping, graphing, and using visual and verbal metaphors. These teachers have explored assignments in metaphor, analogy, and visual design as a way of developing skills in ordering and conceptualizing material. Many secondary teachers have used Hart Day Leavitt and David Sohn's *Stop, Look, and Write* and *Pictures for Writing,* and elementary teachers have used various "art projects" to get the writing going. Drawing for the elementary student is often a map for the writing. Graves (1975) has observed that drawing for the young writer is often not only prewriting—a first draft of the idea—but also a practical necessity for retaining the idea. A child who is writing slowly and with difficulty needs a drawing to retain a memory of the writing's central theme.

Some teachers give students particular techniques for making visual maps. For example, in idea brainstorming, teachers often use a wheel technique (see Figure 2) with one theme at the center and various student contributions in boxes or circles around the center. For narrative discussions (what happens when?), a linear design is often used. An example appears in Figure 3. In the Christensen (1976) approach to paragraph organization, a kind of visual outline is used to make paragraph structure clear:

Coordinate Paragraphs	Subordinate Paragraphs	Mixed
1	1	1
2	2	2
2	3	3
2	4	2
2	5	3
		4
		2

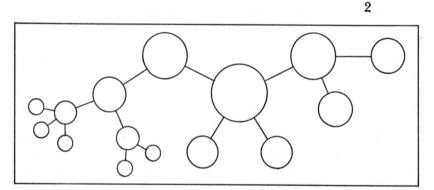

Figure 2. Wheel technique.

In summary, the *processing* approach, as illustrated by the steps and maps methods, provides many classroom lessons using language as an instrument of discovery. In addition, some students seem to have special needs for the *processing* approach. The following essay was written by a ninth-grade student during a fifty-minute class period:

> The person I remember the best was my bestfriend in elementary school she also live up the street from me. She had just move from Danvill. Her dog got lose and I helped her catch him.
> I new her for along time until she move. We still try to keep in touch. But I will never foreget the memories.

The paper has many problems, the most critical of which is fluency. The student should be able to write much more in a fifty-minute period, given the fact that he will "never foreget the memories" (what memories?) and that this person is someone he remembers "the best." The assumption is that prewriting, talking in writing groups, and experimenting with various maps and heuristics (who? what? when? where? why?) will help develop fluency and help break the bottleneck of limited storage capacity in working memory. Any teacher with many students who lack fluency in their writing should consider giving primary emphasis to *processing* approaches.

Distancing: Writing as a Relationship between Speaker and Subject and between Speaker and Audience

Distancing approaches shift the emphasis from text and strategies to the social context. In this approach, teachers organize assignments around the distance between the student-writer and the audience and between the student-writer and the subject. If the student talks to himself or herself, the result is an interior dialogue, a monologue, or diary. If the student talks to an alter ego, the result might be a journal, and a personal message to a friend could be a personal letter. Shifts in the distance from the speaker to the subject can produce similar changes in

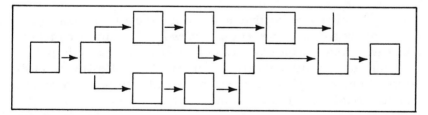

Figure 3. Linear technique.

form. For instance, writing on a close personal subject could result in an autobiography, while a more distant subject could become a biography.

The study of *distancing* leads to a different theoretical framework. *Modeling* has had classical transformational grammar as one of its theoretical frameworks, and Chomsky (1965) has made explicit the theoretical boundaries of that discipline:

> Linguistic theory is concerned primarily with an ideal speaker-listener, in a completely homogenous speech community, who knows its language perfectly and is unaffected by such grammatically irrelevant conditions as memory limitation, distractions, shifts of attention and interest, and errors (random or characteristic) in applying his knowledge of the language in actual performance. (P. 3)

Processing, on the other hand, has had cognitive psychology and the writer's mental map maker as its theoretical framework. Some *modeling* theorists did, of course, contribute to the development of cognitive theory. Chomsky, for instance, distinguished between competence and performance, the underlying language knowledge and the actual word strings spoken or written. Competence and underlying knowledge are a step toward a cognitive theory. But according to I. M. Schlessinger (1971), cognitive theory, unlike classical transformational grammar, includes in its framework the intention behind language performance.

> There is no place for intentions in a grammar, but any theory of performance which fails to take intentions into account must be considered inadequate. The model of a human speaker must, of course, contain rules that determine the grammatical structure of the output. These rules, however, must be assumed to operate on an input which represents the speaker's intentions. (P. 65)

Problem-solving strategies, Gagne's learning hierarchies, which include moving from simple tasks to more complex ones in such matters as adding and subtracting (Gagne et al., 1962), and Piaget's analysis of various tasks, such as those requiring conservation, are all examples of efforts to describe intentions by describing the hypothetical maps that guide learners.

Some theorists, arguing that neither linguistic behavior nor cognitive maps are adequate theoretical frameworks for language production, have introduced the *sociocultural context,* particularly the participant interactions within the context. Breyne Arlene Moskowitz (1978) describes one example of the evidence leading theorists to revised notions about language acquisition:

> A boy with normal hearing but with deaf parents who communicated by the American Sign Language was exposed to television

every day so that he could learn English. Because the child was asthmatic and was confined to his home, he interacted only with people at home where his family and all their visitors communicated in sign language. By the age of three he was fluent in sign language but neither understood nor spoke English. It appears that in order to learn a language a child must also be able to interact with real people in that language. (Pp. 94–94B)

Jerome Bruner (1978) summarizes how the context theory moved away from Chomsky's views:

It has become plain in the last several years that Chomsky's original bold claim that any sample of language encountered by an infant was enough for the LAD (Language Acquisition Device) to dig down to the grammatical rules is simply false. Language is not encountered willy-nilly by the child; it is instead encountered in a highly orderly interaction with the mother, who takes a crucial role in arranging the linguistic encounters of the child. What has emerged is a theory of mother-infant interaction in language acquisition—called the fine tuning theory—that sees language mastery as involving the mother as much as it does the child. According to this theory, if the LAD exists, it hovers somewhere in the air between mother and child. (Pp. 44)

The same theoretical framework is shared by pragmatics, the linguistic point of view that context generates structure. Robin Lakeoff, in a recent lecture on the University of California at Berkeley campus, commented that if generative semanticists had known where their ideas would lead, they would have called their field generative pragmatics. Transformational grammar had difficulty finding some structural explanation for such language as "Will you please pass the butter?" This structure looks like a question, but in social context this structure is a request or even a command. The social context must then be recognized as generating meaning, just as trees from base clauses generated meaning in the old grammar.

The social context has a writer, an audience, a reality, and a message. In rhetorical theory, James Kinneavy (1971) has arranged these four elements in a communication triangle as the framework for his views (see Figure 4). The forms of discourse are shaped by the intentions of the writer and the part of the triangle that gets emphasized, as shown in the following listing.

Purpose	Emphasis	Resulting Discourse
self-expression	writer	expressive (diaries, journals)
convince or persuade	audience	persuasive (editorials, sermons)

convey reality	reality	referential
		(articles, histories)
ordering parts of texts	message	literary
		(drama, songs)

In James Moffett's theory (1968b), discourse is shaped by the distance between the writer and the subject matter. If the writer is focusing on what is happening now, then the form generated is drama and the writer-role is one of recording the "event." If the focus is on what happened, then the form generated is narrative and the writer-role is reporting. Notice that the sequence increases the distance in time and space between the speaker and subject—increasing space because generalizing requires a point of view overlooking all, and increasing time because generalizing requires the temporal shifts from present to past to future.

Distancing assignments are often based on the assumption that writing to a close audience—a friend, an alter ego as in a diary—is a natural place to begin for the young who are, by nature, egocentric. Extending the distance of the audience in a sequence of assignments, moving from writing to a friend to writing for the community at large, requires both a decrease in egocentrism, a natural development as the young mature, and an increase in the child's skills in abstraction, a greater sophistication in selecting what to say and what not to say. This sequence parallels Piaget's findings (1959) about child development and Moffett's theory of discourse. Moffett calls his theory "essentially an hallucination" and says, "Heaven forbid that it should be 'translated' into textbooks." Nevertheless, teacher intuition has developed several sequences that are compatible with both Piaget's and Moffett's theories:

1. From improvisations to panels and trials, in which roles are shifted, developing different distances to subjects

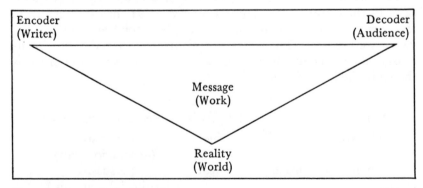

Figure 4. Communication triangle.

2. From journals and diaries to letters and autobiographical incidents, moving the audience from oneself to others and developing a spectator point of view toward one's own experience

3. From interviews and reports to Socratic dialogues and arguments, moving to an anonymous audience in the world-at-large and acting as spectator to the experience of others

The distance from speaker to audience determines questions like diction, punctuation, style, form. A friend requires one logic, a mass audience another. So, too, as noted earlier, does distance from speaker to subject change form. If the speaker records things as if they are happening now, the result is drama. A report of what happened yesterday is narrative. And if the two measures of distance are crossed—writing to a close friend about something that happened in the past—then the juncture produces a particular form—the personal, narrative letter. Assignments compatible with Moffett's theories move students along these two measures of distance. These assignments also create an interacting context in the classroom. Exposition, for example, can begin with two students writing a Socratic dialogue, one on each side of a controversial question. The two students write out their assertions as if they were speaking to each other, handing the paper back and forth, countering each other's arguments. Then the two students review the arguments in their script and, taking one side or the other, write an argumentative essay to the general public of the local community. Argument can also begin as a mock trial or a debate, and biographies can begin as interviews written as scripts.

James Britton's taxonomy of expressive, transactional, and expressive poetic writing (Britton et al., 1975) emphasizes the importance of beginning with personal experience. His view, one that overlaps much of Moffett's work, is that expressive writing (the writing about experience as an expression of self) is basic to any adequate development of skills in transactional writing (writing to convey information to someone) and expressive poetic writing (writing to create a work of art, an object for its own sake). Britton found in London schools an overemphasis on transactional writing and a failure to provide adequate opportunities for expressive writing. He also found that the assignments were weighted heavily toward a teacher-examiner audience.

Some teachers believe that although American schools may emphasize transactional writing in subjects outside English, in English classes the emphasis is on personal writing to close personal audiences. Some teachers report, for example, that in many schools using Moffett's materials, the students always start the sequence again at the beginning of each secondary grade level and never reach assignments in reports or argument.

But Britton et al. (1975) do not decry an emphasis on personal writing. They believe that language production, particularly in writing, whatever the mode, teaches students symbolic skills. In effect, they believe that cognitive theory and contextual theory are not that far apart. If one is producing language in interactions, one is producing maps and symbolic representations in the head. "Language, then," say Britton et al., "is only one way of representing experience, but plays a key role as a means of organizing and storing representations in other modes" (p. 78).

These means of organizing and representing experience have been identified in studies of literary devices. Mark Schorer (1952), for example, describes how a literary technique is both a means of representing and discovering. He describes Emily Brontë as a writer who attempts in *Wuthering Heights* to "lay before us the full character of this passion, to show how it first comes into being and then comes to dominate the world" (p. 193). "This passion" is the love affair of Heathcliff and Cathy. But I feel Brontë has to protect herself from the incrimination, particularly from a minister father and conventional readers who might laugh if they were to see Heathcliff up close, banging his head against a tree. Brontë's solution is to use the very conventional Lockwood as the narrator, and then to screen much of what Lockwood knows through Nellie Dean, the very straight-laced maid. The reader can take the emotional rages of Heathcliff and Cathy as the editorial excesses of Lockwood and Nellie, who would be shocked at anything. Furthermore, Brontë buries the entire story in the past, helping contemporaries to accept what in the present would have been considered "uncivilized" behavior. The selection of the narrative and time helped to tell the story and to protect the author, but later the techniques become a means of discovery for the author. Pushing the events into the past and selecting a narrator different from oneself helps to objectify events. Brontë discovers that Heathcliff and Cathy need the modifications of the conventional world represented by Lockwood and Nellie. Students, too, can use different narrations both to understand their own experience and to hide from the reader when they tell the story. Halfway through the book, Brontë drops Cathy (Cathy dies) and pushes Heathcliff to the background.

One problem in the *distancing* approach is that the teacher does not have easily available a diversity of real audiences and must depend on "pretend" audiences: "Imagine that you are writing to . . ." To meet the need for diversity of audience and new subject matter, many teachers have begun to consider how the community can be used as part of the school curriculum—every parent agreeing to read a letter and respond in some way, student reports on the trial at the local courthouse, neighborhood surveys, and so forth. My impression is that teachers are hungry for writing assignments that use community resources in a manageable fashion, and many useful teaching materials are becoming available (Dandridge et al., 1979).

A second problem, the transition from narration to exposition, is particularly critical in junior high, although high school teachers have had their share of this problem. Students can learn to write rather well on personal subjects to distant audiences. But the shift to distant audiences has an influence on topic selection. For example, "Why I should receive an increase in my allowance" is not an appropriate topic for readers of the *Atlantic Monthly,* unless one is writing satire or using the "I" as a generalizable persona, but "Why teenagers should receive increases in their allowance" is appropriate. The distant audience requires a topic with wider interest among readers. And because the wider interest requires a topic less personal and more general, the student must have some information about teenagers in general in order to generalize about allowances. The greater the distance between writer and audience, the less egocentric the writer must be to bridge the gap.

Reports in junior high on states of the nation, cattle in Argentina, and flax in Egypt are legendary examples of the transitions from close to distant subjects. Year after year these reports pour in. One week the students are writing stories, personal and interesting; the next week they are writing reports, dull and uninspired. What happened in the transition?

Northrop Frye (1957), as Moffett notes, is helpful here. He describes our heroes as first the supernatural or divine, then the mortal who is also miraculous, next the king or exceptional person, and finally the average person and the anti-hero. The sequence parallels what teachers find in student interest: first the fairy tales and talking animals; next the exceptional mortals who can do the miraculous—Spider Man, Bionic Woman, Batman, Wonder Woman; then the heroes like Willie Mays, Julius Erving, Chris Evert Lloyd, and the astronauts; and finally the average person like Mark and Janet or the family in *Sounder,* and the anti-herolike characters from Hemingway and Camus, the latter usually only evident in the eleventh or twelfth grades.

This sequence helps us understand what goes wrong in the transition to expository writing. Young children, beginning as they do with the supernatural, can project their own fantasies into the story and focus their attention on form. Everyone is aware that young children want a favorite story read over and over again, and they will object if the slightest change is made. The pleasure is not in the "facts" of the events. The pleasure is in the form, the opening, "Once upon a time," and the predictable closing, "and they lived happily ever after." In their own writing, young children often finish off their stories by writing in big letters "The End."

The junior high student who is asked to do a report on cattle in Argentina or the history of refrigeration (see Janet Emig, 1971, appendix) is being asked to do two things at once, both of them often new experiences. The student first must write, in a new form, the argument or report, and, second, must attend to "facts" outside an immediate personal experience and put both feet in the "real" world—how many cattle are there in Argentina? But junior high students' natural interests in reading, falling somewhere between *Star Wars* and .James Bond, still allow room enough for personal fantasies so that they do not have to be responsible for real world "facts." *Star Wars* requires one foot in the real world and one foot in dreams and fantasies—very much like the fantasy heroes. Wonder Woman looks mortal—one foot in reality—but she can fly.

One solution is an assignment designed for one foot in the real world and one foot in fantasies. One social studies teacher accomplishes this with an assignment in which the students are told they are going on a cross-country wagon train trip in 1840 and must invent the character they will be on the trip. They can be the Wagon Master, the Gambler, the Cook, the Minister, the Scout—anybody. On the first day they put in their journals their invented names and biographies. On each day thereafter they enter in their journals a description of that day's journey. For instance, on Tuesday the class went from Joplin, Missouri, to Denver, Colorado. Each member was required to use the names of real towns, rivers, mountains, tribes, whatever, in that day's entry. The entry was a fantasy of that day's events, but it had the names of real places. It had to be a convincing lie. In this way, the student is held responsible for "facts," but at the same time is given room for fantasy.

Another solution to this problem of distance to subject matter is to assign students the form and allow any subject whatsoever, no matter how bizarre. In fact, maybe the more bizarre, the better: Why the CIA is presently investigating the school principal, the evidence that extraterrestrial life is now listed on the rolls of the sophomore class, the reasons for the giraffe's long neck. These and other such topics have produced interesting and well-developed arguments. My personal favorite is "Hamlet's problem is overweight," using as evidence the line "Oh, that this too too solid flesh would melt" and others like it. Because the "facts" are beyond dispute, the student can concentrate solely on coherence of form and readability of style. Later, students can do global studies on parking patterns in the school parking lot, the biggest sellers in the school cafeteria, why students get suspended, and student opinions, using polls and surveys.

These subjects obviously bring the "facts" closer to the student's reality, but the student is allowed, even encouraged, to generalize to the student population as a whole and the universe, if need be. Many of the "facts" in such reports are student whim, despite the appearance of data in graphs and charts. I, for one, still doubt that the burritos in the student cafeteria are made out of rat gut.

Asking students to imagine a scene from another point in space is another way to teach *distancing*. Children can be given practice in estimating how spatial arrangements might look from different points of view. One task frequently used to assess children's ability to coordinate visual perspectives involves a miniature landscape with mountains or other large obstructions that can block off certain objects, such as some miniature animals, from the view of a doll placed at a particular point in the tableau. Young children are rarely able to give an accurate assessment of what the doll sees and may respond as if the doll's perspective were the same as their own. The hypothesis is that the children's performance reflects their egocentric thinking (Laurendeau and Pinard, 1970).

I have found that some high school students have difficulty with a similar problem and enjoy trying to write paragraphs explaining what first one point of view might see and then what a different point of view might see. I have stacked things on a lazy Susan at the front of the room—books, pencils, chalk, and whatnot—and, after turning the lazy Susan so that all students see all sides, have stopped the display at a particularly complicated point and asked the students to describe what a student just entering the room would see.

One of the conceptual problems in *distancing* approaches is whether to define writing development as a shift from one mode to another (from oral to written language, for instance) or as a shift from one speech event to another. In the former view, the emphasis is on talk first and writing later and on such rules as "Do not write it the way you say it." In speech-event shifts, the emphasis is on different kinds of talk, conversational first and presentations and ritual later. Speech-event shifts emphasize social context and argue that conversation is not a single mode like oral language but a social form that can occur in both oral and written language. In fact, conversations, according to speech-event theory, have a set of rules that participants must follow. One recent study suggests that a central problem for students writing high school proficiency exams is the selection of the appropriate speech event (M. Myers, 1982). Conversational rules can result in composition failure in such an exam, even though most students are not aware that their conversations have rules. A teaching approach based on speech events might provide students with explicit knowledge about the different rules governing different speech events. Such an approach is only in its preliminary stages and has not as yet been developed.

The following essay was written by a student who would benefit from *distancing* approaches, particularly assignments showing the difference between the rules of conversations and the rules of presentations. The student was asked to write an essay to a general audience on the subject of a favorite person. The student's opening line establishes a letter or oral context instead of a setting for formal, written exposition.

> Hi there! My friend's name is _____. She was born in Hong Kong. She was sixteen years old. This year she was in 10th grade. She was a real smart girl. And she had a big family. You know what I mean!!
>
> In that time I was very happy living with _____ pretty often. She was very friendly and industrious, honest, kinda quiet. Even though she was my real good friend. When I was in Hong Kong I always went to school with _____. We are the same grade. After school she always came to my home to study and helped me. On the weekend we went to the restaurant and went to the theater. We had fun every day sorta.
>
> After that I was very happy. When I came to the U.S. _____ gave me a beautiful jacket for me, and say goodbye. Since she was my good friend. I always send the letters to her. And she sent me a letter that she was very bored. Time passed very quickly. I hoped I'll go back to Hong Kong and have fun with _____ again. I've enjoyed working with my real good friend in Hong Kong.
>
> It was a wonderful day. Really great!!!
>
> Love

Conclusion

Each of the three approaches to composition—*processing, distancing,* and *modeling*—has a long history in the research and teaching of writing, providing coherent theoretical frameworks that can be used to test the findings of both researchers and teachers. The researcher must meet the tests of theoretical consistency and methodological requirements. The research may give clues for teachers to explore, but the researcher cannot provide rules or lesson plans for teachers. The teacher searches for the objective truth of a teaching approach by using the tests of consistency with experience, including both intuition and the various ways of assessing student response, and consistency with a recognizable theory. Theory helps teachers determine whether their intuitions are objectively reasonable. The teacher's findings can provide many valuable clues for testing the validity of researchers' findings.

There is some overlap between the different theoretical approaches to composition. Cognitive psychology has provided a valuable theoretical framework for understanding how *processing* strategies work. But rhetorical studies (Christensen's work, for instance) have been used by cognitive psychologists as a perspective for understanding the *models* that shape the mental maps and guide the mental executive organizers. Some of these maps and executive organizers define relationships among speaker, subject, and audience, and the theoretical framework for defining these *distancing* relationships comes largely from anthropology, pragmatics, and literary criticism.

Many practices also overlap. Writing to an audience has both a *processing* function (the words often flow more easily in social interaction) and a *distancing* function. Imitation of texts has both a *modeling* function (the student is modeling the patterns in the text) and a *distancing* function (the student is adopting a particular point of view). The best classroom techniques probably include all three approaches. Writing groups and a classroom publication program are two ways to combine approaches. Both techniques encourage discussion of the ideas (*processing*), provide an actual audience that one can study (*distancing*), and generate a variety of student models that other students can imitate (*modeling*).

Part Two: Processing

Introduction to Processing

The articles in this section examine three *processing* questions that have been of concern to researchers and practitioners: (1) How does memory work in the writing process? (2) How do children draw? (3) What are the parts of the writing process? What is evident from the three pairs of articles is that the findings of practitioners and researchers, although related, are markedly different. For instance, although Gail Siegel's stages of writing practice are consistent with the research tradition illustrated by the work of D. Gordon Rohman, Siegel's suggested practices and number of classroom steps are quite different from Rohman's. And even though Marilyn Hanf Buckley and Owen Boyle base their suggestions, in part, on the tradition of memory research summarized by Herbert A. Simon, the suggestions of Buckley and Boyle represent a different type of knowledge from that of Simon. Furthermore, neither Siegel nor Buckley and Boyle base their suggestions entirely on research findings. Their experiences as teachers have at least an equal weight (and probably a greater weight) in their conclusions about useful and workable teaching strategies.

How Does Memory Work in the Writing Process?

The research on human memory, as Herbert A. Simon reports in "The Psychology of Thinking," reveals that human beings do not always discover for themselves clever strategies for thinking about a subject and do not always have sufficient means for storing information. Simon also indicates that only a limited amount of information can be stored in short-term memory. Marilyn Hanf Buckley and Owen Boyle, in "Mapping and Composing," present a classroom solution for the memory problem in writing—slowing the task down and providing a strategy for thinking and a means for retaining information. Their mapping approach presented here shows how chunking can be taught in the classroom, thereby helping to solve one of the problems that students have when they write.

How Do Children Draw?

The child first learns to make marks on paper by drawing what Rhoda Kellogg, in a selection from "Understanding Children's Art," calls Basic Scribbles, and from these Basic Scribbles evolve abstract designs, pictures, and letters. Says Kellogg, "Children who have been free to experiment with and produce abstract esthetic forms have already developed the mental set required for symbolic language" (p. 176).

Drawing can also help the young child solve the problem of information overload. For example, Donald Graves (1975) has observed that many children use drawing as a prewriting activity:

> For many children drawing was a major step in the prewriting phase. Michael, the case study chosen for reporting, apparently needed to draw before he was able to write in the composing phase. As he drew he would talk, often making appropriate sound effects to go along with the figure being drawn at the moment. While drawing the dinosaur . . ., Michael made growling noises to simulate the dinosaur's presence. To aid the recording of such data the observer reproduced the drawing, at the same time numbered each operation to indicate the sequence in which the picture evolved. Notable behaviors that accompanied each step were also recorded.
>
> As soon as Michael completed his drawing, he started to write about information contained in the picture. At this juncture he began the composing phase. (P. 231)

Children's art is, then, a record of thought and information, but Rudolf Arnheim (1969) reminds us that it is also a record of other things, including muscle development:

> If one wishes to trace visual thinking in the images of art, one must look for well-structured shapes and relations, which characterize concepts and their applications. They are readily found in work done at early levels of mental development, for example, in the drawings of children. This is so because the young mind operates with elementary forms, which are easily distinguished from the complexity of the objects they depict. To be sure, children often give only rough approximations of the shapes and spatial relations they intend to depict. They may lack skill or have not actively explored the advantages of well-defined patterns. Also, children draw and paint and model not only for the reasons that interest us here particularly. They like to exert and exercise their muscles, rhythmically or wildly; they like to see something appear where nothing was before, especially if it stimulates the senses by strong color or a flurry of shapes; they also like to defile, to attack, to destroy. They imitate what they see elsewhere. All this leaves its traces and keeps a child's picture from being always a neat record of his thought. (P. 255)

In Celeste Myers's description of drawing experiences in preschool, "Drawing as Prewriting in Preschool," the children move from drawing to dictated stories, to playing with plastic letters, and to writing words of their own in their own spelling. Carol Chomsky (1972, 1974) has suggested that children should write before they begin reading:

> If we concede that word recognition, or even just the sounding out of words, appears so much more difficult for children than composing words, why do our reading programs as a matter of course expect children to deal with it first? The natural order is writing first, then reading what you have written. To expect the child to read, as a first step, what someone else has written is backwards, an artificial imposition that denies the child an active role in the whole process. Moreover it takes all the fun out of it. *He* ought to be directing his activities and making the decisions, not you. He ought to pick the words and write them, with your guidance. Or, if you suggest the words, as you will sometimes do, he ought to know that it is up to him to come up with his own spellings. (1972, p. 120)

What teachers need to learn, if they do not already know it, is that invented spelling can be read and can be outgrown. "I kan spil wurdz" does become, in time, "I can spell words."

What Are the Parts of the Writing Process?

D. Gordon Rohman, in "Pre-Writing: The Stage of Discovery in the Writing Process," breaks the writing process into three parts (prewriting, writing, rewriting), and Gail Siegel, in "From Speech to Writing," uses five stages in her lessons (oral language, prewriting, group writing, individual writing, and sharing/rethinking). Siegel's last stage is sometimes called postwriting, the activities that occur after the actual writing is done. Rohman's work has inspired much interest among researchers in prewriting, and in recent years the postwriting stage has become increasingly important to teachers.

In addition to focusing on process while writing is taking place in a single piece, as did D. Gordon Rohman and Gail Siegel, Lester S. Golub, in "Stimulating and Receiving Children's Writing: Implications for an Elementary Writing Curriculum," provides a second perspective—to focus on the writing process throughout several years of a child's life. This developmental perspective shows that the writing problem is not the same at all ages.

2 The Psychology of Thinking

Herbert A. Simon

Herbert A. Simon presents a mathematical problem and discusses several ways of discovering the solution to the problem, showing that the combined system of search and reason, with an emphasis on reason, is the best problem-solving system. In the excerpt that follows, Simon turns to an examination of the bounds and limits on human performance. Ed.

Let us undertake to state in positive fashion just what we think these bounds and limits are, as revealed by behavior in problem situations like this one. In doing so, we shall draw upon both experimental evidence and evidence derived from computer simulations of human performance. The evidence refers to a variety of cognitive tasks, ranging from relatively complex ones (cryptarithmetic, chess, theorem proving), through an intermediate one (concept attainment), to simple ones that have been favorites of the psychological laboratory (rote verbal learning, short-term memory span). It is important that with this great variety of performance only a small number of limits on the adaptability of the inner system reveal themselves—and these are essentially the same limits over all the tasks. Thus the statement of what these limits are purports to provide a single, consistent explanation of human performance over this whole range of heterogeneous task environments.

Limits on Speed of Concept Attainment

Extensive psychological research has been carried out on concept attainment within the following general paradigm.[1] The stimuli are a set of cards bearing simple geometric designs that vary, from card to

Source: Excerpt from "The Psychology of Thinking," in *The Sciences of the Artificial*, 2d ed., by Herbert A. Simon (Cambridge, Mass.: The MIT Press, 1981), pp. 72–98. © 1981 by The MIT Press. Reprinted with permission of the publisher. The notes have been renumbered.

card, along a number of dimensions: shape (square, triangle, circle), color, size, position of figure on card, and so on. A "concept" is defined extensionally by some set of cards—the cards that are instances of that concept. The concept is defined intensionally by a property that all the instances have in common but that is not possessed by any of the remaining cards. Examples of concepts are "yellow" or "square" (simple concepts), "green triangle" or "large, red" (conjunctive concepts), "small or yellow" (disjunctive concept), and so on.

In our discussion here I shall refer to experiments using an N-dimensional stimulus, with two possible values on each dimension, and with a single relevant dimension (simple concepts). On each trial an instance (positive or negative) is presented to the subject, who responds "Positive" or "Negative" and is reinforced by "Right" or "Wrong," as the case may be. In typical experiments of this kind, the subject's behavior is reported in terms of number of trials or number of erroneous responses before an error-free performance is attained. Some, but not all, experiments ask the subject also to report periodically the intensional concept (if any) being used as a basis for the responses.

The situation is so simple that, as in the cryptarithmetic problem, we can estimate a priori how many trials, on the average, a subject should need to discover the intended concept provided that the subject used the most efficient discovery strategy. On each trial, regardless of response, the subject can determine from the experimenter's reinforcement whether the stimulus was actually an instance of the concept or not. If it was an instance, the subject knows that one of the attribute values of the stimulus—its color, size, shape, for example—defines the concept. If it was not an instance, the subject knows that the *complement* of one of its attribute values defines the concept. In either case each trial rules out half of the possible simple concepts; and in a random sequence of stimuli each new stimulus rules out, on the average, approximately half of the concepts not previously eliminated. Hence the average number of trials required to find the right concept will vary with the logarithm of the number of dimensions in the stimulus.

If sufficient time were allowed for each trial (a minute, say, to be generous), and if the subject were provided with paper and pencil, any subject of normal intelligence could be taught to follow this most efficient strategy and would do so without much difficulty. As these experiments are actually run, subjects are not instructed in an efficient strategy, are not provided with paper and pencil, and take only a short time—typically four seconds, say—to respond to each successive stimulus. They also use many more trials to discover the correct concept than the number calculated from the efficient strategy. Although the experiment has not, to my knowledge, been run, it is fairly certain that, even with training, a subject who was required to respond in four seconds and not allowed paper and pencil would be unable to apply the efficient strategy.

What do these experiments tell us about human thinking? First, they tell us that human beings do not always discover for themselves clever strategies that they could readily be taught (watching a chess master play a duffer should also convince us of that). This is hardly a very startling conclusion, although it may be an instructive one. I shall return to it in a moment.

Second, the experiments tell us that human beings do not have sufficient means for storing information in memory to enable them to apply the efficient strategy unless the presentation of stimuli is greatly slowed down or the subjects are permitted external memory aids, or both. Since we know from other evidence that human beings have virtually unlimited semipermanent storage (as indicated by their ability to continue to store odd facts in memory over most of a lifetime), the bottleneck in the experiment must lie in the small amount of rapid-access storage (so-called short-term memory) available and the time required to move items from the limited short-term store to the large-scale long-term store.[2]

From evidence obtained in other experiments, it has been estimated that only some seven items (or perhaps as few as four) can be held in the fast, short-term memory and that perhaps as many as five to ten seconds are required to transfer an item from the short-term to the long-term store. To make these statements operational, we shall have to be more precise, presently, about the meaning of "item." For the moment let us assume that a simple concept is an item.

Even without paper and pencil a subject might be expected to apply the efficient strategy if (1) he was instructed in the efficient strategy and (2) he was allowed twenty or thirty seconds to respond to and process the stimulus on each trial. Since I have not run the experiment, this assertion stands as a prediction by which the theory may be tested.

Again the outcome may appear obvious to you, if not trivial. If so, I remind you that it is obvious only if you accept my general hypothesis: that in large part human goal-directed behavior simply reflects the shape of the environment in which it takes place; only a gross knowledge of the characteristics of the human information-processing system is needed to predict it. In this experiment the relevant characteristics appear to be (1) the capacity of short-term memory, measured in terms of number of items (or "chunks," as I shall call them); (2) the time required to fixate an item, or chunk, in long-term memory. In the next section I shall inquire as to how consistent these characteristics appear to be over a range of task environments. Before I do so, I want to make a concluding comment about subjects' knowledge of strategies and the effects of training subjects.

That strategies can be learned is hardly a surprising fact, nor that learned strategies can vastly alter performance and enhance its effectiveness. All educational institutions are erected on these premises. Their full implication has not always been drawn by psychologists who conduct experiments in cognition. Insofar as behavior is a function of learned technique rather than "innate" characteristics of the human information-processing system, our knowledge of behavior must be regarded as sociological in nature rather than psychological— that is, as revealing what human beings in fact learn when they grow up in a particular social environment. When and how they learn particular things may be a difficult question, but we must not confuse learned strategies with built-in properties of the underlying biological system.

The data that have been gathered, by Bartlett and in our own laboratory, on the cryptarithmetic task illustrate the same point. Different subjects do indeed apply different strategies in that task—both the whole range of strategies I sketched in the previous section and others as well. How they learned these, or how they discover them while performing the task, we do not fully know (see chapter 4 [of the Simon book]), although we know that the sophistication of the strategy varies directly with a subject's previous exposure to and comfort with mathematics. But apart from the strategies the only human characteristic that exhibits itself strongly in the cryptarithmetic task is the limited size of short-term memory. Most of the difficulties the subjects have in executing the more combinatorial strategies (and perhaps their general aversion to these strategies also) stem from the stress that such strategies place on short-term memory. Subjects get into trouble simply because they forget where they are, what assignments they have made previously, and what assumptions are implicit in assignments they have made conditionally. All of these difficulties would necessarily arise in a processor that could hold only a few chunks in short-term memory and that required more time than was available to transfer them to long-term memory.

The Parameters of Memory—Five Seconds per Chunk

If a few parameters of the sort we have been discussing are the main limits of the inner system that reveal themselves in human cognitive behavior, then it becomes an important task for experimental psychology to estimate the values of these parameters and to determine how variable or constant they are among different subjects and over different tasks.

Apart from some areas of sensory psychology, the typical experimental paradigms in psychology are concerned with hypothesis testing rather than parameter estimating. In the reports of experiments one can find many assertions that a particular parameter value is—or is not—"significantly different" from another but very little comment on the values themselves. As a matter of fact the pernicious practice is sometimes followed of reporting significance levels, or results of the analysis of variance, without reporting at all the numerical values of the parameters that underlie these inferences.

While I am objecting to publication practices in experimental psychology, I shall add another complaint. Typically little care is taken in choosing measures of behavior that are the most relevant to theory. Thus in learning experiments "rate of learning" is reported, almost indifferently, in terms of "number of *trials* to criterion," "total number of *errors*," "total *time* to criterion," and perhaps other measures as well. Specifically the practice of reporting learning rates in terms of trials rather than time, prevalent through the first half of this century, and almost up to the present time, not only hid from view the remarkable constancy of the parameter I am about to discuss but also led to much meaningless dispute over "one-trial" versus "incremental" learning.[3]

Ebbinghaus knew better. In his classic experiments on learning nonsense syllables, with himself as subject, he recorded both the number of repetitions and the amount of time required to learn sequences of syllables of different length. If you take the trouble to calculate it, you find that the *time per syllable* in his experiments works out to about ten to twelve seconds.[4]

I see no point in computing the figure to two decimal places—or even to one. The constancy here is a constancy to an order of magnitude, or perhaps to a factor of two—more nearly comparable to the constancy of the daily temperature, which in most places stays between 263° and 333° Kelvin, than to the constancy of the speed of light. There is no reason to be disdainful of a constancy to a factor of two. Newton's original estimates of the speed of sound contained a fudge factor of 30 percent (eliminated only a hundred years later), and today some of the newer physical "constants" for elementary particles are even more vague. Beneath any approximate, even very rough, constancy, we can usually expect to find a genuine parameter whose value can be defined accurately once we know what conditions we must control during measurement.

If the constancy simply reflected a parameter of Ebbinghaus—albeit one that held steady over several years—it would be more interesting to biography than psychology. But that is not the case. When we examine some of the Hull-Hovland experiments of the 1930's, as reported, for example, in Carl Hovland's chapter in S. S. Stevens' *Handbook*, we find again (after we calculate them, for trials are reported instead of times) times in the neighborhood of ten or fifteen seconds for college sophomores to fixate nonsense syllables of low meaningfulness by the serial anticipation method. When the drum speed increases (say from four seconds per syllable to two seconds per syllable), the number of trials to criterion increase proportionately, but the total learning time remains essentially constant.

There is a great deal of gold in these hills. If past nonsense-syllable experiments are re-examined from this point of view, many are revealed where the basic learning parameter is in the neighborhood of fifteen seconds per *syllable*. You can make the calculation yourself from the experiments reported, for example, in J. A. McGeoch's *Psychology of Human Learning*. B. R. Bugelski, however, seems to have been the first to make this parameter constancy a matter of public record and to have run experiments with the direct aim of establishing it.[5]

I have tried not to exaggerate how constant is "constant." On the other hand, efforts to purify the parameter measurement have hardly begun. We do know about several variables that have a major effect on the value, and we have a theoretical explanation of these effects that thus far has held up well.

We know that meaningfulness is a variable of great importance. Nonsense syllables of high association value and unrelated one-syllable words are learned in about one-third the time required for nonsense syllables of low association value. Continuous prose is learned in about one-third the time per word required for sequences of unrelated words. (We can get the latter figure also from Ebbinghaus' experiments in memorizing *Don Juan*. The times *per symbol* are roughly 10 percent of the corresponding times for nonsense syllables.)

We know that similarity—particularly similarity among stimuli— has an effect on the fixation parameter somewhat less than the effect of meaningfulness, and we can also estimate its magnitude on theoretical grounds.

The theory that has been most successful in explaining these and other phenomena reported in the literature on rote verbal learning is an information-processing theory, programmed as a computer simulation of human behavior, dubbed EPAM. Since EPAM has been reported at length in the literature, I shall not discuss it here, except for one point that is relevant to our analysis. The EPAM theory gives us a basis for understanding what a "chunk" is. A chunk is a maximal familiar substructure of the stimulus. Thus a nonsense syllable like "QUV" consists of the chunks "Q," "U," "V"; but the word "CAT" consists of a single chunk, since it is a highly familiar unit. EPAM postulates constancy in the time required to fixate a chunk. Empirically the constant appears to be about five seconds per chunk, or perhaps a little more. Virtually all the quantitative predictions that EPAM makes about the effects of meaningfulness, familiarity, and similarity upon learning speed follow from this conception of the chunk and of the constancy of the time required to fixate a single chunk.[6]

The Parameters of Memory—Seven Chunks, or Is It Two?

The second limiting property of the inner system that shows up again and again in learning and problem-solving experiments is the amount of information that can be held in short-term memory. Here again the relevant unit appears to be the chunk, where this term has exactly the same meaning as in the definition of the fixation constant.

Attention was attracted to this parameter, known previously from digit-span, numerosity-judging, and discrimination tasks, by George Miller's justly celebrated paper on "The Magical Number Seven, Plus or Minus Two."[7] It is no longer as plausible as it was when he wrote his paper that a single parameter is involved in the three kinds of task, rather than three different parameters; we shall consider here only tasks of the digit-span variety. Nor is it entirely clear today whether the correct value of the parameter is seven or four—rather too large a range for comfort.

The facts that appear to emerge from recent experiments on short-term memory are these. If asked to read a string of digits or letters and simply to repeat them back, a subject can generally perform correctly on strings up to seven or even ten items in length. If almost any other task, however simple, is interposed between the subject's hearing the items and repeating them, the number retained drops to two. From their familiarity in daily life we could dub these numbers the "telephone directory constants." We can generally retain seven numbers from directory to phone if we are not interrupted in any way—not even by our own thoughts.

Where experiments appear to show that more than two chunks are retained across an interruption, the phenomena can almost always be explained parsimoniously by mechanisms we have already discussed in the previous section. In some of these experiments the explanation—as already pointed out by Miller—is that the subject recodes the stimulus into a smaller number of chunks before storing it in short-term memory. If ten items can be recoded as two chunks, then ten items can be retained. In the other experiments where "too much" appears to be retained in short-term memory, the times allowed the subjects permit them in fact to fixate the excess of items in long-term memory.

I shall cite just two examples from the literature. N. C. Waugh and D. A. Norman report experiments, their own and others', that show that only the first two of a sequence of items is retained reliably across interruption, but with some residual retention of the remaining items.[8] Computation of the fixation times available to the subjects in these experiments shows that a transfer rate to long-term memory of one chunk per five seconds would explain most of the residuals. (This explanation is entirely consistent with the theoretical model that Waugh and Norman themselves propose.)

Roger Shepard has reported that subjects shown a very long sequence of photographs—mostly landscapes—can remember which of these they have seen (when asked to choose from a large set) with high reliability.[9] When we note that the task is a recognition task, requiring storage only of differentiating cues, and that the average time per item was about six seconds, the phenomenon becomes entirely understandable—indeed predictable—within the framework of the theory that we are proposing.

In the remainder of his chapter, Simon examines the organization of human memory and the mental processing of language. Ed.

Notes

1. This account of concept attainment is based on the paper with my late colleague Lee Gregg, "Process Models and Stochastic Theories of Simple Concept Formation," *Journal of Mathematical Psychology, 4* (June 1967): 246–276. See also A. Newell and H. A. Simon, "Overview: Memory and Process in Concept Formation," chapter 11 in B. Kleinmuntz (ed.), *Concepts and the Structure of Memory* (New York: Wiley, 1967), pp. 241–262. The former paper is reprinted in *Models of Thought,* chapter 5.4.

2. The monograph by J. S. Bruner, J. J. Goodnow and G. A. Austin, *A Study of Thinking* (New York: Wiley, 1956) was perhaps the first work to emphasize the role of short-term memory limits (their term was "cognitive strain") in performance on concept-attainment tasks. That work also provided rather definite descriptions of some of the subjects' strategies.

3. The evidence of the constancy of the fixation parameter is reviewed in L. W. Gregg and H. A. Simon, "An Information-Processing Explanation of One-Trial and Incremental Learning," *Journal of Verbal Learning and Verbal Behavior*, 6 (1967): 780–787; H. A. Simon and E. A. Feigenbaum, "An Information-Processing Theory of Verbal Learning," *ibid.*, 3 (1964): 385–396; Feigenbaum and Simon, "A Theory of the Serial Position Effect," *British Journal of Psychology*, 53 (1962): 307–320; E. A. Feigenbaum, "An Information-Processing Theory of Verbal Learning," unpublished doctoral dissertation, Pittsburgh: Carnegie Institute of Technology, 1959; and references cited therein. All these papers save the last are reprinted in *Models of Thought*.

4. Herman Ebbinghaus, *Memory* (New York: Dover Publications, 1964), translated from the German edition of 1885, especially pp. 35–36, 40, 51.

5. B. R. Bugelski, "Presentation Time, Total Time, and Mediation in Paired-Associate Learning," *Journal of Experimental Psychology*, 63 (1962): 409–412.

6. Most of the experiments against which EPAM has been tested employ recall tasks rather than simply recognition. EPAM contains two subprocesses that are implicated in fixation: a process of learning to differentiate and an image-storing process. Since recognition involves largely the former rather than the latter, it is possible that study of recognition tasks may reveal a fixation parameter smaller than five seconds per chunk. Indeed experiments reported to me by Walter Reitman and by Dr. Mary Potter (private communications) suggest that the time required to store the fact of having just seen familiar objects or pictures of them may be on the order of a second or two.

7. *Psychological Review*, 63 (1956): 81–97.

8. N. C. Waugh and D. A. Norman, "Primary Memory," *Psychological Review*, 72 (1965): 89–104.

9. Roger N. Shepard, "Recognition Memory for Words, Sentences, and Pictures," *Journal of Verbal Learning and Verbal Behavior*, 6 (1957): 156–163.

3 Mapping and Composing

Marilyn Hanf Buckley and Owen Boyle

What is a map? A map is a graphic representation of a written or oral composition, often including only key words. Using a map, students organize ideas; produce and receive information; and think, imagine, and create a product uniquely their own. Mapping aids composing and comprehending because it teaches students to differentiate among primary, secondary, and tertiary ideas; it is a simple and useful procedure for the organization of classroom activities in speaking, writing, listening, and reading.

When students make maps of books, essays, or lectures they discover that the process makes the work accessible to them for longer periods because retention becomes easier. Mapping can precede and improve oral discussions which are important in preparation for writing. Mapping can be a prewriting, revising, or postwriting activity assisting students in organizing, composing, and evaluating compositions. Mapping and outlining help students organize, but mapping has six advantages over outlining:

Mapping is easy to share.

Mapping illustrates relationships.

Mapping presents a whole structure.

Mapping is personal and idiosyncratic.

Mapping is easily learned.

Mapping moves students from fluency to form.

Mapping adds a visual dimension to our students' thinking; students gain greater control and fluency in their thinking with both visual maps and verbal exchange than with either maps or verbal exchange alone.

Source: Adapted from "Mapping and Composing" in Marilyn Hanf Buckley and Owen Boyle, *Mapping the Writing Journey*, Curriculum Publication no. 15 (Berkeley: Bay Area Writing Project, University of California, 1981), pp. 8-36. Used with permission of the Bay Area Writing Project.

Student Maps

Throughout this article are examples of maps which represent first attempts by students. These maps were selected for the wide range in ability and age of the authors, and they illustrate how easy it is for students with varying abilities to learn mapping.

The map in Figure 1 illustrates a seven-year-old girl's first attempt at making a map for composing. The map was planned orally; first the teacher illustrated how maps work by mapping a sample letter, then the girl and the teacher talked about what the girl wanted to say to her grandfather and grandmother. The teacher made a few suggestions, but the map was formed and written by the student. The girl used the map to start her writing; as she made discoveries about her subject, she enlarged her map. The map aided her in fluency, helped her make discoveries about her subject, and facilitated form. The first page of her five-page letter follows.

> Dear Grannie & Gramps
> Thank you for writing me that letter. Thank you for being so nice to me while we were visiting you. My mom figured that you woud send my sock because she cound'nt find it before we left. Could you

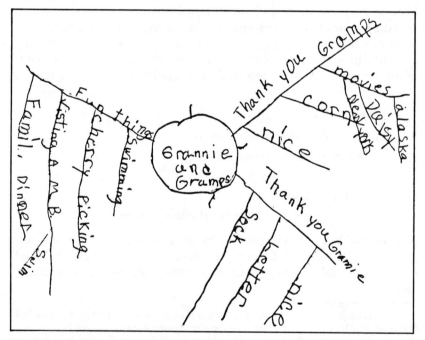

Figure 1. Map prepared by seven-year-old.

call Antie Louie and tell her that the pictures are on there way.
Gramps It was fun planting the corn with you.
I enjoyed your moveis . . .

A Mobile Map for Oral Composition

The map in Figure 2, by a fifteen-year-old student, was created in the
form of a mobile for use by a teacher of elementary children to facilitate
oral composition. Children use the mobile to remind them of the
important parts of the story as they tell it to their classmates. Later the
students make personal maps to illustrate their own oral book reports
or stories.

Mapping for an Autobiography

A useful first assignment to familiarize students with mapping is to
have them make a map to plan the writing of an autobiography. Using

Figure 2. Mobile map prepared by fifteen-year-old.

a known subject facilitates their mapping. Students place a controlling idea in the center of their map and use brainstorming techniques until they have many childhood memories for their paper. They select their "best" incidents for the map, with the central idea in the middle and supporting incidents or ideas on the extensions. The teacher lets the students know that as they make new discoveries they may add to or delete from their maps.

When students complete their maps, they tell their stories to a group or a partner; students should have opportunities to relate their stories orally before they write. While they tell their stories, listeners are mapping to give information to the speakers, who can then reevaluate their organization. Figures 3 and 4 are maps representing the first efforts of two high school students. One is more creative than the other, but each follows the rules of mapping to make an autobiographical map which is unique. These two maps were made following a brief introduction to mapping by Dr. Marilyn Buckley.

Group Composition and Mapping

One way to introduce students to mapping and composing is to involve them in writing a group essay. Groups select topics; or, for the

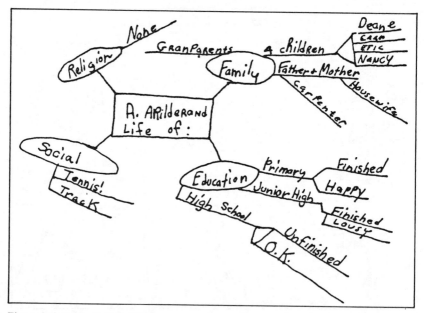

Figure 3. Autobiographical map.

purposes of comparison, the teacher can give groups the same assignment. This assignment helps students become aware of the processes of writing, revising, and editing; and, because they have to make group decisions, students discuss word choice, organization, and style. Mapping the assignment facilitates organization and revision by allowing the students to watch the structure change as they get new ideas for their papers.

A group reads its assignment, brainstorms, and begins selecting key words for the map. When students have their map drawn on poster paper, they begin talking about their ideas and expand or contract their structure. Students work on a topic sentence and on the first paragraph; an adult moves from group to group giving assistance. Groups com-

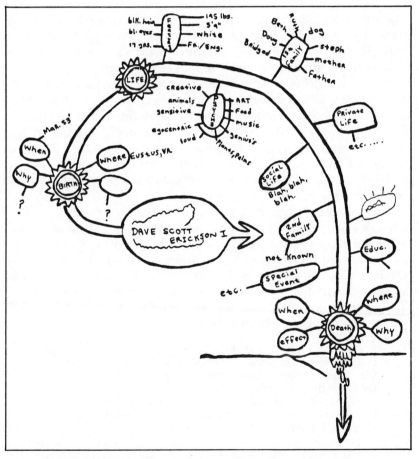

Figure 4. Autobiographical map.

plete the first draft, give it to another group for discussion, and revise the paper before reading it to the entire class.

In this exercise, mapping facilitates interaction and leads students through the process of writing an essay. After mapping in groups, students will be better prepared to write their own essays.

When the first drafts are complete, students read and edit their papers in groups using guidelines the teacher presents to the class. This is done before the teacher reads any of the papers thoroughly. The lesson is over after the teacher shows successful essays, using the overhead projector.

Mapping a Research Paper

Many students merely copy information from encyclopedia articles for research papers because they don't know how to paraphrase or get the main idea of an article. Mapping can help students overcome these deficiencies by forcing them to read for key words and ideas.

Students first brainstorm to generate words about a subject, categorize their words, and begin to arrange them in a map. Following this exercise, they go to the library to get more information on the subject, or the teacher may distribute an article to the entire class. Students map this article and rely only on their maps to recall information they want to use for their papers. After practicing with this article, students should have a good idea of how to cull information from primary and secondary sources.

The following paper by a nine-year-old girl is a good example of what can happen when a map is used to do a research paper and of what can happen when a map is not used. The girl mapped the first parts of her paper (see Figure 5), but neglected to map the last part. The result is original writing in the first part of the paper, followed by copied polysyllabic words which were incomprehensible to the girl. The mapped part of her essay is clear and original, and the unmapped part is simply copied. This part of Jenny's paper was mapped first:

> George Seurat did not paint pointillism, he called his painting divisionism and it often got mixed up with pointillism. Pointillism leaves white sections on the canvas. And George Seurat painted with out leaving spaces.
>
> In his pictures he uses very many colors. Especially in his sky, here are the colors he uses: green, blue, light blue, white, gray. But all the different colors blend together to make one color.
>
> He paints of outdoor places and at the places the people are having fun. Here are the places he paints, parks, beaches, picnics and lakes. You see in his pictures people sailing, people strolling,

children bouncing balls and holding their mother's hand, and
people with their pets, people in shade under their umbrellas
people fishing and canoeing.

This is the part of the paper which Jenny did not map:

Impressionist art is natural and direct. Seurat's paintings are stiff,
and figures seem immovable.

In the painting Courbevore Bridge the striking power of colors
based on the contrast of tones is sustained by a pattern of aspiring
verticals broken only by the hazy, distant horizontal of the bridge
and the dark diagonal of the riverbank.

The last paragraph above was copied directly out of the encyclopedia
and is incomprehensible to the girl who wrote it. Fortunately, she
ended in her own words:

I think Georges Seurat's paintings are good because of the
colors he uses and the way he uses them.

George Seurat died of diptheria at the age of 31. George Seurat
knew a lot about dots and now so do you.

Jenny, Age 9

Conclusion

Mapping is a powerful new tool used in writing, reading, listening,
and speaking. In the last few years mapping has been used by professional writers such as Robert Pirsig, *Zen and the Art of Motorcycle
Maintenance,* Douglas Hofstadter, *Gödel, Escher, Bach,* and Peter
Russell, *The Brain Book,* and it has been used by educators in England
and the United States. It is being used with students of varying
intellectual capacities in all grade levels. Mapping is one of the tools
which all teachers should have in their repertoires.

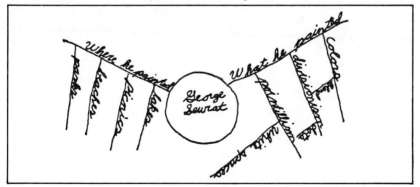

Figure 5. Map for research paper prepared by seven-year-old.

If we want students to generate words easily, if we want to help students organize their essays or stories efficiently, if we want students to write coherently, then mapping is one of the tools we will teach. As a prewriting activity, mapping helps students start writing easily; as a shaping activity, mapping helps students form their ideas; as a holistic activity, mapping helps thinkers synthesize ideas. Because it takes advantage of our verbal and visual abilities, mapping adds a new dimension and power to all language activities. This simple visual technique, taught in just a few minutes, can help all our students write better.

4 Understanding Children's Art

Rhoda Kellogg

Rhoda Kellogg was first attracted to children's art more than thirty years ago when she noticed that the three-year-olds in her pre-school were drawing mandalas, designs based on a crossed circle and considered by Carl Jung to be of great human and psychological significance. She focuses her attention on preschoolers' scribbles, which she called "self-taught child art," and concludes that these "early scribblings are essential to understanding all forms of graphic art as well as child art" (p. 172). Ed.

Basic Scribbles

Every form of graphic art, no matter how complex, contains all the lines found in children's work, which I call the 20 *Basic Scribbles:* vertical, horizontal, diagonal, circular, curving, waving or zig-zag lines, and dots. [See Figure 1.] Basic Scribbles can be made whether or not the eye controls the movement of the hand, for scribbles are the product of a variety of directional muscular movements which human beings make even before the age of two. Basic Scribbles are not learned from adults—they are spontaneous human "events" which take place when a finger or marking instrument moves over a surface and leaves a record of the movement. Not until I had studied child art for many years did I realize that though these early scribblings are visually meaningless to adults, they are visually significant to the child who makes them.

The Basic Scribbles are the building blocks out of which all graphic art, pictorial and non-pictorial, is constructed. And when the child looks at his scribblings, he sees them as visual wholes or entities.

Source: Excerpt from "Understanding Children's Art" in *Readings in Psychology Today* (Del Mar, Calif.: CRM Books, 1969), pp. 172-76. Reprinted from *Psychology Today Magazine.* Copyright © 1967 Ziff-Davis Publishing Co. Figure numbers have been added.

Before young children can draw the figures called a "man," a "horse," "a dog," and so forth, they will not only have scribbled, but will have constructed many abstract components and designs. I now know that children's first pictorial drawings are not early attempts to draw specific objects as the sight of those objects registers in the mind. Instead, children gradually realize that certain objects resemble their own designs, and observe that adults call some of these designs "houses," "boats," "people," "flowers." Thus children learn which drawings are pictorial and which are not. Drawing "from life" comes at a much later time. All children spontaneously scribble and make designs, but adults must teach them how to "copy nature."

It is difficult for adults to appreciate and understand self-taught art because the minds of children and of adults are so different. Through years of living, adults have accumulated a store of rich associations which children have yet to acquire. For example, when a child looks at an ◯ he has drawn, he sees only a round form, or gestalt, but the adult may see this as a scribble, a letter, a circle, an ornament, a symbol, a sign, a wheel, a ring. . . .The famous psychologist, Arnold Gesell, once said that our knowledge of the child is about as reliable as a 15th-century map of the world. The scribblings of children can help adults gain a more reliable map.

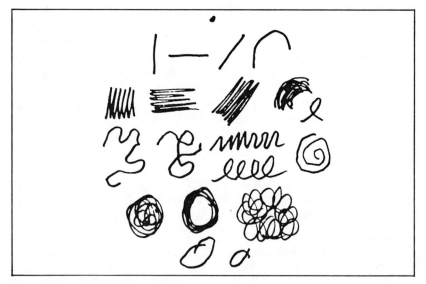

Figure 1. 20 Basic Scribbles.

Sequential Development in Self-Taught Art

As children progress from scribbling to picture-making, they go through four distinguishable stages: the Placement Stage, the Shape Stage, the Design Stage, and the Pictorial Stage.

Placement stage. Even the very earliest scribblings are not placed on the paper by happenstance. Instead, most of them are spontaneously drawn on the paper in *placement patterns,* that is, with an awareness of figure and ground relationships. I have detected 17 different placement patterns. The Spaced Border Pattern is shown below, and six others are shown in [Figure 2]. The 17 patterns appear by the age of two, and once developed are never lost.

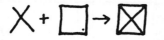

Shape stage. Placement patterns produce overall gestalts, or forms, which result from the location of the scribblings on the page. These gestalts contain implicit shapes. For example, the Spaced Border Pattern usually implies a rectangular shape:

By age three, most children can draw these implied shapes as single-line outline forms, called *diagrams,* and have reached the Shape Stage. There are six diagrams: circles (and ovals), squares (and rectangles), triangles, crossses, X's, and odd forms. [See Figure 3.]

Design stage. As soon as children can draw diagrams, they almost immediately proceed to the Design Stage in which they put these simple forms together to make structured designs. [See Figures 4 and 5.] When two diagrams are united, the resulting design is called a *combine:*

$$\times \ + \ \square \ \rightarrow \ \boxtimes$$

and when three or more are united, the design is called an *aggregate:*

$$\times \ + \ \square \ + \ + \ \rightarrow \ \boxtimes$$

Pictorial stage. Between the ages of four and five, most children arrive at the Pictorial Stage, in which their structured designs begin to look like objects which adults can recognize. [See Figure 6.] The Pictorial Stage can be divided into two phases: the first contains *early pictorial* drawings, and the second contains *later pictorial* drawings.

The early pictorial drawings differ from the gestalts of the Design Stage in that they are suggestive of "human figures," "houses," "animals," "trees," and the like. The later pictorial drawings are more clearly defined and are easily recognized as familiar objects by adults. The later pictorial drawings do not necessarily represent a more advanced stage of artistic development; they are merely those pictorial drawings which adults recognize and approve of.

In his pictorial drawings, the child is not necessarily trying to draw representationally, but is more concerned with creating esthetically satisfying structures. For example, a Multiple-loop Scribble (smoke) might appear more pleasing to him if it circles around a square aggregate (a house). Logical consistency does not become his concern until adults restrict his expression along lines considered to be "proper."

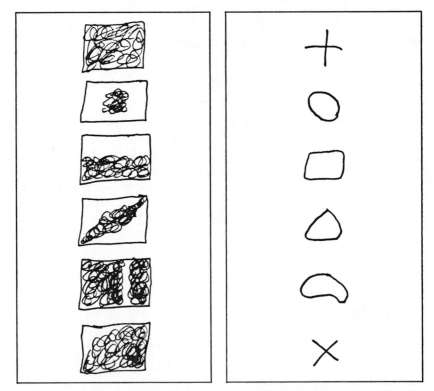

Figure 2. Placement patterns drawn by children in the Placement Stage, ages 2-3.

Figure 3. Diagrams drawn by children in the Shape Stage, ages 3-4.

From Humans to Rockets

The child's first drawings of the human figure look very odd to adults; the figure is round like a ball and the arms come out of the head. The reason for this lack of likeness is that the child is not drawing persons as seen, but is modifying the mandalas and suns of the late Design Stage in order to give his familiar gestalts a new look.

Mandala is a Sanskrit word denoting a "magic circle," though crossed squares and concentric circles or squares are also mandalas. The distinguishing characteristic of a mandala is its perfect balance, and mandala balance is dominant in self-taught art. The child's mandalas are prominent in the combines and aggregates, and are a departure point for proceeding to draw suns, radials, and human figures. [See Figure 7.] The mandala gestalt (1) suggests the sun gestalt (2) and the two of them evolve into the first human figure (3). In the first drawings of humans, the arms are attached to the head and there are

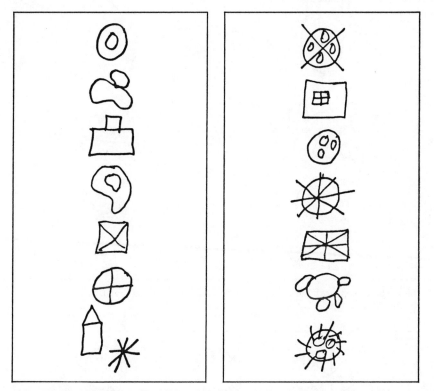

Figure 4. Combines drawn by children in the Design Stage, ages 3-4.

Figure 5. Aggregates drawn by children in the Design Stage, ages 3-4.

markings on top to balance the legs. Later the child omits arms from his drawings, perhaps in the effort to relieve the monotony of mandala balance. But actually almost all drawings of humans that children create before age six do fit nicely into an implied circular or oval shape, no matter what distortions of anatomy are required. This leads me to conclude that the child is not at all concerned with trying to draw his "humans" so that they look like people; he is striving for variety within a set of esthetic formulas.

Figure 6. Early pictorial drawings and later pictorial drawings drawn by children in the Pictorial Stage, ages 4–5.

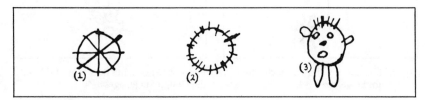

Figure 7. Mandalas drawn by children.

Drawings of human figures are followed by drawings of animals which are only modified gestalts of humans. For example, when the ears are on top of the head the human becomes what adults call an animal.

In the same way, the "buildings" which children spontaneously draw are not attempts to depict real houses. Instead, these gestalts are interesting variations on designs made up of squares and rectangles. This applies to drawings of boats, cars, trees, airplanes, and rockets.

Before age five there are no differences between art gestalts produced by boys and girls. From then on, however, cultural influences lead them to draw different subject matter.

Is Picasso Right about Child Art?

The child's production of art gestalts collides head-on with the conception of art which adults have learned after age six and have passed on from one generation to another, according to the approved formulas of the local culture. Adults who coach children to draw real-life objects are not really being helpful; they may even be causing harm. The child's purpose is not that of drawing what he sees around him; rather, he is probably a very experienced master of self-taught art, concerned primarily with the production of esthetic combinations which are often the envy of adult artists. In fact, Picasso says that adults should not teach children to draw, but should learn from them.

It is very difficult to convince adults that art is not essentially a matter of portraying reality. A deep appreciation of art derives from an appreciation of both the explicit and the hidden esthetic gestalts present in all art; the pictorial aspect of art is important, but it is not the ingredient which separates mundane art from great art.

Children left alone to draw what they like, without the interference of adult "guidance," usually develop a store of gestalts which enable them to reach the culminating stage of self-taught art. From there, if they are especially gifted, they may develop into great artists, unspoiled by the stenciled minds of well-meaning adults. Few children, however, are given this opportunity, and most relinquish art after the first few years in school.

Child Art and Learning to Read

Failure to allow self-taught art to take its natural course of development after age six causes confusion in the child mind and misunderstandings between children and adults, both of which interfere with learning and discipline in school. The child whose ability to create art gestalts has been developed usually learns to read quickly and well. Since neither parents nor educators know the value of scribbling, they fail to provide a place, under proper supervision, for the very young to scribble. This is unfortunate, because scribbling and drawing develop the child's ability to perceive abstract gestalts, an ability so necessary for learning to read. The teaching of reading and writing has never been based on any awareness of the child's interest in abstract expression. Children who have been free to experiment with and produce abstract esthetic forms have already developed the mental set required for learning symbolic language.

As the child learns to read, he is expected to comprehend difficult systems of gestalt-making, each with its own order and rules: (1) the written and printed language system of the culture; (2) the simple art gestalts that teachers and parents make and which the child is supposed to copy; (3) adult art used as illustrations in books; (4) gestalts as they appear in photographs, movies, and television; and (5) gestalts as they appear in charts, graphs, diagrams, and maps.

Reading and writing primarily involve visual skills, yet prevalent teaching methods emphasize association of the spoken word with the graphic symbols for those words. I believe that teaching the alphabet and stressing phonetics may be the wrong approach. Reading can better be taught by recognizing the importance of the child's inherent gestalt-making system as it is developed in self-taught art, and then by building upon it. Allowing a child to draw what he likes for at least 30 minutes every day in school might very well free him to continue developing his capacity to perceive abstract gestalts. This would lay the groundwork for improving his reading, and would improve his writing ability also, because scribbling and drawing develop the fine muscle skills required for making precise markings on paper.

Kellogg's essay closes with a discussion of using child art as a means of testing intelligence and concludes that children's early abstractions (and their later pictorial drawings) "are the products of innate patterns of neurological growth and human development" (p. 179). Ed.

5 Drawing as Prewriting in Preschool

Celeste Myers

In preschool activities, children ages three to five years learn how to make marks on paper. The children's growth in the motor skills of handling crayons, pencils, and felt-tip pens can be easily assessed if portfolios are kept of student work. The fact that children grow in their drawing skills and, as a correlate, grow in their storytelling skills is suggested by the four drawings presented here. In Figures 1 and 2, the children drew the pictures and then dictated the stories. In Figures 3 and 4, the children drew the pictures and then wrote the stories. Both assignments had a theme phrase: *It's spring* for the first two and *Someone special* for the second set (C. Myers, 1976).

The child who dictated only the theme phrase and "It's raining hard" had very little to use as a resource in the drawing. The child who dictated "It's spring and a flower is coming for a little walk. It rains and the sun dries up the rain," on the other hand, had many more details in the picture to use as a resource. The same is true in the second pair of first-grade pictures on someone special. In fact, the one child has extended the assignment to a series of pictures, each making a different point about "my mom." The captions for the individual pictures are a form of prewriting. To write the final draft, the child shifts the tense of the captions from progressive present (*is kissing, is hug*) to the simple, habitual present (*kisses, hugs*) and adds connectives (*becase, and*).

The drawing-storytelling lessons in preschool usually have four steps: (1) the teacher presents a story structure, either a theme (*Someone special, It's spring, Santa Claus*) or setting; (2) the children orally give details about the theme, usually answering the questions who, what, when, where, and why; (3) the children draw their stories about the theme; and (4) the children dictate their stories to the teacher, who writes the stories on the drawings, or the children write their stories on their drawings. Often the children talk to themselves about their story or object as they draw it. The following lesson, using the theme *Behind the door*, illustrates these four steps:

Materials

Premade books with six or eight pages and a colored paper cover;
felt-tip pens; sample book

Procedure

The cover of the book should draw children into the story and
encourage them to expand on the theme. A possible theme is
Night. "You wake up and it's dark in your room. You see a door—
one you have never seen before—you open the door and go
through it. . . ." A cover for the *Night Book* might be a house cut
from black construction paper with the words *Night Book* printed
on it.

1. Get the children excited (and perhaps worried) about what is
   behind the cover picture. Before they even open the book, have
   them brainstorm for story possibilities.

Figure 1.

2. Ask the children to open the book and go inside. They may draw a picture story about what they see or what happens "behind the door." Ask each child in turn to describe what she or he is drawing and write the story at the bottom of each page. If the story is very complicated, you may want to limit the picture caption to main ideas only. As much as possible, write the story verbatim as the child dictates it.

3. If there is time later in the day, read the stories to the whole group.

Variation

1. A book in the shape of a tepee for an Indian story: "One day when out walking you find a tepee and go inside. . . ."

2. After a field trip or special holiday, make a cover in the shape of a fire engine, pumpkin, etc., and have each child recall and draw in sequence that special event.

Figure 2.

Someone   Special

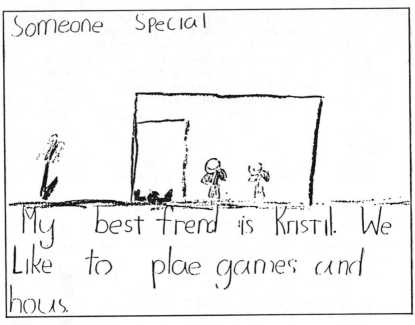

My   best frend is Kristil. We
Like   to   plae games and
hous.

Figure 3.

Someone   Special
(1:)   (2)
I'm fowsing my mom to   My . mom is kissing   My mom is huy
make my own brecfast   me.   me   (huging)

My   mom   is   special   becase   she
kisses   me   and   she   hugs   me   and
(she)
IC   dusin't   make   me   make   my   own
brecfast   but   Somerimes (she can be a grouch.)

Figure 4.

Another useful theme is *Me,* as illustrated by the *Me Book* lessons:

Materials

Folders made from large sheets of construction paper folded in half; felt pens; paper. Note: Folders should be attractive and durable. Use adhesive-backed paper or other art supplies to decorate and reinforce the folders. Children should be able to look at their books as often as they wish.

Procedure

1. Gather children at a table and allow each child to choose a favorite-colored folder. Explain that they will be able to make a book about themselves. Tell children that the folders will be kept at school and worked on each day until the books are finished.
2. Print *Me Book* on a piece of paper for older children to copy at the top of their folders. For younger children, print the words in pencil or chalk for them to trace. Have children put their names at the bottom of the folders. Give help as needed. (Save space in the center of the front cover for child's picture.)
3. Give each child a piece of paper and ask him or her to draw a self-portrait.

At subsequent times continue to add to each child's *Me Book* with the following activities:

Families

Pass out pieces of paper and ask children to draw their families. Discuss sizes, ages, pets, etc. Ask each child to identify family members in the picture. Label the picture as each child dictates.

My Room

Ask children to draw their rooms. As children draw, ask questions about their rooms: "Do you share your room? What size window does it have? What color is the room? What color are the curtains? Is there a big or little bed? Are there toys? Are they kept in a toy box or on shelves?" Encourage children to draw and describe with as much detail as possible.

Over a period of time, add other materials to the *Me Books* (see C. Myers, 1976, for additional variations):

1. Ask parents to send baby pictures.
2. Take Polaroid pictures or snapshots of children at school to put on the cover of the books. (Or ask parents for a recent photo.)
3. Cut a small snip of the child's hair to tape in the book.
4. Make hand- and footprints.
5. Let children go through magazines and cut out pictures of favorite things.

Each *Me Book* will be different. Children should include things important to them, and nothing has to be put in except the things they want. When completed, send the *Me Books* home. Consider letting children mail their books home.

Sometimes the themes for drawing-storytelling are organized around a social action such as making a holiday card which is mailed home, making exhibits for parent night, or making signs for the child's bedroom area at home. *Making movies* is an example of such a lesson:

Materials

Medium-sized box with rectangle cut from the bottom of box for movie screen. Cut holes below screen for dials. Large pieces of paper from paper roll; felt pens; crayons; magazines for cutting out pictures; scissors; glue.

Procedure

1. Settle children around a table that has moviemaking materials on it. The movie screen might be on a nearby table for easy viewing by those at the work table. This is an imaginary screen, perhaps a cardboard box with screen area and dials. Explain to the children that they can be moviemakers and make their own movies. Demonstrate by turning on the pretend screen, putting a picture on the screen, and telling a story about the picture.

2. Have each child take large pieces of paper and draw a movie. Have magazines available for those children who wish to choose pictures, cut them out, and glue them to papers for their movies.

3. As the children finish making their pictures, one child at a time can put his or her picture(s) on the movie screen, push the dials, and tell the others the story—describe what is happening, name the objects in the pictures. Teachers can help with language and imagination by asking who, what, why, and how questions. Help each child sequence his or her story by asking what happened first, next, last. Younger children might simply name what they have drawn. Encourage questions and comments to the "producer" from the audience.

Variation

On long strips of butcher paper, children can draw a sequence of large pictures. By installing these on dowels in the screen box and cranking the dowels, the movies pass before the eyes.

Drawing and writing are visual records of the intellectual growth of small children. The physical growth is evident in the shoes that no longer fit, the diapers that are now pinned on dolls. But the record of intellectual growth is lost if the drawings and writings of children are not saved. Schools can help maintain some of this record if collections of children's work are saved each year. The seven drawings in Figures

5-11 illustrate the developmental patterns of composition in children ages three to five years.

The drawing in Figure 5 looks like a fairly typical two-year-old's scribble. The child started, however, with a vertical line which extends about halfway down the page. Another line in another color is drawn parallel to the first and goes all the way to the bottom of the page. The concepts related to long, high, tall, etc., are being rehearsed in the child's eyes and muscles. These vertical lines are done in bland pink and grey. The child then abandons the effort to make long lines in favor of producing a vivid scribble pattern all in red.

Figure 6 shows the significant control that a few months of growth and experience bring. This drawing shows mastery of essentially all

Figure 5.

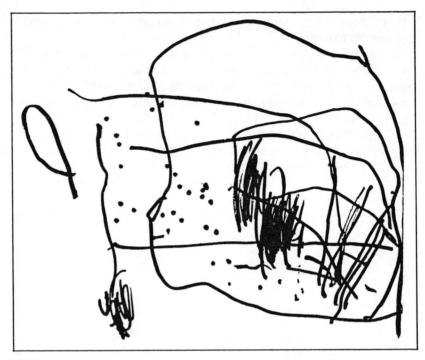

Figure 6.

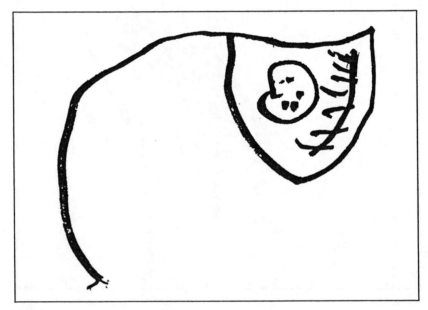

Figure 7.

basic strokes—horizontal, vertical, curved, intersecting, and straight lines, enclosed and closed figures, dots and scribbles. The drawing was accompanied by a narrative on an event in the child's immediate experience, the first rainfall of the season. Several aspects of the rain narrative are superimposed on each other as the drawing and narration proceed. It's common for children to illustrate their stories with several "pictures," one on top of the other, as shown. This child, in fact, talked about the raindrops, the water in the street, and the falling rain while drawing the picture.

The child who made the drawing in Figure 7 not only exhibits the full range of basic strokes shown in the previous drawing but also experiments with composition and editorial skills. He knows where he wants the lines and dots to go, he leaves some spaces empty, and when the picture was completed, he announced, "I'm done, teacher." This picture was, in fact, one of a series of three by this child.

Figures 8-10 show three patterns of organization in the drawings of young children. All three patterns have their recognizable parallels in written composition. The drawings, all by children between four and five years old, were drawn in response to a request by the teacher to "draw a picture of your family." Figure 8 is typical in that the mother is the largest figure and closest to the child, and the child draws herself with greater detail than the other figures. Figure 9 is a more literal family portrait. The figures are drawn with geometric shapes—circles, squares, rectangles, and lines—and are rather stiff "stick figures." In contrast, Figure 10 never quite gets to the "assignment" because the child becomes engrossed in describing where she lives, how to get there, and what one sees along the way. Her drawing is part family, part story, and part map.

In both Figures 9 and 10, the children wrote their own names. The names become part of the drawings, and the style is exactly like the drawings. Bridget prints her name in careful, geometric shapes, while Melinda expands her marks to fill the space available and to complement the composition of the picture. In Figure 11, the words and the drawing become fully integrated.

Figure 8.

Figure 9.

Figure 10.

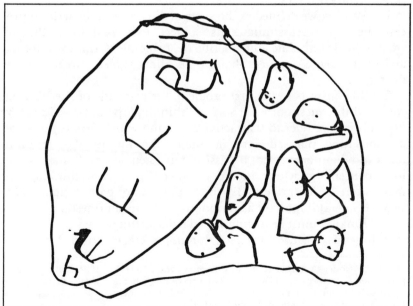

Figure 11.

6 Pre-Writing: The Stage of Discovery in the Writing Process

D. Gordon Rohman

I. The Principle

Writing is usefully described as a process, something which shows continuous change in time like growth in organic nature. Different things happen at different stages in the process of putting thoughts into words and words onto paper. In our Project English experiment,[1] we divided the process at the point where the "writing idea" is ready for the words and the page: everything before that we called "Pre-Writing," everything after "Writing" and "Re-Writing." We concerned ourselves mainly with Pre-Writing for two reasons: it is crucial to the success of any writing that occurs later, and it is seldom given the attention it consequently deserves.

Pre-Writing we defined as the stage of discovery in the writing process when a person assimilates his "subject" to himself. In our Project, we sought (1) to isolate and describe the principle of this assimilation and (2) to devise a course that would allow students to imitate its dynamics.

To find answers to the first problem, the principle of Pre-Writing, we asked the question: what sort of "thinking" precedes writing? By "thinking," we refer to that activity of mind which *brings forth* and develops ideas, plans, designs, not merely the entrance of an idea into one's mind; an active, not a passive enlistment in the "cause" of an idea; conceiving, which includes consecutive logical thinking but much more besides; essentially the imposition of pattern upon experience.[2] Several important assumptions underlie our question:

a. Thinking must be distinguished from writing.

b. In terms of cause and effect, thinking precedes writing.

Source: College Composition and Communication 16 (1965): 106–12. Reprinted by permission of the National Council of Teachers of English. Some usages that appear in this article are not consistent with the present NCTE Guidelines for Nonsexist Use of Language; they have not been changed in this reprint.

c. Good thinking can produce good writing; and, conversely, without good thinking, good writing is impossible.

d. Good thinking does not always lead to good writing; but bad thinking can never lead to good writing.

e. A failure to make a proper distinction between "thinking" and writing has led to a fundamental misconception which undermines so many of our best efforts in teaching writing: if we train students how to recognize an example of good prose ("the rhetoric of the finished word"), we have given them a basis on which to build their own writing abilities. All we have done, in fact, is to give them standards to judge the goodness or badness of their finished effort. *We haven't really taught them how to make that effort.*

f. A knowledge of standards is not enough to produce good writing; in practice such critical principles usually have a *negative* value: students are enabled to recognize more vividly their own inadequacies.

g. From a creative point of view, the standards established by the rhetoric of the finished word are too remote, too abstract. It is not enough to know *about* goodness; we must know it from experience. Whereas the classical practice of imitation held up the finished masterpiece for the example, we sought ways for students to imitate the creative principle itself which produces finished works. Unless we can somehow introduce students to the dynamics of creation, we too often simply discourage their hopes of ever writing well at all. As Jerome Bruner writes in *The Process of Education*, the way to make schooling "count" is to give students an understanding of the fundamental structure of whatever subjects they take.[3]

In writing, this fundamental structure is *not* one of content but of method. Students must learn the structure of thinking that leads to writing since there is no other "content" to writing apart from the dynamic of conceptualizing. "You can't write writing," as one critic once wrote. But can you isolate the principle that underlies all writing? And can you then practice that principle in whatever "subjects" you may choose?

Because this stage we call Pre-Writing is within the mind and consequently hidden, it must necessarily be what John Ciardi calls a "groping." Ciardi describes the process introspectively as without end, "but in time the good writer will acquire not only a sense of *groping for* but a sense of having *groped to:* he begins to know when he has finally reached whatever he was reaching for."[4] The paradox gives us an important clue, we believe, to the principle of Pre-Writing: writers set out in apparent ignorance of what they are groping for; yet they recognize it when they find it. In a sense they knew all along, but it took some sort of heuristic process to bring it out. When it is "out," they have discovered their subject; all that's left is the writing of it.

Pre-Writing, then, is that stage which concerns itself with "discovery." But we must attempt to state the principle objectively to throw as much light as possible upon Ciardi's term "groping." Discovery of what? Not of some*thing* at all, but of a pattern of somethings. Bruner, again, says in his essay "The Act of Discovery," that "Discovery, whether by a schoolboy going it on his own or by a scientist cultivating the growing edge of his field, is in its essence a matter of rearranging or transforming evidence in such a way that one is enabled to go beyond the evidence so reassembled to new insights."[5] It is more useful to think of writing *not* as made up of words but of *combinations* of words. The meaning of writing is the meaning of the combination, the pattern that the meanings of the many words make when fused by a writer's consciousness in the moment of "discovery." What the writer is groping for (in Ciardi's term) is that combination that "clicks" for him; an arrangement that will fit his subject to him and him to his subject.

So far we have attempted to describe the formative stages of any writing; we must add now that we believe "good writing" is that discovered combination of words which allows a person the integrity to dominate his subject with a pattern both fresh and original. "Bad writing," then, is an echo of someone else's combination which we have merely taken over for the occasion of our writing. "Bad writing" is the "Letters for All Occasions" sort of book: writing problems identified and solved in advance of any person's encountering them, a specific collection of models of "good form" (i.e., manners) ready-cast. But we contend that "good writing" must be the discovery by a responsible person of his uniqueness within his subject.

By "person" we mean one who stands at the center of his own thoughts and feelings with the sense that they begin in him. He is concerned to make things happen and not simply to allow things to happen to him; he seeks to dominate his circumstances with words or actions.

Another way of putting it would be to say that every writing occasion presents the writer with two contexts to discover: one we might call the "subject context," that is, some *things* about a "subject" that may be learned in an encyclopedia. But obviously reading an encyclopedia does not enable one to write essays. The writer has a second, more crucial, context to discover, what we might call the "personal context": that special *combination* of words which makes an essay his and not yours or mine. We submit that "good writing" is that which has involved a writer responsible enough to discover his personal context within the "subject context," and "bad writing" is that which has not.

(In neither case is "correctness" an issue. "Bad writing" can be, often is, flawlessly "correct.")

The late Dorothy Sayers described as "conversion"what she thought happened within persons in the formative stages of their writing.[6] An "event" was converted into an "experience." An event she distinguished as something that happens to one—but one does not necessarily experience it (like the "subject context"). He only experiences a thing when he can express it to his own mind (the "personal context"). A writer, she goes on, is a man who not only suffers the impact of external events, but experiences them. He puts the experience into words in his own mind, and in so doing recognizes the experience for what it is (for him, we might add). To the extent that we can do that, we are all writers. A writer is simply a man like ourselves with an exceptional power of revealing his experience by expressing it, first to himself (Pre-Writing), and then to others (Communicating) so that we recognize the experience as our own too. When an "event" is so recognized, it is converted from something happening *to* us into something happening *in* us. And something to which we happen. The writer gropes for those words which will trigger this transformation.

A good deal of behavioral research, in writing as well as in other things, has attempted to ignore the reality of the conscious, responsible, willing person. We cannot commit this fundamental error as researchers of the writing process. Without a person at the center, the process is meaningless; prose without a person *in*forming it could better be written by a computer programmed with all the stereotyped responses of our culture. A fundamental question faces those in English and those in the government who support its research: to what end do we teach writing? If it is to "program" students to produce "Letters and Reports for All Occasions," it is not only ignoble but impossible. The imp of the perverse in students will simply thwart any attempts to reduce them to regimented sentences. However, if it is to enlighten them concerning the powers of creative discovery within them, then it is both a liberal discipline and a possible writing program. We must recognize and use as the psychologists do in therapy, a person's desire to actualize himself. Such a desire makes mental healing possible; such a desire makes writing possible since writing is one important form of self-actualization. What we must do is place the principle of actualizing in the minds of students and the methods of imitating it in their hands.

II. Imitation

Our practical problem was to devise ways that students might imitate the principle of Pre-Writing. We employed three means chiefly: (1) the keeping of a journal, (2) the practice of some principles derived from the religious Meditation, and (3) the use of the analogy.

Because we assumed that the process of transformation was nothing if not personal, we began our course by asking students to "collect themselves" in a journal. We demanded daily performance of some sort, although we did not specify length. We mimeographed a long list of questions that we hoped would provoke our students to some discovery of what they believed, what they felt, what they knew. In the process of introspection, formalized by the daily writing in the journal, we hoped to mobilize the consciousness of every student writer. If writing is a groping process for what it is in us that "tallies" with a subject, then the more familiar we are with ourselves, the better the chances of our "groping to" some discoveries in writing. To guide our students somewhat, we reprinted for them several entries from Henry Thoreau's journal which concerned the art of keeping a journal; such entries illustrated as well as described the process of self-discovery.

The great majority of students came to value their journal above anything else in the course. Perhaps for many it was the first time they had ever been encouraged to get themselves stated. As one student wrote, "I established a discovery of myself *for myself,* a feeling for language in my journal entries. . . . I learned through the use of perspective to see the subject as it appears from a personal sense of what is real." Another wrote, "I wrote in my journal for several weeks before I realized that I was doing so far more than just a course. It began to mean something to me. It became more than just a proving ground for my themes. . . . It became a vital part in my whole life." We are convinced that the journal *works* as a "method"; more important, we are convinced that good writers are persons with a *real involvement* in their subjects and in themselves. Is not one of the basic curses of typical writing courses their pervasive sense of "phony involvement," not only of the student with the set topics of his themes, but of the teacher with an approach wholly outside and tangential to the problem? The journal was one way we sought to make the course *real* to students; it also made it real to teachers because the writing in the journal was, more often than not, worth reading.

The second technique was to use some principles taken from the religious discipline of the Meditation. Our assumption, you will recall, is that writing is a personally transformed experience of an event. Bruner quotes from the English philosopher Weldon: "We solve a problem or make a discovery when we impose a puzzle form on a difficulty to convert it into a problem that can be solved in such a way that it gets us where we want to be. This is, we recast the difficulty into a form that we know how to work with—then we work it. Much of what we speak of as discovery consists of knowing how to impose a workable kind of form on various kinds of difficulties."[7]

We were attracted to the Meditation because it seemed to provide us with a model or "*puzzle* form" that might give students an inner knowledge transforming their "events" into "experiences." Our use of a method as rigid in outline as the Meditation to provoke spontaneity and originality may seem paradoxical. The solution of the apparent paradox lies in the word "original": we sought not "novelty" but "reaction from the origins." The personal, patterned response that characterizes Pre-Writing issues from the same sort of dynamic interplay of self and world that the Meditation depends upon. The Meditation, like a puzzle, asks its questions in such a way that they can be solved by us. As Erich Fromm writes in his essay "The Creative Attitude," to be original does not primarily mean to discover something new, but to *experience* in such a way that the experience originates in me. The Meditation was precisely designed to achieve this effect: to experience religious doctrine in such a way that the experience no longer merely happens *to* you but *in* you. The Meditation involves the willful employment of the mind in progression of stages on a process of transformation of religious "subjects" into personal experiences. Its whole intention is to make personally real what Whitehead would call the "inert" ideas of religious doctrine. The typical Meditation begins by assuming that the most obvious entry into a person's consciousness is through his senses. And in the "Composition of Place," the person meditating must seek to bind his subject to some definite picture which illustrates it. He must give to airy nothing a local habitation; must find the "objective correlative" of dogma; must imagine himself present and aware in scenes that embody principles. Whereas, before, he has an "outsider's" disengaged knowledge, he now seeks that "insider's" knowledge which binds him in heart and soul to the subject being meditated, so as to set the will on fire with the love of God. Not the specific skills of this or that school of meditation, but the principle of "discovery" that lies within all the schools of meditation attracted us to this ancient art. The Meditation was designed to be a heuristic model, something which served to unlock discovery. We adapted the discipline to our use to give students both a sense of direction to their groping, and an actual "puzzle" to impose on their writing problems. First, we said, compose a "place" for your subject, one where you can "live." Keep composing until you reach the point that your understanding of your "subject" is experienced within, until, in other words, the "event" of your subject happening *to* you becomes an "experience" happening *within* you. With such a discovery, the urge to "get it down" usually increases to the point that the will directs the actual writing of words to begin.

We assume, in using the Meditation, that knowledge must become personal and that one effective way of achieving this is by insisting that knowledge become concrete, since persons react more to the concrete than they do to the abstract. In addition, by returning our students to the concrete world of the five senses, we encourage them to "earn" their abstractions. We insist that they escape from the thought clichés which pass for "writing" and "thinking" in our culture by a return to the thing freshly experienced. Within this real encounter lies hope for creative surprise and new insight "to set the will on fire" to write.

Student comments indicate that the process of Meditation can give them the *experience* of insight. "Once I started to 'see' the concrete details within my subjects," wrote one student of the "Composition of Place," "the writing process became easier for me, for I could 'respond' more fully to the subject." Another wrote, "This course also taught me to look at things as if it were the first time and I had never seen them before." Another concluded, "I now think of subjects in relation to my experiences."

The third major approach we used to allow students to imitate the dynamics of "Pre-Writing" is the analogy. The journal encouraged students to discover themselves; the meditation put into their hands a "puzzle form" of discovery. The analogy, we hoped, would illustrate the "bisociation" of all experience. That is, as human beings, we are enabled to know anything in our present simply because we have known similar things in our past to which we compare the present. Each act of present "knowing" associates the present with the past as another instance. That is why we say that a writer is one who recognizes present events as special cases of transformed "experience" known before. Writers are people who *recognize* things, and their life is full of the "shocks of recognition" when what they are "groping for" becomes finally something "groped to." Miss Sayers observes that "the perception of likenesses, the relating of like things to form a new unity, and the words 'as if'" pretty well describe the creative process of writing.[8]

The analogy also gave us another "puzzle form," a "converting mechanism" to allow students to imitate the dynamics of transformation that we believe are at the heart of Pre-Writing. Analogy illustrates easily and to almost everyone how an "event" can become an "experience" through the adoption of what Miss Sayers called an "as if" attitude. That is, by arbitrarily looking at an event in several different ways, "as if" it were this *sort* of thing, or that *sort* of thing, a student can actually experience transformation from the inside. We ask students to choose an analogical "vehicle" which has already been an "experience" for them, that is, something already converted from "outside" to "inside." Then we ask them to apply this "vehicle" to the as yet undiscovered possibilities of their subject. The analogy functions both as a focus and a catalyst for "conversion" of event into experience. It also provides, in some instances not merely the heuristic for discovery but the actual pattern for the entire essay that follows. The creative mind, as we have assumed throughout this paper, works not primarily by analysis or measurement of observables as machines work, but by building images of unity out of what William James called the blooming, buzzing confusion of events. "Creation," as Denis de Rougemont writes, is not "something from nothing" as with the Deity, but rather is better comprehended as a different arrangement of elements already known according to laws known or knowable. Therefore it is better understood as composition. Art that is, represents reality. And the analogy reproduces the "re-presentation" process in miniature. By rearranging and reassembling the focus of our experience of things, analogy puts into our hands a ready-made model of pre-writing discovery. In addition, analogy also provides practice with the concrete world of the five senses, and, by enlisting the student writer in a personally-experienced encounter with his subject freshly seen from the perspective of a new analogy, we have provided him with the "motor" to make his subject "go" for him.

As one student wrote of the analogy, "When one approaches a topic, he needs an 'angle' or a concept for approach. If he looks into his more familiar and concrete world, he can find a number of things he knows well. If he sets these up alongside of the broader topic, relationships will evolve. His thoughts will be directed; his language will be freshened. . . . Analogy is an exploratory device; it can be a structuring and unifying device." Another wrote, "The analogy approach stresses organization and growth—perhaps the most important part of thought —rather than layout." Another confessed, "To my surprise, the analogical approach worked, and I've gained new insights. . . ." Another wrote of the analogy, "It is a technique that seems to bring an abstract subject closer to the reader, and the writer too, for that matter. . . . For not only did the subject seem clearer to me, but through an interesting perspective, writing actually was fun. I learned to 'play' with ideas, to let myself go, to gain new insight. . . ." Another concluded that analogies "help to achieve new and significant thought, lead you through some kind of structured thought, giving you a unity of order in the paper, and provide you with a language to work with."

III. Conclusion

To conclude: in our brief project research, we sought to isolate the structuring principle of all Pre-Writing activity and then to devise exercises to allow students to imitate that principle in their own "Pre-Writing." Ours did not pretend to be a complete course in writing: the rhetoric of effective communication needs to follow any discovery of a structuring concept. But without the rhetoric of the mind, it seemed to us, no course in the rhetoric of the word could make up for the fact that the writer has discovered essentially nothing to say. In fact, to continue to teach rhetoric without attention to discovery reinforces that indifference to meaning that characterizes the modern world of politics and advertising. We have sought, in other words, not only to identify and practice a principle, but to insist that the principle is valuable only when alive and used within the consciousness of an aware, responsible person.

The kind of writing that our project produced was that which immediately follows the discovery of fresh insight; it was not necessarily a kind of writing suitable to all possible occasions for written discourse. We believe, however, that writing grounded in the principle of personal transformation ought to be the *basic* writing experience for all students at all levels, the propaedeutic to all subsequent and more specialized forms of writing. The evidence of our testing programs clearly shows that writing produced under these conditions is, first, good in itself. Our essays showed a statistically significant superiority to essays produced in control sections. But more important to our way of thinking are the indirect effects of this approach which introduces students to the dynamics of creative response itself:

a. It can lead students to produce writing good in itself.

b. It can train students to creative discovery in other fields, since the psychology of creative surprise is not restricted to writing.

c. It makes writing of a worthwhile kind *possible* to more students than traditional modes, especially those based upon imitation of the finished product ever could. And by making writing possible to average students, we also make it more desirable. Our students more often than not ended up our course liking to write; perhaps for the first time they felt within themselves, along their pulses, that sense of power, of self-fulfillment, which the psychologists call "self-actualization."

As one student wrote, "I felt compelled to write, but not because it meant a grade, rather because I did not want to disappoint the professor or myself." As another put it, "I was made to feel that I was capable of creating something new. I was brought to an awareness of the world about me that I had just taken for granted. I really began to 'see'." These must ultimately be the major reasons we teach persons to write: the renewed sense of self, the renewed vision of things.

Notes

1. "Construction and Application of Models for Concept Formation in Writing," U.S. Office of Education Cooperative Research Project Number 2174.

2. We shall be talking about two different and distinct kinds of structure: that which Jerome Bruner refers to as the fundamental organization of a subject such as mathematics or biology; and that pattern of meanings which a writer gives to a subject. To keep the two separate, we shall use "structure" to refer to the characteristic combinatorial principle of Pre-Writing; and we shall use "pattern" to refer to the individual organization that every writer imposes upon his work.

3. (Cambridge, 1962), p. 11.

4. *Saturday Review*, XLV (Dec. 1962), 10.

5. *On Knowing: Essays for the Left Hand* (Cambridge, 1962), pp. 82-83.

6. Dorothy Sayers, "Towards a Christian Aesthetic," *The New Orpheus: Essays Towards a Christian Poetic*, ed. Nathan A. Scott (New York, 1964), pp. 14-15.

7. *On Knowing*, pp. 93-94.

7 From Speech to Writing

Gail Siegel

"How do you spell 'oranges' without the 'o'?" a child asked me.
"What?" I said.
He repeated the question. I remained baffled. Finally he showed me
his paper and I realized that he knew how to spell the "o." It was the
"ranges" of "oranges" that he was struggling with.

For me, the anecdote illustrates an important lesson. Young children must learn the delicate synchronization of mental and motor skills
required for writing. But the most difficult task is translating ideas into
words. The child above knew what he needed from me, but not how to
express his need to me.

I find it useful to view young writers as passing through a series of
developmental stages:

1. Transcribing Stage
2. Re-copying Stage
3. Sentences/Whole Phrases Stage
4. Independent Stage

The stages aren't rigid; they have soft edges. Some children pass
from stage two straight to stage four. For others, stages three and four
happen simultaneously. In a kindergarten, first, second, or third grade
class, I expect to find some children at every stage, depending on their
individual maturation and writing experience.

I also find it useful to consider the developmental stages as coincid-
ing with the linear progression from fluency (ease and confidence with
language) to coherence (making formal and grammatical sense) to correctness (punctuation, paragraphing, etc.).

Source: Excerpt from "From Speech to Writing," in *Sequences in Writing, Grades
K-13* by Gail Siegel, Lynda Chittenden, Jean Jensen, and Jan Wall, Curriculum Publica-
tion no. 13 (Berkeley: Bay Area Writing Project, University of California, 1980), pp. 1–8.
Reprinted with permission of the Bay Area Writing Project.

Transcribing Stage

Pre-writers need to have their spoken language transformed into writing by an adult. The children tell a teacher, aide, or parent volunteer what they want to say, and the adult transcribes the children's words into writing. The sequence is as follows:

1) Child talks, adult writes, child illustrates; or 2) child illustrates, child talks, adult writes.

Children at this stage want to illustrate what has been written for them. Transcribed speech, or pre-writer's "writing" usually involves simple sentences, while the pictures may be quite detailed. Pictures illustrate the feelings and details not expressed in the language.

For instance, one six-year-old dictated: "I feel bad because my Mommy and Daddy went away." Her picture shows a lone child standing in the open doorway of her home. The parents are leaving, holding packed suitcases. The little girl in the picture has big tears rolling down her cheeks. Her face is obviously forlorn as the parents wave good-bye. The reader feels the emotion and impact from the picture, not from the transcribed writing. There is a narrative quality to a child's illustration.

In a primary classroom, particularly kindergarten or first grade, it helps to have several adults or older children available during the writing worktime to take dictation. Young children often have short attention spans and need someone to listen to them when they have ideas. Although children are not actually writing during this phase, they are developing foundations upon which writing will later build.

The following are further examples of transcribed speech of five and six year olds:

> Today we painted boxes for the Halloween play.
>
> At art we made a map of Ross and we put our houses on it.
>
> My Dragon—he lives in the sea. He is green and he likes to drink water. He cracked out of an egg. He likes to eat grass. He flies. When he flies he swoops down and catches birds and eats them. Sometimes he goes in the water and eats fish.
>
> My Magic machine makes bubble gum and it crushes up rocks. They're not wrapped yet. Then they're wrapped and then they're put in the box. It doesn't have a special flavor.

If these children are asked, they may be able to give more detail, but normally there is little "meat on the bones" at this stage. They tell stories about real or imagined events in short, simple sentences.

Re-Copying Stage

It is not long before children move into stage two and become re-copiers. This usually happens sometime during the first semester of first grade. During the new phase, children still dictate, but they are able to re-copy what an adult writes. They can read, know the alphabet, and can hold a pencil. They feel an enormous sense of accomplishment when they can write on their own. They begin to view themselves as writers.

For children at this stage, the physical task is arduous. Holding a pencil, using an eraser, thinking of words and actually writing can be overwhelming to children. I frequently have them cross out each word they copy to help them keep track of where they are.

"Re-copy" writing has many similarities to the language of children in transcribing stage. It is generally first person experiential or fantasy writing. Usually it is declarative and lacks detail, color, and substance.

A sample of class journal entries, as told to the teacher and then re-copied by the children:

> Robbie said in science that our heart is like our motor and the food is the gas.
> My Grandmother came to the play. I think she likes it a lot.
> Our Christmas banners are hanging all around the room and they are so pretty and green and sparkle and we can do more.
> We all learned our parts for the Christmas play and Mrs. Safford was happy. The boys do not want to be wearing tights.

Again the illustrations (and children's sound effects and verbalization during drawing) have the action and detail that the writing lacks. These children are given plenty of time and experience with telling and re-copying. Their writing is read aloud, displayed, published, and enjoyed. Gradually they gain the tools and confidence to pass on to stage three.

Sentence/Whole Phrases Stage

Children at this stage of development know what they want to say and are able to write down some of their thoughts independently. They are eager to write for themselves and are learning to be comfortable with words and thoughts, and consequently less dependent on adult help. Adults are available for help with phrases or whole sentences as the child needs them. For instance a child at this stage may ask the teacher to write "once upon a time," but that same child will then finish the sentence independently. Their writing sounds much like their speech and has characteristics of the first two stages of writing:

> I wonder how the raining got up in the sky so it could fall. I like rainy days because my Mom sometimes gives me hot cocoa.
>
> Yesterday I made a pre school for my brother we sang and played it was fun we have candy cans the end.
>
> last night is was raining so hard that our lights went out I had to get our hoemkeper I went out in the rain I went in my bare feet.

These children have the confidence to write even though they are making errors in spelling and grammar. What matters to them now is that they can write. Correctness and neatness can be considered after the initial writing is on paper. More importantly, fluency is now developing. Stage three writers are exploring how the language works and can translate their ideas onto paper. The task of transforming mental images and language into written words becomes less burdensome. Like new walkers, they slowly forget the awkward mechanics and get from one point to another with less conscious effort. The more frequently these children write, the easier it becomes to write. They begin to add flavor, color, detail, action, and characters to their writing.

Independent Stage

At some point during the sentence/phrase level, children begin to rely on themselves almost completely and may only ask an adult to supply an occasional word for their writing. As they become independent writers, many children gain fluency and begin to work for greater coherence. Young writers working to become coherent are concentrating on making sense and building structure and sequence into the writing. They may not be conscious of this process, but the writing shows evidence. During this period writers need to be able to hear their work and to have an opportunity to re-draft the pieces of writing. Of course these young independent writers may still struggle with either fluency or coherence:

> I like books because I like reading what most like the pictures what I like are the *"Where's Wallace?"* and *Curious George* and *Spiders,* and *Miss Nelson is missing* and *a Great Day for Up* and *Here Comes the Strike Out.*
>
> Seven Year Old

This child is having difficulty with fluency. The thoughts are flowing so quickly in his head that it is impossible to get all of the necessary words on paper. As the student has the opportunity to share his writing, he will notice gaps, or the teacher or writing group will point them out.

Another example, this time of a child working on coherence:

> Last night I had a dream. That a big fercious monster came and
> took me to a planet called Pluto. And then he took me to see the
> king. The kings said you are on the plant Pluto. Do you have any
> sweters I said. No he said. I better go home and get my sweter. O.k.
> he said Zoink take her back to get her sweter so Zoink went back to
> my house and I got my warmest sweter on and went back to Pluto
> and saw the king. He said you a going to help us do experiment
> were going to turn the statue of liberty into a flying diamond so we
> can go back to pluto.

Eight Year Old

The author has little difficulty with fluency, although there are some minor omissions. She needs some work on sequence and structure, so that her story is clear and has purpose. She will have a chance to read her dream aloud to the class and then, after some peer and teacher response, she can make any changes she feels are necessary to complete this story.

Although both of these children are fairly independent writers, they need to hear their writing read orally so that they develop an ear for the sound of the language. Eventually they will learn to correct omissions and add missing thoughts as they experience this group sharing.

Sequential Teaching Strategies for Writing

I find it helpful to view the steps I use in teaching writing as a sequence. These are not ironclad rules; rather they are processes which encourage and facilitate writing. This is the sequence: oral language, pre-writing, group writing, individual writing, and sharing/re-thinking. I use these strategies for children at any of the stages of writing development, whether they are transcribing or independent writers.

Oral Language

For many writers, particularly young children, the initial touching of pencil to paper seems like crossing the Himalayas. Constant pencil sharpening, playing with the eraser, getting the right paper, and other delaying tactics seem necessary. I have found that oral language experience prior to writing is of primary importance. Once children have a fund of vocabulary, it is much easier to begin writing.

The oral language part of writing involves developing a bank of key words which can be used in the children's writing. A young writer needs these words to draw from, just as a builder needs bricks.

If my class is going to write about "Fall," we brainstorm for several days. Children suggest words or short phrases such as "leaves turning colors," "crisp," "horseback riding on trails," "scrunching leaves on my way home," "crunchy apples in my lunch," "walnuts," "Halloween," and so on. These words are recorded on the board or on butcher paper and displayed for several days as additional words come to mind. The wealth of vocabulary that the children already know is tapped before the act of writing. When the actual writing takes place, many of the necessary words and phrases have already been "rehearsed."

Pre-Writing

Pre-writing is all of those experiences that the teacher plans for the class before they write. It may include reading aloud selections by other children or authors on the particular topic. As they listen to what someone else has written, children can consider the wide range of possibilities open to them. Films, experiments, cooking, art, or personal experience all provide illustrations from which young children may draw when they are ready to write. My class wrote easily about trees after we had taken tree walks, listened to tree poems, discussed familiar trees, and looked at tree bark in the microscope.

> A tree is the best place for building a fort, because it is cozy. No one can find you there.
> Seven Year Old

> A tree is nice because if something rolls down the hill, a tree can stop it.
> Six Year Old

> Trees live almost anywhere, in streams, or lakes. Trees are important for food. We could not live without trees. They are good to live in or to use to build your house.
> Seven Year Old

I have found that writing facilitates the teaching of other subjects such as science and vice versa, an effective symbiosis. As part of a science unit, my class studied seeds and plants. The writing that took place prior to our study was non-descript, one-dimensional:

> a seed is a small thing

> seeds make plants

> You put seeds in dirt and they grow

After our science study, the children's writing flowed more easily and was more vivid because the children had had numerous experiences with plants and seeds. Seeds had been soaked and cut; they had sprouted and were then planted. Logs were kept about these experiments. The children had become observers. Plant word lists were on the walls. Through writing, they were then able to explore what they had learned and experienced as well as what they thought:

> A seed is part of our food chain to live. A seed is something that lives. We can eat seeds. Seeds grow and make plants. You have to have seeds to make a new plant.
>
> Seven Year Old

> A seed can grow into a big bush in many months. A Seed can have a maroon coat that protects it. If you soak a seed in water overnight, it will get very wrinkled and the coat will be light. I have grown a bean plant and a corn plant from seeds.
>
> Seven Year Old

The children's experience is reflected in their writing. Exploring what they know, young writers may try a more poetic form:

> If I was a seed . . . If I were a seed, I would be protected by my cover. My little red thing around me. When my cover turned wrinkly, I would be scared half to death.
>
> Eight Year Old

> If I was a seed, I would stretch and grow my leaves. I would wish my owner would not be clumsy. I would want a nice owner who would talk to me. If a farmer picked me and cooked me with my other bean friends, that would be sad.
>
> Seven Year Old

When oral language and pre-writing are part of a writing lesson, the final writing is like a well rehearsed play. The language and experiences are part of the practicing.

In the remainder of her article, Siegel describes her approach to group writing (suggesting that students describe a field trip, keep a class journal, create a class play, or write a letter to the principal), individual writing (using such modes as reports, stories, haiku, poetry, jingles, plays, fables), and sharing/re-thinking (where students read their writing aloud in groups to spot unclear passages or incomplete information and then reformulate or revise their writing). Ed.

8 Stimulating and Receiving Children's Writing: Implications for an Elementary Writing Curriculum

Lester S. Golub

"Above everything else I would like to see our schools staffed by men and women who have poetry in their souls."

Sybil Marshal, *Adventure in Creative Education*

Why not poets in the classroom as well as firemen, astronauts, physicists, candy makers, and lion trainers? But, the poet is different. He makes his living by writing, by stirring the reader's imagination by using his own imagination, by manipulating language. He is expendable in our pragmatic society, but without him there would be no song, no discovery of the inner voice of man that is in all of us. And that is what writing is all about, discovering our inner voice and expressing it in such a way, with language, that it stimulates some sort of sensitive, creative response in the listener or the reader. This explanation of writing must be kept in mind as we teach children to write, since it is the stimulating of this inner voice and the response it creates in others which becomes our teaching goal. In a way this goal will be too simple for those who teach from traditional language arts textbooks, where grammar, mechanics, and usage predominate. For the sake of this discussion, let us discard these texts and look squarely at the problem of stimulating and "receiving" children's writing which is their thinking in their most intimate voice.

In discarding the mechanical and grammatical dictates of language arts texts we are left face to face with the child of nine through twelve who has learned to read some simple and not so simple prose, who has learned to manipulate the pencil at an excruciatingly slow rate and who

Source: Elementary English 48 (1971): 33–49. Reprinted by permission of the National Council of Teachers of English. Some usages that appear in this article are not consistent with the present NCTE Guidelines for Nonsexist Use of Language; they have not been changed in this reprint. The writing samples have been transcribed into print. Misspellings and sentence fragments have been retained, with periods added.

has thoughts on his mind which he *wants* to express. Not only do the children in grades three through six with whom we have worked *want* to express their ideas in writing, they also *like* to express their thoughts in writing. Once the writing is done, they want to express themselves aloud with members of the class. Why, then, do children grow to detest writing in the upper grades? Can it be that their linguistic imagination and their inner voice which permit our students to know themselves have been extinguished?

Writing as a growth process. Although most children, by the time they begin school, know how to structure the English language using the rules of an introductory text in transformational grammar, rules pertaining to declaratives and interrogatives, affirmatives and negatives, active and passive voice, simple sentences, conjoined sentences, and embedded sentences, they have no explicit grammatical or rhetorical knowledge. This preschool linguisic genius still communicates like a child.

Giving a very simple stimuli of asking a child to describe a picture so that another child can identify it will offer the following difficulties for the child: (1) He will have difficulty relying exclusively on language. He wants to use his whole body for expression. (2) He will show egocentrism by using terms and experiences not shared by the listeners. (3) He will fail to use contrasts so that the listener can associate similarities and differences, assuming that the listener knows much more about the subject than he actually does.

This simple discourse situation presented to a preschool child illustrates to the teacher of children's writing just how deeply embedded are the writing difficulties which we attempt to alleviate in the process in teaching writing. In asking a nine-year-old child to tell a story he has heard, the teacher must be aware of the child's ability to order information so that the reader has consecutive information at each point of the narration, the teacher must be aware of the child's ability to embed sentences to convey likely figure-ground relationships in his linguistic and psychological subordination, the teacher must be aware of the child's logical conjoining of words and sentences by the use of coordination, the teacher must be aware of the child's production of a sequence of thoughts that describe a line of thought, the teacher must be aware of the child's ability to shift styles depending upon his intended reader, and the teacher must be aware of the child's ability to use metaphor to capture similarities and differences in a situation. None of these writing abilities are dependent upon grammatical knowledge, none are well developed in early childhood or in early and late adolescence. There are no definitive limits to any of these skills, and even professional writers struggle to maintain or reach these mentalistic behaviors. The struggle which professional writers encounter in surmounting these problems are at the rhetorical level rather than the grammatical level. A case in point is illustrated in Jack London's semi-autobiographical novel, *Martin Eden.*

In spite of all that we know about the structure of English, there is very little which we can do to make a child write or talk like an adult, a first grader like a fourth grader, a seventh grader like a twelfth grader, and a twelfth grader like a professional contributor to *Atlantic* or *Harper's.* Yet children who are learning to read can and must simultaneously be learning to write. It does not take the child long to realize that the style of a note to Grandmother explaining that he will take off from school the day before Thanksgiving in order to have a longer visit with her is different from a note containing the same information but directed to the school principal. Even a supermarket list can be ordered in a logical order so that merchandise can be picked off the shelves in the most expedient way. In the classroom, stimuli for eliciting children's writing should in some way permit the child and the teacher to become aware of the rhetorical problems in writing. The quasi-linguistic problems such as spelling, capitalization, and punctuation, so apparent when an adult looks at children's writing, must be de-emphasized by the teacher. Rather, the teacher should attend to the child's linguistic and rhetorical development which is as inevitable as the child's physical development.

The following samples of children's writing will illustrate growth patterns in linguistic and rhetorical thought problems encountered by children at different grade levels. At each level, the stimulus for eliciting the written response was different and can be inferred from the response.

These children are retelling an experience from their reading. How might the teacher "receive" these two samples? Children 1A and 1B have done well. Linguistic errors are negligible. In reading child 1A's sample, the teacher senses an omission in the logical development in the sequence of events. This problem was not unique to child 1A. However, child 1A is able to place a time sequence in his passage with the word *then.* Child 1B allows the reader to make this logical connection by placing his sentences in a logical order. Needless to say, both children have good kernel sentence sense. The teacher need not state all of these facts to the children, but he now has a beginning for further language exercises with the children. The teacher is beginning to "receive" the children's writing. The special meaning of "receive" as used here implies that the teacher listens to or reads the child's message, he accepts the message in the mode in which it is delivered without criticizing the language of the message, and then responds to the message in such a way that his response suggests a stimulus to which the child can once again respond in either the oral or written language mode. With this communications process, the dialogue between the child, his peers, and the adults in his environment remains open and continuing.

The first impression in comparing grade one with grade two is that grade two has more information packed into each writing sample. However, syntactically they are not very different. The information is apparent in the vocabulary, the coordination, and the metaphor. Student 2A is having difficulty in ordering events and in placing referents and their modifiers. Student 2B demonstrates the problem of egocentrism. The babies and the rabbit family exhibit human emotions such as love and pride and finally the student forgets the rabbits completely and is preoccupied with her friends, especially Patty. The child is no longer able to identify with the animals. As children start to write about themselves, "receiving" their writing becomes more difficult for the teacher.

The difference between thought and language in grades two and three is astounding. By grade three the child is writing cursive, he is using coordination and subordination to express relationships. His egocentrism appears appropriate to the writing stimuli offered the child. Here the teacher's knowledge of literary analysis will help him see that a value system is being displayed by both student 3A and 3B. Other people's value systems are not always easy to accept. Student 3A expresses a value in being trusted, permitted to show responsibility and to grow up so that she can do the exciting things big people do. Will the teacher's value system and the child's clash at this point if the teacher cannot understand the child's world view? How will the teacher receive these values? Student 3B expresses another set of values. First, he is impressed by the importance of decisions in his life ambition, to

---

1A

If you want to catch a Leprochaun you must go to a dark woods. Plant a mousetrap. Put hay over it. Then he will get caught in the trap.

1B

If you want to catch a leprochaun you must go to a dark.woods. Make a hole and put a box over the hole. Put sticks over it and grass. He will come out and fall in the hole.

Figure 1.

be a winning quarterback. He also shows appreciation for other boys who are good football players. There is a complete lack of the competitive spirit in the paper. The competitive spirit is a highly praised American value. How will a teacher receive these values? Grade three appears to be the place to start teaching writing as encoding.

In these two fourth grade samples [Figures 4A and 4B], the reader can grasp the writer's sense of audience and his ability to express his own voice. Time sequences become better defined as the children learn to control grammatical past and present tense. A real effort is made to

---

2A

Peter Rabbit

Once upon a time there lived a rabbit his name was peter. He lived with his mother and father under the big tree. He has wiskers as big as my little finger. Then his mother died and his father did to. He has blue eyes. He has long Pointed ears and he is Pink.

The End
Rusty

2B

Mr. and Mrs. Rabbit had 5 babys

Mrs. Rabbit is a Rabbit.
She had 5 babys. Mr. Rabbit like the little babys. I my Pord of Mrs. Rabbit. I think they are Pretty. Mr. and Mrs. Rabbit sould be Pord Too. one baby has blue eyes. two has pink eyes. two has black eyes. They are very Pretty. I Love Mr. and Mrs. Rabbit and the 5 babys they like my very best friend. She is Patty. I have a lots of friend. But Patty is my very best friend.

The End

Figure 2.

3A

    I like being eight and nine because you get to do stuff *exciting*. And join clubs you want to be in. And in brownies you fly up to girl scouts. You are trusted more often when you are eight and nine years old. You get to do things that big people do.

3B

    What are you going to do. Laterl throw the baum or go for it. To be a winning Quarterback your going to think about those things. I was once a quarterback but I threw quick, and got yardeg. My team was pleased wiht me. But when Dean F. came in boy did he do a good job. But when you grow up go out for football. and Dan G. boy did make a run back.

Figure 3.

control and order the sequence of events. These papers will not be difficult for the teacher to receive. The problem in receiving these papers is to receive them in such a way as to create a new stimulus which will elicit a more personal response to the next writing activity.

Something important happens between the fourth and the fifth grade in the development of the child's thought and language process. There is a complexity of events in the child's expression which is also obvious in his complex sentence structure. However, the complex of ideas seems to lack a psychological depth of field which can be obtained through a skillful use of coordination and subordination. Student 5A is involved in a cause and effect type of relationship which is somewhat successful. Student 5B might have wanted to indicate some causal relationships, but these sequences are not successfully conveyed since there are big gaps in the student's perceptions of a world of experience probably known only through vicarious experience. The teacher has to receive the values expressed by student 5B with different psychological and sociological judgments from those used for receiving similar values expressed by a mature writer.

The thought and language growth between the fifth and sixth grades is not so striking as that between the fourth and fifth grades. If one criteria of the word "creative" is imaginative or different, this sign of creativity is present in these two writing samples. Perhaps a better sign of creativity in children is the ability to order their thoughts. This

---

4A

Paul Bunyan And His Ox
Most of you know Paul Bunyan. He way the man in the world. He liked to work on roads. Did you know he luilt a brige across the Pacific Ocean. It only took him one mouth. He started in March and ended in Apirl. Babe his blue ox cut the trees. Then he hald them down to the river. Paul Bunyan lifted them up. Then he nailed them together. He got into the muttle of the Ocean and lifted it up.

The End

4B

In The Woods
One day when I was walking in the wood's I saw a great big thing. I didn't know what it was. So I started to walk toward it. I saw that it was Paul Bunyan's pipe. I knew it was his because it was so big. Then I walked a little bit more in the woods and do you know what I saw then? It was Paul Bunyan's axe. So I walk ahead a little bit. And then I saw Paul Bunyan in person.

The End

Figure 4.

is also evident in these two writing samples. Creativity should not be confused with the bizarre and teachers should not resort to all kinds of gimmickry as stimuli for eliciting bizarre responses from their student writers. For the purposes of stimulating responses and receiving written responses from children, the most effective criteria of creativity should be the child's expression of his sincere individuality, his ability to order his perceptions and his language, his ability to obtain a psychological depth of field to obtain meaningful relationships, and to test hypotheses and to reach generalizations which lead to further hypothesis testing.

In sample 6A, there is a degree of the rebel and the social critic coming through. The student is testing social values, especially the superficial ones. In sample 6B, there are signs of fear and anxiety, emotions which seem different from the secure emotions of love, friendship, pride, respect, and cooperation which were apparent in the lower grades. These less welcome but important emotions are difficult for teachers to receive and deal with in class.

5A

The First Elephant

It was July 9, 423 B.C. when a little elf was swimming in Bula Bula creek. Then all of the sudden a Bula Bula monster sprang out of the water. A Bula Bula monster looks like a tuna can on its side with a car running over it. The little elf swam as fast as he could to shore but he was'nt fast enough. The monster threw a rock at the elf and hit him in the head. The elf got so mad that he tryed to put a spell on the monster but rock took all his powers away. So he climbed up a tree. After the Bula Bula monster left he climbed down. But without his powers he couldnt get home. So he spent 180 years eating ants. After 180 years he got so big and fat you could'nt see around him. Later scientists found out what happened so they called it a elfant because it ate so many ants. Later his name was changed to an elephant.

By Craig

5B

Flower Power!

One dull day I sat down in our racky rocker and started to read the News Paper. One page 4 it said join the cools at the Super Sonic Sack. So at 4 minutes after 1 minute I went to the sack and I was able to join. One Tuesday I went to the Super Sonic Sack and we just sat around and told jokes and riddles and this cool kid said "Experience is a teacher, But here's what makes me burn, He's always teaching me things I do not care to learn. On Wild Wednesday we went camping to visit Flower Powered Boys!

Figure 5.

This discussion of the development of elementary children's thought and language has deliberately not been a statistical one. Computer programs are available for obtaining word and structure counts to measure children's language growth. These language responses must be correlated against thought responses before we can completely "receive" and understand children's writing.

Children's Writing in the Elementary Curriculum. In our research on children's writing,[1] we have discovered that stimulating children to write at the third through sixth grade is not a difficult problem. Certainly any kind of experience which stimulates a child's imagination will serve as a stimulus for oral or written discourse, be it a picture, a film, an experience from life, a retold narrative, a dialogue, a moment of creative dramatics, or simply the presence of another receptive person. In the research described here, we used picture stimuli and accompanying directions. The research was also concerned with some pedagogical questions about the pictures such as: Does it matter if the pictures are black and white or color? Does it matter if the directions

---

6A

Clarence the Crosseyed Principal

One day there was aman looking for a job. He went to school to make a teleaphone call and he heard a hello in the backround and it was a music teacher a crosseyed one. He was terified so he ran down the hall and the other prin Mr. Peabody went out of saw him and he had to sit in the corner with a dence cap on. Then the music teacher started to sing and Mr. Peabody went out of his mind.

So then Clarence became principal. He made new rules for the school, some were Do not walk in the halls, but run. The girls couldn't ware long dresses and the boys had to ware long hair. One day there was a fire alarm and he put on a raincoat. So the town's people named the school Crosseyed school of Clarenceville.

6B

The Seceret Cave

One night when Kevin was sleeping he heard the strangest sound. It souned like it was coming from the Seceret Cave. So Kevin got up and dressed and went to the Seceret Cave. When he got to the cave there was a bat in the doorway. He was screaming. We scared him away. Then we went in and looked around. Down in the water hole was a young boy. He was dead. Someone had trough him in the hole. And held him there for a while. But who? Keven thought. Kevin went home and told his dad. And he asked Kevin if he had touched it. I said No. In the morning we called the police.

Figure 6.

are general or specific? Does it matter if the pictures are abstract or concrete?

A set of large color photographs and paintings was duplicated in black and white as well as color. A set of general and a set of specific directions were prepared to accompany each picture. The pictures were then rated on an abstract-concrete scale.

Results of our study show that the black and white-concrete pictures were more successful than black and white-abstract, color-concrete, or color-abstract. The children who received a black and white-concrete picture wrote more and tended to see the narrative-descriptive possibilities in the picture. These students produced more subordinate adverbial clauses, used more adverbs other than time, place, and manner modifiers, and more medial adverbs. They tended to use fewer nouns per T-unit (a T-unit is a main clause with all of its related modifying phrases and clauses), fewer words per clause, fewer words in fragments, and fewer coordinated nouns. They also tended to tell a story rather than simply describe what they saw on the page. Apparently the black and white-concrete picture provided enough stimulus to energize and to direct the students' creative and linguistic imaginations. The difficulty of using a picture, a film, a play, or a literary work which is a completed composition in itself as a writing stimulus is that it does not energize the student's creative imagination even though it does produce a complete and satisfying aesthetic experience.

The type of directions, general or specific, used to accompany the stimulus makes no difference at all. The stimulus generally will capture the child's attention, and he will do what he will and can with it, no matter what the directions tell him to do.

By contrasting black and white pictures to color pictures, the black and white pictures produced fewer adjectives but these pictures produced more adverbs, more clauses but shorter ones, more types of kernel sentences, more single-base transformations, more modals, and more clauses per T-unit, thus producing longer T-units.

As one would expect, the girls wrote more than the boys, but when an adjustment was made for amount, there were fewer if any differences in structural variables. If our goals in teaching writing are clarity, economy, and directness of expression, the boys have it over the girls.

Receiving the child's written response to the stimulus is a more difficult matter and not so amenable to experimental research. However, certain conclusions from examining the development of children's writing as illustrated by the samples in this paper imply certain guidelines in receiving children's written expression.

The teacher who receives children's writing must be both a literary analyst and a psychologist. Like the literary analyst and the psychologist, the teacher must know: (1) the history of the life and times of the author, (2) what the author is actually saying on the page, (3) the psychological development of the author and the psychological clues to an interpretation of what the author is saying, and (4) the social and cultural background of the author.

The teacher cannot receive a child's writing by verbalizing to the child a historical, psychological, or sociological analysis of the child's content. Nor can the teacher receive a child's writing by criticizing and attacking the child's language. Not even a friendly, penning in red, "You have made nine spelling errors!" at the end of a child's journal entry is appropriate. The teacher must respond first to the child's writing by accepting it. The writing can be read aloud, put on an audiotape, acted out, pinned on a wall, or stenciled and published in a school or classroom publication. In order to keep the children from going dry, the teacher must continually enrich the child's experience in the nonverbal world through art work, museum exhibits, and creative dramatics. These activities might actually result in less time for writing but in most instances they are worth the time. For example, a young child who had just read a poem about a cat and had participated in an oral vocabulary building association drill preferred to draw all of the soft, warm objects he could call to mind including his mother. Museums are nearer to our door than might be expected, especially historical, natural, and industrial museums which suit our purposes even better than art museums. Dioramas in these museums can easily be interpreted by a child's linguistic imagination.

The teacher must continually enrich the child's experience in the verbal world by reading poetry and stories, and discussing current interests and events. In providing this type of verbal and nonverbal enrichment, the teacher and the children must make a deliberate and difficult attempt to stay away from the ready-made word and symbol world of advertisements so that "Let Johnny put you in the driver's seat" doesn't suddenly and seriously appear in a child's tall tale. The child's symbols must be his own so that his teacher and his peers can understand the child's true thoughts.

Frequently the symbols in the form of figurative and unique language will not be the immediate result of a stimulus. The child's inner voice may be put in after the public voice is expressed and the child can see that he has something personal to say. This should be the primary purpose of rewriting, not necessarily the cleaning up of spelling and punctuation errors.

The writing stimulus given the child must also be related to the teacher's purposes. If, for example, the teacher is attempting to evoke and analyze symbolism in the children's writing, stimuli such as apple, fire, flag, snake, lighthouse, birds can be used in a number of forms in order to observe if and how these potential symbols might manifest themselves in the children's thought. Metaphor and similes might be evoked by offering the child contrasting stimuli so that similarities and differences can be observed and figures of speech unconsciously produced.

If the teacher's purpose is to help the child understand what sincerity of expression is and to help the child discover his own inner voice, the writing stimuli might be simply forcing the child to write a parody or to imitate an easy piece such as "Casey at the Bat." A child's ability to handle realism can be examined by taking the child's treatment of a subject and contrasting it with the treatment given it by another writer. For example, a child's treatment of a topic such as "An Old Man I Knew" can be contrasted with a passage from *The Old Man and the Sea* or "The Man with a Hoe."

Children should also be provided with emotional human problems as their stimuli. If teachers shy away from such stimuli as a family argument, poverty, drunkenness, close personal relationships, hatred, and death, with what adults will the child ever discuss these human problems? Certainly not his parents. Discussing these human emotions with children is difficult for most teachers and can best be attempted in indirect ways such as dramatics, story telling, dialogue, and plot synopsis. Frequently, creative dramatics can get at these emotions without words before they are verbalized, but here the teacher must be a skillful director.

In the intellectual history of education, instruction in writing has been reserved for the economic and intellectual elite, whereas instruction in reading has been a central goal in the education of the masses. As a result, the ability to write has become a caste and class marker. In discussing the lower working class pupils, Bernstein[2] states:

> Such children will experience difficulty in learning to read, in extending their vocabulary, and in learning to use a wide range of formal possiblities for the organization of verbal meaning; their reading and writing will be slow and will tend to be associated with a concrete, activity-dominated, content; their power of verbal comprehension will be limited; grammar and syntax will pass them by; the propositions they use will suffer from a large measure of dislocation; their verbal planning function will be restricted; their thinking will tend to be rigid—the number of new relationships available to them will be very limited.

Bernstein concludes that these features of lower working-class pupil language "is a culturally induced backwardness transmitted and sustained through the effects of linguistic processing."

This linguistic, caste-class marker promises to remain in the United States as long as elementary education is directed toward reading with little or no classroom time or financial assistance given to writing. Writing instruction cannot await the last two years of high school; then it is too late to learn how to express one's thoughts in the written code. Writing instruction, the process of encoding, must begin with reading instruction, the process of decoding. Our definition of literacy must be reshaped to include reading and writing and only then will we be on the road to reducing the shocking number of illiterates (more than three million) in the United States. A child's concept attainment ability can grow only in proportion to the growth of his oral and written language ability.

Resources

Brown, Rollo W. *How the French Boy Learns to Write* (Champaign, Illinois: National Council of Teachers of English, 1965).

Cofer, Charles N. and Musgrave, Barbara S., ed. *Verbal Behavior and Learning* (New York: McGraw-Hill, 1963).

Conlin, David A. and Herman, George R. *Resources for Modern Grammar and Composition* (New York: American Book Co., 1965).

Creber, J. W. Patrick. *Sense and Sensitivity* (London: University of London Press, 1965).

Dunning, Stephen, ed. *English for the Junior High Years* (Champaign, Illinois: National Council of Teachers of English, 1969).

Holbrook, David. *Children's Writing* (Cambridge: Cambridge University Press, 1967).

Marshall, Sybil. *Adventure in Creative Education* (New York: Pergamon Press, 1968).

Menyuk, Paula. *Sentences Children Use*, Research Monograph No. 52 (Cambridge, Massachusetts: Massachusetts Institute of Technology, 1969).

Moffett, James. *Teaching the Universe of Discourse* (Boston: Houghton Mifflin, 1968).

Murray, Donald M. *A Writer Teaches Writing: A Practical Method of Teaching Composition* (Boston: Houghton Mifflin, 1968).

Passow, A. Harry, Goldberg, Miriam, and Tennenbaum, Abraham J. ed. *Education of the Disadvantaged* (New York: Holt, Rinehart and Winston, 1967).

Spolin, Viola. *Improvisation for the Theater* (Evanston, Illinois: Northwestern University Press, 1963).

Sweet, Henry. *The Practical Study of Languages* (London: Oxford University Press, 1964).

Whitehead, Frank. *The Disappearing Dais* (London: Chatto & Windus, 1966).

Vygotsky, Lev S. *Thought and Language* (Cambridge, Massachusetts: Massachusetts Institute of Technology, 1962).

Notes

1. L. S. Golub and W. C. Frederick, "An Analysis of Children's Writing under Different Stimulus Conditions," *Research in the Teaching of English,* 4 (Fall, 1970) 168-181.

2. Basil Bernstein, "Social Structure, Language, and Learning," *Educational Research,* 3 (June, 1961) 163-176.

Part Three: Distancing

Introduction to Distancing

Distancing refers to the relationships among writer-speaker, audience-reader, and subject. For the beginning writer, there may be an added problem, distance to task. That is, the writer must somehow get into the writing task at hand. Distance to task involves many of the same issues that were explored in the previous section on *processing*. Sometimes a beginning writer gets into the task by talking about it or mapping it or drawing it. Beginning writers who are having trouble often begin their essays with statements like "I am writing about my favorite person," or even "I am writing a paper for my third period class on the subject of what caused World War I." This problem of how to start is a central concern in the theory and practice of Robert Zoellner's talk-write paradigm. The other articles in this section examine the problems of distance-to-subject and distance-to-audience.

Distance to Task

Robert Zoellner, in a selection from "Talk-Write: A Behavioral Pedagogy for Composition," agrees with D. Gordon Rohman that thinking must be distinguished from writing. But while Rohman turns to journal writing, analogies, and meditation, Zoellner turns to talk. In fact, Zoellner argues that talk *is* thought, that thinking something and saying something are one and the same thing. For Zoellner, changing from *think-write* to *talk-write* shifts "our pedagogy from that which is empirically inaccessible to a phenomenon which is observable and manipulatable" (p. 274). One thing that is observable in talk is the strategy a student uses to solve problems. Herbert A. Simon (1981) argues that in most problem situations, such as those found in writing, the solution or response used is usually not an optimal or best answer, only a reasonably satisfactory one. Says Simon, "we only rarely have a method of finding the optimum." Simon labels this acceptance of the satisfactory as "satisficing," a combination of *sufficing* and *satisfying*. This strategy is evident in the student exchanges reported by Vincent and Patricia Wixon in "Using Talk-Write in the Classroom." In talk-write both the writer and the questioner are "satisficing" as the writing develops.

Distance to Subject

The writer must not only get into the task but also establish some distance to subject. Emily Brontë's *Wuthering Heights* is a good example of a writer trying to find an appropriate distance. If Brontë had written a personal letter to Heathcliff to declare her love, then one would say that she had, in James Britton's terms, written transactional prose. That is, she had written from the point of view of a participant in the action. But Brontë wrote the tale from the point of view of a male named Lockwood and sometimes from the point of view of the maid as reported by Lockwood. In Britton's terms, telling the story through Lockwood puts the writer in a spectator role and establishes a poetic mode. In a selection from "An Approach to Function Categories," Britton, Tony Burgess, Nancy Martin, Alex McLeod, and Harold Rosen report that English secondary schools assign primarily transactional writing, some poetic writing, and almost no expressive writing. Expressive writing is basic in Britton's theory because it is the form of writing in which the writer represents an experience personally.

Arthur Applebee (1977) modified Britton's theory by adding two dimensions—one for conversion and another for articulation:

Conversion

(Animal Farm)	*(Modest Proposal)*	*(The Origin of Species)*
Poetic	Expressive	Transactional
(myth)	(confessions)	(textbooks)

Articulation

James Pierce's article, "Composition Course: Pursuit of Ideas," gives examples of writing assignments that are poetic (an imaginary dialogue between two people) and transactional (a letter). This lesson, leading students through a variety of types of writing and beginning with materials from the students' direct experience, seems to answer the perennial question from teachers, "How does one get from personal experience writing to exposition?"

Distance to Audience

James Moffett, in "Rationale for a New Curriculum in English," describes the universe of discourse as the venerable trinity of *I, you, it*—informer, informed, and information. Moffett's views have helped English teachers shift their attention from strictly textual matters (introduction, body, conclusion) to the relationships among participants in a communicative event. One of these relationships is the distance to the audience—how far away is the audience in space, how well does the speaker know the audience, and how well does the audience know the speaker?

The lessons presented here by Mary K. Healy, in a selection from *Using Student Writing Response Groups in the Classroom,* and Miles Myers, in "The All-City High Project," illustrate how sensitivity to audience can be developed in various classroom assignments. Healy's writing response groups can be established in any classroom, and if the teacher is patient and careful, these groups can begin to have a powerful influence on student writing. The lessons from Myers grew out of an effort to give students direct experiences with new audiences and new subjects outside of school. In these assignments, students write to a jury they have watched, write to stockholders whom they have seen in the offices of brokers, and write thank-you letters to adults they have interviewed. In addition, students are asked to do face-to-face interviews with adults in many different types of agencies.

9 Talk-Write: A Behavioral Pedagogy for Composition

Robert Zoellner

Robert Zoellner's article begins with a short discussion of instrumental metaphors or conceptual constructs that shape the English teacher's thought process and approach to teaching and to research. Zoellner then examines the thesis that "theory and practice in English composition is presently dominated by such an instrumental metaphor" and that "this metaphor is outmoded, grossly simplistic, and inhibitory of genuine progress in teaching students on any level to write effectively" (p. 269). Ed.

The pervasively defining instrumental metaphor in our teaching of composition and rhetoric can be easily and succinctly stated: it asserts that *the written word is thought on paper*. In slightly different terms, it equates *the act of thought with the act of writing* in the sense that the scribal stream "symbolizes" both vocal utterance and the thought which generates it. We English teachers do not, of course, adhere consistently to this metaphorical equation: we have all told students, for example, to "think before they write," an admonition which at least in temporal terms makes thinking separate from and anterior to the act of writing. But this non-metaphorical formulation solves no problems and indeed raises another question: if writing is not thought in some form, then what is it? If we answer that obviously writing is the *expression* of thought we are still in a corner, for this suggests that expression is somehow non-mental, perhaps simply physiological. Their humanistic commitment will prevent most English teachers from being comfortable with such a conclusion.

Generally, however, we adhere—sometimes consciously but more often unconsciously—to an instrumental metaphor which establishes

Source: College English 30 (1969): 269–74, from a longer article that appeared on pp. 267–320. Reprinted by permission of the National Council of Teachers of English. Some usages that appear in this article are not consistent with the present NCTE Guidelines for Nonsexist Use of Language; they have not been changed in this reprint. The notes have been renumbered.

some largely undefined one-to-one relationship between the thinking process on the one hand and the written word on the other. This equivalence is evident, for example, in the majority of the textbooks that we assemble for our students. One could easily fill a five-foot bookshelf with high school and college texts which ignore entirely the *act* of writing, which have little or nothing to say about the *action* which stands as a central term between thought on the one hand and the written word on the other. The writer-as-actor seldom appears. Overwhelmingly, our textbooks—and the theory which produces them—are product-oriented rather than process-oriented, taking for the most part an artifactual and textual approach to the *written* (past tense) word and to the logical and intellective imperatives which we assume can account entirely and completely for its genesis. The student is burdened with long chapters on "clear thinking" and "logical analysis"; we divert him with the Aristotelian elegancies of the outline, and immerse him in undistributed middles, ladders of abstraction, and squares of opposition. In all of this we are assuming that if we can somehow get the student to think clearly, he will thereupon write clearly. This is not only our great metaphor. It may also be our great myth.

When we return an "F" theme to the student, we are likely to tell him in our written comment that we failed the theme because he had not "ordered his thoughts properly" or had "expressed himself obscurely," forgetting entirely that these are mentalistic assertions which Pavlov (among many others) deprecated because of their logical circularity. To tell a student that his theme is unclear and disorganized because his thought is faulty is roughly the same as asserting that "Fred ate a big meal because he was hungry," or that "Frank struck out with his fists because he was angry." Such explanations explain nothing because we have simply substituted one verbal formulation for a given segment of human behavior for another verbal formulation of the same segment.

I do *not* suggest that as English teachers we stop talking about planning and organization; nor am I saying that logical thought has nothing to do with the compositional process. I am only suggesting that our present "think-write" instrumental metaphor ignores or glosses over certain central elements of the *act* of writing. What some of these elements are can be easily ascertained by simply observing a group of students writing an in-class theme or an hour's essay test. Here, for instance, is Student A, a bright and articulate senior: we are only twenty minutes into the hour, but already she has covered five bluebook pages, her pen moving effortlessly, swiftly, and without pause over the paper. Next to her sits Student B. From earlier class discussion I know that he is even more insightful and articulate than Student A; his vocal comments have suggested to me that he may be of graduate caliber. But something is wrong. He sits hunched intensely over his desk, laboriously *drawing* each word rather than *writing* it. He has covered only two bluebook pages, and I can tell from the expression on his face that he knows he's not cutting it. Student B is therefore a puzzle: he walks, he talks, he acts with a facility equal to that of Student A; indeed, if it were otherwise, if he spoke, or opened doors, or tied his shoe-laces, or drove a car as haltingly and painfully as he writes, *I would send him to a hospital.* I am absolutely certain that he thinks with rapidity and precision. Why can't he write that way?

· Student C, in the back of the room, will be more successful as a housewife than as a Ph.D. candidate—but a couple of office conferences have made it clear that her mind is more than adequate, her vocal facility unexceptionable. Yet there she sits, locked hopelessly in an obsessive and circular little ritual. She writes a sentence, and then she reads it over, her lips moving soundlessly—and then she reads it over again, and then again. She re-dots her "i's" and re-crosses her "t's," as if putting the final touches on an oil painting. She reads the sentence over *two more times,* and then at long last plunges ahead. This is not a caricature: while I have no hard data on scribal ritualism in college students, unobtrusive eye-movement counts during test periods make it clear that many students cannot write a sentence until they have re-read the previous sentence from three to ten times.

In even worse shape is Student D; half way through the hour, when he ought to be warmed up and moving along rapidly, I find his desk covered with springs and ink-cartridges. He has instituted a thousand-mile overhaul of his ballpoint pen in the middle of the test. Student E, female and feminine, spends a six full minutes (I time her)—ten percent of the available test time—addressing herself to the cuticle-and-hangnail problem. Yet I remember that both of these students had things to say on the "Queen Mab" chapter of *Moby-Dick* which would have held a creditable place in a published article.

These students must be distinguished from Student F, who presents no problem. He has been cutting class and is obviously hung-over, in no shape to write anything. But Students A through E, multiplied by the thousands, constitute a massive indictment of current teaching methods in English composition at *all* levels, if only because large numbers of them have a 3.0 or better grade-point in those courses where the objective test has replaced the essay. They are intelligent, articulate, and vocal—but much evidence suggests that they write as badly when they leave college as they did when they entered.

It is time we explored the possibility that these failures have their source in the massive deficiencies of our instrumental think-write metaphor, which furnishes us with a pedagogy exclusively intellective and mentalistic, and therefore comfortably in consonance with our humanistic commitment. This is perhaps the nub of the problem: our humanism may be getting in the way of our common sense, which should have told us long ago that the writing difficulties I have just described cannot be due entirely to "poor preparation" or "faulty thinking"—whatever these vague and empirically inaccessible entities may be—but rather to *faulty or maladaptive behavior*. There would appear to be a concrete, discriminable, and empirically accessible behavioral dimension to the *act* of writing to which we have insufficiently attended.

One need not, however, confine oneself to classroom observation of the student actually engaged in scribal activity. The papers that come out of the theme or test situation—if viewed in a certain light—provide copious evidence of the existence of a behavioral dimension in the scribal act. But rather than inflict upon the reader yet another dreary catalog of horrible examples of student writing, I would rather suggest very quickly the practical difficulties of our think-write metaphor. When, for example, a student tells me that in Philip Freneau's "The House of Night," "everything is so dreary and foreboding that the story is told in a dreary setting," and later in the same essay asserts that the Romantic stress on imagination "tends to make the poetry more lively and give more life to the poem," I may mark in the margin, "wordy and repetitive." Here I am concentrating on the "write" half of the metaphor, or more precisely, the *written* word as artifact. The difficulty is that in telling the student that he is wordy and repetitive I am revealing the pervasive *textual* bias which is the logical concomitant of the instrumental metaphor; I am directing both my attention and the student's to a certain characteristic of the text-as-product rather than to the characteristics of the *scribal act* which produced it. I am dealing with an effect, and adroitly avoiding the problem of cause altogether.

Similarly, when a sophomore tells me that he thinks Benjamin Franklin "would be very hard to have for a friend, for he was definitely a self-made man with little formal education and he let everyone know it," I may comment in the margin, "personalistic, subjective, and irrelevant." The referents for these three evaluative terms are obviously logico-mentalistic, and assume the presence of something called "faulty thought"—but it is just as credible to assume that the student's comment is a specimen of learned behavior, and that the student is *responding* to "Benjamin Franklin" *in the only way he knows how*. The same problem appears with the student who defines *tabula rasa* as the idea "that Man's soul was a blank sheet of paper and it was Man's idea to keep it that way." If I write "comic-book oversimplification" in the margin of the test, I am again positing the presence of faulty thought processes. But we must address ourselves to the possibility that the student's version of *tabula rasa* represents a reductive pattern of response which is behavioral rather than intellective. Many students have told me that they "knew better" or "didn't mean to say that"—and it is possible we ought to believe such assertions.

The crucial question of belief in the average student's intellectual integrity—as well as the question of reading the evidence properly—is best highlighted by what might be called the behavioral "happenings" which are such a common feature of office interviews with students. Miss X told me earnestly in a theme that "one of the nicest things about Denver is that everyone has a nice place to live." When, during an office conference, I twitted her about this greeting-card assertion, she became visibly irritated. Well, if I was going to be *that* way about it, of *course* she knew that everyone in Denver did *not* have a nice place to live—did I take her for a fool? Miss X thought me the most unreasonable of men: I was taking her scribal assertions seriously, thus substituting new ground-rules for the ones to which she was clearly accustomed. The significant thing here is not so much the scribal artifact that Miss X produced, but rather her *behavior*, the pattern of responses that she brought to bear in the writing situation.

A similar problem arose with Miss Y, a senior who signed up for my Composition Analysis class because she was an English certification candidate. When I asked the class to compose a series of topic sentences on subjects of "urgent interest" to the average high school student, this future English teacher came up with this: "A happy person is one whose inner beauty shines through." When in conference I asked Miss Y if she *really* believed that the average high school student—involved in 300 cubes with four on the floor, the atonalities of Simon and Garfunkel, and the sexual urgencies of adolescence—would find "inner beauty" a compelling theme topic, she found the idea laughable. Actually, she said, she hoped to focus her professional career on special education for delinquent adolescents, and she knew perfectly well that she would "probably have to yank the marijuana cigarettes out of their mouths before I can ever get them to talk about 'inner beauty'." But when I asked her why she did not draw on this hard-nosed realism when formulating theme topic assignments, she was unable to give an account of her behavior.

Miss X and Miss Y may or may not be typical of college writers—but it would appear to be entirely hopeless to insist endlessly and ritualistically on the priority of clear thought and the instrumental utility of the think-write metaphor if in actual fact we are on the college level encountering significant numbers of students who have been taught—or conditioned to—a *behavioral* pattern of responses to the writing situation which involves the conscious or unconscious dissociation of what the student really thinks on the one hand, from what he actually writes on the other. Before we commit ourselves irrevocably to a totalistically intellective pedagogy, we ought to first ascertain whether thought stands in immediate relation to scribal activity, or whether there exists an intervening behavioral term which, in the phrasing of the information theorists, constitutes a quantifiable and manipulatively accessible amount of "noise in the channel."

The solution, of course, may be to exploit other available channels. Indeed, the most compelling and suggestive office-interview "happening" occurs when I read the student's utterly opaque and impenetrable sentence or paragraph aloud to him. "Mr. Phillips," I say, "I simply can't make head nor tail out of this paragraph; what in the world were you trying to say?" When I pose this question in this situation, large numbers of students, certainly a majority, respond with a bit of behavior which I suggest may be of immense significance for the teaching of composition. They open their mouths, and *they say the thing they were unable to write.* "Well, Dr. Zoellner," they usually begin, "all I meant to say in that paragraph was that . . . ," and out it comes, a sustained, articulated, rapid-fire segment of "sound-stream," usually from five to fifteen seconds' duration, which communicates to me effectively and quickly what they "had in mind" when they produced the impenetrable paragraph I hold in my hand. And all I had to do to elicit this fascinating bit of behavior was to ask them *to shift from the scribal modality to the vocal modality.*

These explanatory segments of sound-stream, which a linguist would call free utterances, I call "cortical utterances," or, in the case of some topics and some students, "visceral blurts." I think they are important for two reasons. In the first place, I wonder if the cortical utterance or visceral blurt does not shoot a large hole in our instrumental think-write metaphor. If Mr. Phillips' paragraph does not communicate to the reader, most of us would assert that Mr. Phillips obviously hadn't "taken enough time" to sort out and order his ideas. But when I ask him what he meant in the paragraph, his vocal response to this question is characterized by alacrity and immediacy: there is generally little hesitation, little fumbling, and no discernible time-segment when he might be assumed to be re-thinking the paragraph. In fact, the reflexive rapidity of the cortical utterance suggests strongly that Mr. Phillips *had* thought it out, and that if the paragraph is opaque the problem lies not in the realm of thought, but elsewhere.

In the second place, I suggest that the cortical utterance or visceral blurt is important because it may possibly provide us with a *point d'appui* from which to build a new instrumental metaphor and a new pedagogy which will be, in Theodore Sarbin's phrase, "more in keeping with concurrent scientific vocabularies." The cortical utterance is, of course, vocal rather than scribal. Consequently, as a communicative unit, it exhibits all the lingual and paralingual characteristics of the sound stream which are not available in the scribal modality. But when we strip these vocal characteristics away we are frequently if not always left with a word-pattern substrate which is (a) *protoscribal* and (b) *rhetorically viable*. It won't do as writing, but it may furnish us with a behaviorally derived datum which we can use to begin to teach writing. Even more important, by shifting our attention from thought process to operative utterance we shift our pedagogy from that which is empirically inaccessible to a phenomenon which is observable and manipulatable. Finally, for the generalized and abstractive imperatives of thought we substitute *the behaving student* in all his uniqueness and individuality.

But if the cortical utterance gives us a *point d'appui* for a new pedagogy, it does not, of itself, give us a rationale for that pedagogy. For this we must turn elsewhere, and I now propose to take the reader through a quick review of certain principles underlying what behavioral psychologists call "learning theory." This can best be accomplished by turning our attention to the behavior of infrahuman organisms such as the white rat in a "learning situation," and then making the extrapolation—perhaps successfully and perhaps not—from rodent to student.[1]

In the remaining pages of his article, Zoellner provides a detailed discussion of the application of operant conditioning theories to the current think-write pedagogy in English composition and proposes classroom techniques incorporating these principles of operant learning into a talk-write pedagogy. Ed.

Note

1. For a general behavioral discussion of learning, addressed to student teachers and using a vocabulary somewhat different from what I shall employ here, see James M. Thyne, *The Psychology of Learning and Techniques of Teaching* (New York, 1963).

10 Using Talk-Write in the Classroom

Vincent Wixon and Patricia Wixon

In 1969, Robert Zoellner filled nearly an entire issue of *College English* describing a behavioral approach he was using in teaching composition, one he called talk-write. He saw that students often could talk very clearly and fluently, explaining meaning in their incoherent and graceless prose, so he got his students to revise by having them say aloud what they meant to write. We have adapted Zoellner's ideas for our classrooms, believing that students improve their skills by talking out their writing. And they improve while getting help *during* the writing process.

The talk-write method is simple. Pair students (or let them pair themselves) and give each team a wide felt-tip pen and a section of butcher paper or newsprint taped to the wall. The large writing area helps students escape the blank 8½-by-11-inch paper syndrome. With butcher paper, they are more apt to experiment, change words, and cross out what they don't like, realizing language is to be played with; it's not unchangeable once written.

Each team has a writer and a questioner. The writer will talk out what he or she wants to write with the questioner encouraging, helping to bring out material by asking natural questions like, "What happened next?" or, "I don't follow; tell me more." Once the team decides it has enough information, the writer will start writing, talking out each section (perhaps a sentence at a time) before writing. While the writer is writing, the teammate serves as adder and clarifier, helping the writer remember the details and order by asking pertinent questions. Also, the teammate-questioner helps the writer change confusing details or references, and the questioner's positive cues keep the writer talking. The questioner assists but doesn't dominate. When the com-

Source: Adapted from "Getting It Out, Getting It Down: Adapting Zoellner's Talk-Write," *English Journal* 66 (1977): 70–73 and "An Update on Talk-Write in the Classroom," *Oregon English* 2 (1980): 23–24, 35. Used with permission of the National Council of Teachers of English and *Oregon English*.

129

position is complete, it will probably look messy with sentences crossed out, sections reorganized, changes in spelling and mechanics. But while reading it aloud, the writer should hear just what he or she intended to say. Then the questioner should read it aloud so the writer can hear it in another voice. Next the partners switch roles and begin with a fresh piece of paper.

An example of a descriptive writing assignment and the talk-write process could begin with the teacher saying:

> Think back to the places you have lived. Now think of your favorite of these places, perhaps a favorite room or a spot outside that place. Now describe it. You should try to use all the senses. You might include what the room smelled like, how the lighting affected seeing in the room, what the floor felt like. Describe each part completely enough for us to feel we are there. You should write at least two paragraphs.

The teams will then go to their papers and begin. The writer, Eric, talks out his whole idea. Eric may say to his teammate, "I want to write about when we lived in this big house that used to be a barn."

To which Beth may reply, "A barn! Where was that?"

"Oh, it was by this steep hill in Portland."

"What did you like so much about that barn-house?"

"Well, it had these neat stairs."

"What was so neat about the stairs?"

"Well, they came out. They were built so they kinda swerved around."

"I'm not sure what you mean. Like a circular stair?"

"No, I mean they went up, then there was a wide place where they turned—I guess it's called a landing. Then they went up some more and we used to put an old army blanket across the railing and we'd play army games."

"Who is 'we'?"

"Oh, my brother and me."

"Was he older or younger than you?"

"Two years older."

"Sounds good. Why don't you write that down."

"Okay. I'll start with, 'I remember when I was seven and my brother was nine and we lived in a big house that used to be a barn.'"

"Is it important to say where this house was?"

"Yeah. I'll say it was by a steep hill in Portland, and there was this window that if you stretched up to it you could see over the top of the hill."

"Are you going to put that part about the window in your writing?"

"Yeah. I'll say there was this small window up high above the stairs and you could see over the top of the hill out of the window. Oh, and the stairs were real dark 'cause we couldn't reach the socket to put a lightbulb in."

"Anything more about the stairs?"

"Yeah. They were steep and the landing was about four feet wide. We'd put this blanket up and pretend we were in jail. The railings on the stairs were the jail bars, ya know. And we'd sit and watch the rain hit that high window and we'd plan how we were going to escape out that window."

"Okay, sounds like you're ready to write. How are you going to begin?"

Eric writes down his ideas, reads them aloud, and makes changes with Beth's help.

> When I was seven and my brother was nine, we lived in a big house that used to be a barn, it was by a steep hill in Portland and it had a small high window in the dark stairs where you could see over the top of the hill.

He then moves to the interior of the house, following the same technique of writing, reading aloud, and rewriting until he is pleased with the writing.

> The stairs were very steep and we played on them when it was raining. We hung a scratchy old army blanket across the wood railings on the stairs landing. We fastened the blanket with pieces of string on one side and a stack of old magazines on the other. The blanket was the ceiling of the enemy jail we were trapped in.

Through the talk-write dialogue the students use each other's strengths. Beth may know how to spell some words that Eric cannot; Eric may be excellent at supplying detail. And by reading aloud and listening, both students will catch mistakes in construction they might otherwise miss in silent reading.

Eric finishes his writing and revises the final sentence:

> We huddled on the musty floor of our prison and looked through the bars, watching the rain come down the high window and we devised complex escape plans.

Near the end of the talk-write assignment, the teacher, who has been working with other teams, arrives with words of encouragement, praising Eric and Beth for the details and organization. The teacher may remind Eric to try to use active verbs, perhaps to describe how the rain is coming down the window. The teacher avoids negative criticism, especially early in using talk-write, but may find this the perfect time to work with the comma splice in paragraph one.

After the writings are complete, the teacher guides the class around the room, pointing out good things in all the writings or focusing on a few student papers. The teacher emphasizes choices the writer made in the order or in the details and points out well-written sentences and mature punctuation. Using the paper as part of a longer assignment might also be discussed.

With talk-write, writing becomes public. Each student is a model of the writing act for others, and students can walk around, reading and commenting on others' work, receiving, in Frederick H. Kanfer's terms, vicarious reinforcement—"that which increases the probability that we will do 'what we see others doing successfully.'"[1] This public aspect gives the writer a stake in writing; the student is producing it for peers—not just for the teacher. Even students with poor basic skills will write better and more interestingly. Not only will they help each other, but basic students will often write more using talk-write than they will when working alone. If a basic student is paired occasionally with a responsible better writer, gentle suggestions from the better writer can help the basic student make strong writing improvements.

Allowing students to use their vocal skills to improve their writing skills produces other benefits. In speaking, a student has a unique voice that is often washed out in writing. Talk-write can help give writing a truer voice while at the same time it improves speaking, making it more precise. Also, the student's talk is the specification for writing. An "outside" vocabulary is not imposed—words spring from the student's existing way of saying things. The student attains writing competence by constantly and critically listening to herself or himself.

In using talk-write for the first time, teachers frequently wonder about the ability of students to act as competent questioners. The class may benefit from a demonstration of the dialogue between the writer and the questioner, performed either by the teacher and a student or by two students the teacher trains. The proficiency of the questioner will quickly improve as the assignment is repeated.

Talk-write should be considered a first draft and should reflect the multitude of changes seen on any first draft. Therefore, talk-write should not be graded. (If necessary, students can be given points for participating, but what they write should not be graded or many of the benefits of using this process will be lost.) The talk-write assignment should be short, a paragraph or two in length, so that there will be enough time for both partners in a team to serve as writers and ques-tioners during a single class period. Also, the method is intense with the questioning, clarifying, and rewriting, so it is difficult to sustain for a long time.

Talk-write works for a variety of assignments at nearly every grade level. The assignment might be a self-contained exercise to develop fluency, it might be saved for comparison with other student writings, or it might be used as part of a larger assignment.

One typical second-grade talk-write assignment is writing a thank-you letter. Jayne Freeman of Lewelling Elementary School in Milwaukie, Oregon, introduces this assignment in early January while students have a fresh memory of a holiday gift for which they can write a thank-you note. She models the letter form on a large sheet of butcher paper and leaves it on display for students to refer to while they work in pairs.

Julie Hadley was hired midyear as a fourth-grade teacher at Richmond Elementary School in Salem, Oregon. About four weeks after she began, she asked her students to think back to the first day she met them and to talk-write a paragraph on their observations of her that first day. Hadley was delighted with the wide variety in her students' descriptions: the jewelry she wore; her long, dark hair; her smile and laugh; her sitting close and listening. The assignment proved to be a strong beginning lesson on describing a person. By putting the paragraphs together, the class produced a composite characterization.

DeEtta Scarborough, a sixth-grade teacher at Central Point Elementary School in Central Point, Oregon, has used talk-write with her classes for three years. The first week of school she has students write a paragraph about a memory of something that happened when they were in kindergarten or first grade. By starting the year with talk-write, Scarborough's students know immediately that she values writing, that they will be writing often in her class, and that they will share much of their writing. The students accept her approach and are not self-conscious about their writing. Two typical first-week-of-school talk-write paragraphs follow.

Kindergarden
When I was in Kindergarden we had to make a cake all by our self. so while I was mixing it the bowl droped. I didn't know what to do so I just put the batter back in the bowl & went ahead and made a cake with it. . . . . . . it tasted awful.

Dianne Bo

Wash Out
Once in first grade a boy would always be mean or bad to someone so the teacher would wash his mouth out with soap and I would always feel good that it was not me but I would feel sorry for him but I guess thats what he gets..
THE END
Mandy Boyum

Scarborough saves these early talk-write papers to compare with later writings so students and their parents can see how the writings have improved. Before Halloween, she has the students write about a Halloween memory, and before Christmas they write "A Christmas Memory." Students frequently write about grandparents, as this student did:

Christmas with our Grandp and Grandma!
On Christmas day we go over to our Grandp and Grandma to have
a Christmas party. Everbody is in vited to come which is alot of
people. There is alot of food and in the corner there is a small tree
all decorated. With lots of presents under neath the tree. After
supper we pass out the presents. Some gifts are hand made which
are really pretty. We all have a good time at our Grandpa and
Grandma.

Mandy Boyum

In secondary school, talk-write is a good method to use for writing
assignments in subjects other than language arts. Research shows that
writing is an important learning tool and that the more opportunity
students have to write in any subject area, the better their chances to
learn. Some successful talk-write assignments with junior high and
middle school students are a song-writing competition for which students talk-write lyrics and a chorus, step-by-step first-aid procedures,
and a description of a science observation. Barbara McDougall, drama
teacher at McLoughlin Junior High School in Medford, Oregon, uses
talk-write to introduce script writing for puppet shows. Students work
in pairs to come up with a story, then write out the idea in script form
on large sheets of butcher paper taped to the classroom wall. McDougall moves around the room checking each team's work within a single
hour, spotting immediately where teams have not included enough
action. Students then rewrite their scripts on 8½-by-11-inch paper to use
during their puppet show. After the performance, students rewrite their
script, adding what they feel would have improved the show. They
turn in this final paper for grading.

Because it is social, involving sharing and public writing, talk-write
can draw students together. For her Family Living class at Phoenix
High School in Phoenix, Oregon, Agnes Chirgwin uses a talk-write
assignment asking students to describe a time when their families felt
especially close. She does this assignment the first week of class,
quickly building strong ties among the students. A sample student
paragraph follows.

When I was 14 my dad bought our first dragster. We took it to the
races. We didn't think to highly of it. Well when my dad took first
place it made the whole family have a special place in their heart.
Now we all think very highly of it. It has made our family closer,
by going places.

K. K.

Talk-write has also been a successful part of a high school unit on
aging. Students are assigned to interview someone over sixty-five, then
to write up one of the experiences told to them. To help establish the

character of the person telling the memory, students talk-write a descriptive paragraph. If each student wrote this assignment privately, the teacher might receive thirty nearly identical paragraphs: "The person I talked to had white hair, many wrinkles, old skin," and so on. Using talk-write, students can see where they need to add concrete details to recreate a unique person. They get help from their partners and from other paragraphs in progress around the room. These descriptions are then inserted in the interviews, adding a lively element to their accounts.

Several high school teachers have found talk-write works especially well for beginning expository assignments. Introductory paragraphs, with work on thesis statements, can be done easily with this team process—and the teacher can look around the room, see common problems, and deal with these problems as a group. Students can use talk-write to identify the main points and supporting information, to discuss the best order, and to write the first paragraph or so. Their writings can be left on the wall for other students to read and comment on. Then the authors can incorporate classmates' ideas into their papers as they work alone.

As these assignments show, talk-write is not an exclusive method of teaching composition, but one that can be used as part of nearly any kind of writing assignment. It is simple and effective, gets students to help each other, makes writing social rather than solitary, allows for natural and positive discussion of the writing, and integrates language skills to the benefit of both speaking and writing. It is a technique that we and many other teachers have found useful.

Note

1. Robert Zoellner, "Talk-Write: A Behavioral Pedagogy for Composition," *College English* 30 (January 1969): 310.

11 An Approach to
Function Categories

James Britton, Tony Burgess, Nancy Martin, Alex McLeod, and
Harold Rosen

James Britton and his coauthors turn to function categories in an
attempt to provide a framework for the question "Why are you
writing?" They recognize that both the writer's intention and the
effect upon the reader are factors, and a single piece of writing may
serve several purposes. The authors embrace the concept of a
hierarchy of functions, with some functions serving a more
predominant role than others, and incorporate this concept in
their function categories. Ed.

Clearly, any attempt to set out functional categories for utterances must
rest upon a theory as to how language works: will constitute, in fact, a
way of looking at language in operation. Our scheme derives from
some important general ideas upon which scholars in many fields seem
to have converged in the past fifty years or so.

Ernst Cassirer[1] pointed out in 1944 that, of all the animals, man
alone responds with systematic *indirectness* to the signals he receives
from the world around him. All creatures have systems of nerves bringing in such signals, and other systems carrying out their responses. In
man, however, there is as it were a third system shunted across those
two—the 'symbolic system'. From the incoming signals man *represents
to himself*, cumulatively, what his world is like, and his responses are
thereafter mediated by that world-representation. Thus what is from
one point of view a storehouse of past experience for the individual is
from another point of view a body of expectations regarding his future.
Accumulating a 'retrospect', he projects also a 'prospect'. His response
to signals from his immediate environment is to generate a hypothesis,
from past experience, and put that hypothesis to the test.

Source: Excerpt from "An Approach to Function Categories," pp. 77-83. Reproduced, by permission, from *The Development of Writing Abilities (11-18)* by James
Britton et al. (Schools Council Research Studies, Macmillan Education, 1975). The notes
and figures have been renumbered.

Susanne Langer's *Philosophy in a New Key* sets the theory out in detail. Her 'new key' is the notion that man possesses a new need, over and above the biological needs he shares with the other creatures—the need to symbolize. Sapir makes the point again, and places language among the means by which man represents experience to himself:

> It is best to admit that language is primarily a vocal actualization of the tendency to see realities symbolically . . . an actualization in terms of vocal expression of the tendency to master reality not by direct and *ad hoc* handling of this element but by the reduction of experience to familiar form.[2]

And Georges Gusdorf[3] has epitomized the idea as follows: 'Man interposes a network of words between the world and himself and thereby becomes the master of the world.'

Bruner,[4] taking up the work of Piaget, sets out the three principal systems of representation, genetically developed in this order: *enactive* —a representation in terms of movement-cum-perception; *iconic*—a representation in terms of perception freed from movement; and *symbolic*—linguistic representation.

Language, then, is only one way of representing experience, but plays a key role as a means of organizing and storing representations in other modes. Vygotsky's *Thought and Language* is a brilliant exposition of this idea.

The American psychologist, George Kelly,[5] making his own approach, takes the scientist as his model for man and sees learning, not as a special kind of human behaviour, but as behaviour at its most typically human. Man is born a predictor, forever framing his hypotheses from past experience, submitting them to the test of actuality, and modifying his predictive apparatus in the light of what happens. A man's 'personal construct system', to use Kelly's term, is his world representation.

In recent years, sociologists have arrived at similar conclusions and in doing so enriched our understanding of what is involved. Their emphasis, necessarily, is upon interactions between people and the co-operative building of a common world. Where the psychologist has looked at an individual successively construing his confrontations with the world, the sociologist focuses upon situations, encounters between people, and looks at the way individual representations fit into the jigsaw of a social reality. Thus, for example, Berger and Luckmann:

> The most important vehicle of reality maintenance is conversation. One may view the individual's everyday life in terms of the working away of a conversational apparatus that ongoingly maintains, modifies and reconstructs his subjective reality.[6]

The effect of this convergence of thinking has been enormously powerful. One general effect is to set up, alongside a sense of the importance of language as a means of communication, a sense of its value *to the user*. With a communicative incentive, that of sharing experience, the speaker *shapes* experience, makes it available to himself, incorporates it, so shaped, into the corpus of his experience. Children using language in school are busy structuring their own experience and weaving into its fabric the experience of others.

The Role of Participant and the Role of Spectator

It is an essential feature of this idea that in successively representing to ourselves our contacts with the world we are not simply making ourself into receptacles for past experience, but are actively concerned to maintain an ever-improving predictive apparatus. Our orientation is to the future rather than to the past. Behaviour, as George Kelly has shown, is experimental, and our past experiences provide the hypotheses. Thus every new experience must be taken as a challenge to the established order of our past experience: and every experience must be followed by modification or reinforcement of that order. In general, we make the necessary adjustments as we proceed: if, on the other hand, what happens is too unlike our expectations, we shall not be able to adjust in our stride. We participate as best we can, but after the event we are left with the adjustment still to make. And this we ordinarily do by going back over the experience—in mind, in talk, or (if we are young enough) in make-believe play. Our re-enactments are likely in some degree to distort the experience in the direction of what is acceptable to us, or what is intelligible to us.

This process of re-enactment in order to 'come to terms' is essentially similar to the process by which we enter into imagined experiences, either in day-dreaming or in reading fiction. In terms of an abstract model we might put it this way: given that man constructs a representation of the world as he has experienced it *in order to operate in it,* an alternative kind of behaviour is then open to him: he may manipulate the representation *without seeking outcomes in the actual world.* The first of these two kinds of behaviour (operating in actuality via the representation) we would call behaviour *in the role of participant,* and the second (working upon the representation without seeking outcomes in actuality) we want to call behaviour *in the role of spectator.* To be in the role of spectator is, in one sense, to generate hypotheses without the present intention of putting them to the test.

D. W. Harding, the British psychologist, made a distinction of this kind as long ago as 1937.[7] He took first the example of an actual spectator looking at a building site or a street accident. The spectator takes up this role, Harding suggested, because what he sees 'discloses or makes more vivid to him some of the possibilities of his surroundings'. He is not concerned simply to perceive and understand, for what he sees engages his feelings and invites him to apply his sense of values. Of course, when we participate in events we evaluate in order to act, but 'it is as onlookers that we can most readily endure the penetration of general principles among our sentiments.' Harding is saying, we suggest, that 'the onlooker sees most of the game' *because* he is not called upon to meet the demands made upon the players. It is not simply that the spectator situation offers him an opportunity to try out his evaluations of 'the possibilities of his surroundings', but that a prior need to work upon the evaluative aspects of his world-representation encourages him to seek out those opportunities in which, because he is not committed to any action *vis-à-vis* the situation he is observing, he may do so with single-minded attention to principles— ethical, moral, social, aesthetic or any other. It is for some such reasons as these that Harding defines a spectator's response to events as a 'detached evaluative response', and goes on to claim that 'if we could obliterate the effects on a man of all the occasions when he was "merely a spectator" it would be profoundly to alter his character and outlook.'

But the claim does not rest solely upon occasions in which we are onlookers in a literal sense. Harding goes on to see day-dreaming and fantasying as 'imaginary spectatorship', and neighbourly gossip about events as 'social imaginary spectatorship', and suggests that what is afoot is essentially a traffic in values. In telling his tale, the speaker offers (both in what he selects and the way he recounts it) his own evaluation of the events narrated, and invites in return the evaluation of his listeners. Such a testing-out or sanctioning of our value systems provides what Harding has elsewhere called a 'basic social satisfaction'.[8]

Our final step, for which Harding also prepares us, is to bring into the category of 'social imaginary spectatorship' the work of the novelist, playwright and poet. Literature constitutes one kind of 'written language in the role of spectator' and presents in a highly developed form our social traffic in values. We have suggested so far that the spectator, being freed from the practical and social demands made of a participant, uses that freedom to focus upon evaluating the possibilities of experience. We must now add another use to which we believe he puts his freedom: he *pays attention to forms* in a way he is not able to as a participant: the forms of the language used, the pattern of events in a narrative, the dance-like movement of thought and, in particular, the pattern of feelings expressed. As participants, our feelings will tend to be sparked off in action; as spectators we are able to savour their quality *as feelings*. As participants we are caught up in a kaleidoscope of emotions; as spectators we have these emotions in perspective. This is a point we shall return to shortly.

In a very general way the distinction between the roles of participant and spectator is the distinction between work and play: between language as a *means* (to buy and sell, to inform, instruct, persuade and so on) and an utterance for its own sake, no means but an *end:* a voluntary activity that occupies us for no other reason than that it *preoccupies.*

The Function Categories

On the distinction between participant and spectator we have based our scheme for distinguishing the principal functions of written utterances. The scheme has three main categories, which are shown in diagrammatic form in Figure 1.

As mentioned earlier [page 10 of the Britton et al. book], 'expressive', the central term in the model, is taken from Edward Sapir, who pointed out that ordinary face-to-face speech is directly expressive and carries out its referential function in close and complex interrelationship with that expressive function.

> It is because it is learned early and piecemeal, in constant association with the colour and the requirements of actual contexts, that language, in spite of its quasi-mathematical form, is rarely a purely referential organization. It tends to be so only in scientific discourse, and even there it may be seriously doubted whether the ideal of pure reference is ever attained by language. Ordinary speech is directly expressive and the purely formal pattern of sounds, words, grammatical forms, phrases and sentences are always to be thought of as compounded by intended or unintended symbolisms of expression, if they are to be understood fully from the standpoint of behavior.[9]

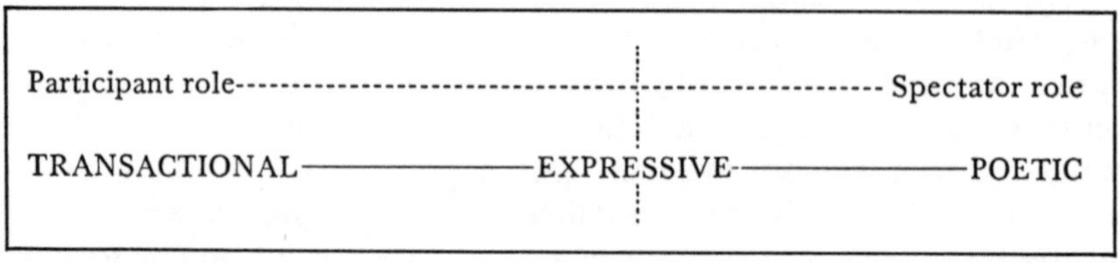

Participant role--|---------------------- Spectator role

TRANSACTIONAL————————EXPRESSIVE————————POETIC

Figure 1. The three main function categories.

An expressive utterance, for our purposes, is one in which the expressive function is *dominant*—whether we have in mind Sapir's 'patterns of reference and patterns of expression', or the whole hierarchy of functions set out by Jakobsen [see page 14 of the Britton et al. book]. We would describe it as an utterance that 'stays close to the speaker' and hence is fully comprehensible only to one who knows the speaker and shares his context. It is a verbalization of the speaker's immediate preoccupations and his mood of the moment. Centrally (that is, in its purest form, for the horizontal lines in the diagram are intended to represent a continuum), it is utterance at its most relaxed and intimate, as free as possible from outside demands, whether those of a task or of an audience. It is, at this central point, free to move easily from participant role into spectator and *vice versa:* mutual exploration, the pursuit of 'togetherness', may proceed equally by the pleasurable reconstruction of past experiences—a traffic in values—or by the exchange of opinions about the world and information with autobiographical relevance, and the borderline between the two modes will be a shadowy one.

It must be admitted that the more we worked on this idea of the expressive function, the more important we felt it to be. Not only is it the mode in which we approach and relate to each other in speech, but it is also the mode in which, generally speaking, we frame the tentative first drafts of new ideas: and the mode in which, in times of family or national crisis, we talk with our own people and attempt to work our way towards some kind of a resolution. By analogy with these roles in speech it seemed likely to us that expressive writing might play a key role in a child's learning. It must surely be the most accessible form in which to write, since family conversation will have provided him with a familiar model. Furthermore, a writer who envisages his reader as someone with whom he is on *intimate* terms must surely have very favourable conditions for using the process of writing as a means of exploration and discovery.

It is certainly not the case that every child's first attempts at writing are expressive according to our definition of the term, and to suggest that it is a 'natural' way to start probably raises more questions than it answers. But it must be true that until a child does write expressively he is failing to feed into the writing process the fullness of his linguistic resources—the knowledge of words and structures he has built up in speech—and that it will take him longer to arrive at the point where writing can serve a range of his purposes as broad and diverse as the purposes for which he uses speech.

This, at all events, provided us with a major hypothesis regarding the development of writing ability in school: that what children write in the early stages should be a form of written-down expressive speech, and what they read should also be, generally speaking, expressive. As their writing and reading progress side by side, they will move from this starting point into the three broadly differentiated kinds of writing—our major categories—and, in favourable circumstances, their mode of doing so will be by a kind of shuttling between their speech resources on the one hand and the written forms they meet on the other. Thus, in developmental terms, the expressive is a kind of matrix from which differentiated forms of mature writing are developed—see Figure 2.

The more fully an utterance meets the demands of some kind of participation in the world's affairs, the nearer will it approach the transactional end of the scale: the more fully it satisfies the spectator-role demands, the nearer it will move to the poetic end. The move in both cases is from an intimate to a more public audience (and this change should be reflected in our classification by sense of audience).

In all other ways, however, the two moves are very different in character. Let us take 'informing' as an example of a typical task for language, a way of participating, a type of transaction. As expressive writing changes to meet the demands of this task, it will become more explicit: that is, it will supply more of the context, will reflect a concern for accurate and specific reference; it will seek the kind of organization that most effectively carries out such a task, and will exclude the personal, self-revealing features that might interfere with it.

To move in the other direction, however—to satisfy in full the demands of the spectator role—an utterance must become a 'verbal object', a construct. Language forms and *the forms of whatever is represented* become, as we have suggested, the objects of attention and contribute to the 'import' of the work. What is afoot is evaluation, so that the embodiment by the writer of feelings and beliefs becomes paramount, and what is included in the utterance may be highly personal. It will be made accessible to an audience of strangers through the complex and subtle internal structure of the artefact: inner experience is, so to speak, given 'reasonance' within the structure, and the whole

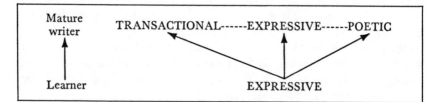

Figure 2. The expressive as a matrix for the development of other forms of writing.

becomes *an experience of order.* A poetic utterance may be said to be a special kind of self-presentation: not so much the embodiment of local or particular feelings as a glimpse into a 'lifetime of feeling', to use Susanne Langer's phrase.[10]

We have been describing the poetic 'pole', the verbal object as work of art: what we need above all to develop is a recognition of writings along the whole spectrum from expressive to poetic—a recognition of the principles upon which the work of literature is constructed, and the application of those principles to less highly organized kinds of writing, the 'art-like'. The work of Susanne Langer is pioneering the way.

In subsequent chapters the authors introduce a set of function categories to cover the range of writings in general use in our society and present the results of a study in which the function categories were applied to student writing samples. Ed.

Notes

1. Ernst Cassirer, *An Essay on Man.*
2. E. Sapir, *Culture, Language and Personality,* pp. 14–15.
3. G. Gusdorf, *Speaking,* p. 7.
4. J. S. Bruner et al., *Studies in Cognitive Growth.*
5. G. Kelly, *The Psychology of Personal Constructs.*
6. P. L. Berger and T. Luckmann, *The Social Construction of Reality,* p. 172.
7. D. W. Harding, 'The Role of the Onlooker'.
8. D. W. Harding, *Social Psychology and Individual Values.*
9. Sapir, *Culture, Language and Personality,* p. 10.
10. S. K. Langer, *Mind: An Essay on Human Feeling,* p. 112.

12 Composition Course: Pursuit of Ideas

James Pierce

The course Pursuit of Ideas was developed in order to provide a bridge from writing about personal experience to writing about ideas. Grounding the student's writing in personal experience is sound, I believe, because it helps generate sensory detail, specificity, and concreteness—antidotes to the thin generalizing characteristic of much adolescent writing. Yet there is still a need to go beyond the experience itself to an analysis or assessment of the experience, to an attempt to fit the experience into a larger whole—traditional expository demands. My assumption was that the student's fondness for and skill in recreating personal experience could be used as the foundation for helping the student gain some ease in writing about ideas. The customary sequence for the assignments listed under each general topic in the course outline is from recreating an experience to analyzing the experience to, finally, reflecting on the experience. Thus, the experience the student recreates becomes part of a larger whole—evidence of change over time, a contrast of attitudes, and so forth.

The general topics used to organize the writing assignments are purposely broad. They identify large areas of experience within which each student can usually be counted on to recall or imagine a specific happening. The topics listed in the following course outline—working, family relationships, school, and the future—are indeed sample topics. Some other topics colleagues and students have suggested and worked with are sports, vacations, pets, and festive occasions.

A. Working

1. Some readings:

    a. Selections from Studs Terkel's *Working*:
       "Who Spreads the News" (boys with paper routes)
       "Supermarket Box Boy"
       "Waitress"
       "Spot Welder"

"Film Critic" (Pauline Kael)

"Introduction"

b. Chapter one of Margaret Bourke-White's *Portrait of Myself*

c. "Jobs," chapter one of Paul Goodman's *Growing Up Absurd*

2. Sample assignments

a. Describe a specific job you have had. What did it feel like to engage in this work? What sights, sounds, smells, tastes, tactile impressions did you experience while doing this work? Re-create the experience of this job in sufficient sensory detail so that a reader may, in a sense, participate in it.

b. Now reflect on this job and write an explanation of what it *meant* to you. Of what significance was this job in your life? Show how the thoughts, the feelings you have about this job evolved from the concrete impressions described in your first paper.

c. Now take a step back from this job. Look at it not from your own personal point of view, but from a wider angle of vision. Where does a job or an experience like this fit in? For example, what point can you make about young people and working or about this kind of job and the function it serves, say, in your family or your community? Use the job you have described as one specific example illustrating the point you are making.

B. Family relationships

1. Some readings:

a. "Printer's Measure"–Paddy Chayefsky

b. "Still Stands the House"–Gwen P. Ringwood

c. "Ship of Dreams"–John Hughes

d. "The Happy Journey"–Thorton Wilder

e. "The Blanket"–Floyd Dell

f. "Snake Dance"–Corey Ford

g. "Paul's Case"–Willa Cather

h. "My First Two Women"–Nadine Gordimer

2. Sample assignments

a. Create a dialogue in which two members of the same household are involved in an argument of some kind. It can be a mild argument, an explosive one, or somewhere in between. Points to keep in mind for your readers: (1) Is the situation clear? (or the circumstances, the setting) (2) Are the characters in the dialogue clearly differentiated? Can the reader always tell who is speaking? (3) Is the dialogue realistic? (4) From the argument, can one gain some understanding of the underlying conflict between the two characters? While the specific argument may be resolved in your dialogue, you should leave the impression that the underlying conflict is not.

b. Have one of the characters in the dialogue write a letter to a third party explaining his or her view of the conflict and asking for advice. Have the third party write an answer to this letter.

c. Have a third party, one with a fairly objective view, interview the two people in conflict and attempt to bring them to some resolution of the conflict.

d. Have this third party, now in the role of a professional counselor, write a letter to a colleague describing the conflict between the two people as a case this counselor is working on.

e. Make a general observation about family life or about family relations, and use the incident depicted in your dialogue as one of a number of examples or pieces of evidence illustrating the general observation. (Some sample general observations: "In family relationships, the year is always zero."–Arthur Koestler. "The commonest axiom of history is that every generation revolts against its fathers and makes friends with its grandfathers."–Lewis Mumford. "The fundamental defect of fathers is that they want their children to be a credit to them." –Bertrand Russell.)

C. School
  1. Some readings:
    a. "Lost at C"–Jean Shepherd
    b. "The Idealist"–Frank O'Connor
    c. "All Things Bright and Beautiful"–Nancy Hale
    d. "Such, Such Were the Joys"–George Orwell
    e. "Who Is to Blame for the Current Mess in Education?"–Clifton Fadiman
    f. "You Force Kids to Rebel"–Steven Kelman

  2. Sample assignments

    a. Describe an incident, one that sticks in your mind—funny, sad, serious—that you experienced at school. This can be something that happened to you or that you observed happening to someone else. You may tell this in narrative form or write it as a factual reminiscence.

    b. Now write a paper explaining why this incident stuck in your mind. What is its special significance? Is it significant only to you, or is it an instance of a general truth about school or about young people at a certain stage?

  c. Describe a series of happenings occurring over a period of time that makes a point about some "phase" of your school life. Use the incident described in the first paper as one of these happenings.

D. The Future[1]

  1. Some readings:

    a. "By the Waters of Babylon"–Stephen Benet

    b. *Rite of Passage*–Alexis Panshin

    c. "My Planet 'Tis of Thee"–Isaac Asimov

    d. *The Limits of Growth*–Meadows, Meadows, Randers, and Behrens

    e. "Alternative Lifestyles"–Meadows et al.

    f. "A List of Predictions for the Future"–Meadows et al.

  2. Sample assignments

    a. Select one of the alternative lifestyles. Imagine a particular person living this lifestyle. Now narrate a day in the life of this person. His or her actions and behavior should illustrate the characteristics that predominate in this lifestyle.

    b. From the list of predictions for the future, select the five that you most want to happen. Now narrate a scene in the future that would reveal how these predictions would concretely and practically influence one's life.

    c. After the groups in the class have selected the five predictions for the future they most want to happen and the five they least want to happen, write an interpretation of the class's preferences. First, which predictions predominate? Second, what trends in preference are revealed by these choices? Third, what values seem to be behind the preferences?

The chart in Figure 1 describes the composition sequence in a slightly different way (it includes the prewriting stage) and likens the task of the writer to that of the detective. The detective, like the writer, is confronted with a problem or puzzle and must go through a period of discovery (prewriting stage); the detective gives the confusing experience shape (analytic stage); and often the detective gains fresh insight into or new knowledge about a general human problem (reflective stage). A Holmesian view might be a welcome assist to those patiently investigating the impenetrable mysteries of student compositions.

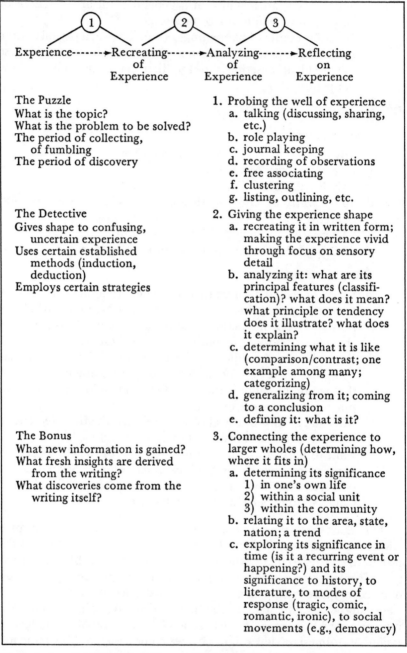

Experience- - - - - - →Recreating- - - - - →Analyzing- - - - - - →Reflecting
                       of   of   on
             Experience   Experience   Experience

The Puzzle

What is the topic?

What is the problem to be solved?

The period of collecting,
   of fumbling

The period of discovery

1. Probing the well of experience
   a. talking (discussing, sharing,
      etc.)
   b. role playing
   c. journal keeping
   d. recording of observations
   e. free associating
   f. clustering
   g. listing, outlining, etc.

The Detective

Gives shape to confusing,
   uncertain experience

Uses certain established
   methods (induction,
   deduction)

Employs certain strategies

2. Giving the experience shape
   a. recreating it in written form;
      making the experience vivid
      through focus on sensory
      detail
   b. analyzing it: what are its
      principal features (classifi-
      cation)? what does it mean?
      what principle or tendency
      does it illustrate? what does
      it explain?
   c. determining what it is like
      (comparison/contrast; one
      example among many;
      categorizing)
   d. generalizing from it; coming
      to a conclusion
   e. defining it: what is it?

The Bonus

What new information is gained?

What fresh insights are derived
   from the writing?

What discoveries come from the
   writing itself?

3. Connecting the experience to
   larger wholes (determining how,
   where it fits in)
   a. determining its significance
      1) in one's own life
      2) within a social unit
      3) within the community
   b. relating it to the area, state,
      nation; a trend
   c. exploring its significance in
      time (is it a recurring event or
      happening?) and its
      significance to history, to
      literature, to modes of
      response (tragic, comic,
      romantic, ironic), to social
      movements (e.g., democracy)

Figure 1. A sequence for composition comparing the role of the writer to the role of the detective.

Note

1. "The Future" turns the process around. No one has experienced the future, but we can all imagine it. The first stage in this sequence is to express what we imagine happening in the future by supplying the concrete details and specific happenings that would be likely and appropriate for our vision. Notice that assignment *c* is an expository activity: an analysis of the class's preferences, the "evidence" supplied by the class itself.

13 Rationale for a New Curriculum in English

James Moffett

Unlike other animals, the human baby cannot for some time do for itself. During the first months of utter helplessness and the following years of extreme dependence, the child must get others to do for it. Thus we learn at the outset of life the tremendously important art of manipulating other people. This is the genesis of rhetoric—and it begins before we learn to speak. Crying soon becomes a means of summoning the milk supply or the dry diaper. Later the rhetorical repertory of the child includes vomiting, holding breath, throwing temper tantrums, evacuating inappropriately, whining, wheedling— and obeying. But if this is so, what do we mean when we say we are going to teach rhetoric to students? They are past masters before they even come to school.

To be worth discussing at all at a convention of English teachers, rhetoric must mean something more than forensic argumentation, as it did for Aristotle, and something less than effective communication, as it does for many educators today. The one conception falls far short of the needs of an English curriculum, and the other virtually becomes a synonym for it. For me rhetoric refers to the ways one person attempts to act on another, to make him laugh or think, squirm or shiver, hate or mate. Acting on others through words is merely one species of instrumental behavior in general. Our talk about the world is in the world and of the world; the use of language is a motivated drama. (I'm not speaking to you on this occasion for nothing.) So I assume that there is no such thing as a discourse without a rhetoric, however

Source: Robert M. Gorrell, ed., *Rhetoric: Theories for Application* (Champaign, Ill.: National Council of Teachers of English, 1967), pp. 114-21. Reprinted by permission of the publisher. Some usages that appear in this article are not consistent with the present NCTE Guidelines for Nonsexist Use of Language; they have not been changed in this reprint. This study was made possible by funds granted by Carnegie Corporation of New York. The statements made and views expressed are solely the responsibility of the author. For further reading on the topic, the author refers readers to his *Active Voice: A Program for Writing Assignments* (Montclair, N.J.: Boynton/Cook, 1981) and *Teaching the Universe of Discourse* (Boston: Houghton Mifflin, 1968).

unconscious or naive it may be; that except for exercises in English courses, every discourse is motivated by something in the speaker and directed toward an audience on whom it is meant to have an impact.

I cannot hope to say anything new to you about rhetoric, however, unless I utter it in the same breath with abstraction. How A tries to act on B through language simply cannot be detached from that whole logical and cognitive operation by which we abstract reality into symbols. Rhetoric is a variable factor of total process. *What* A is saying is some abstraction of the world. But at the same time we abstract *from* we abstract *for*. Whether I call the green film on the surface of a pond "spring algae" or "scum" is of great rhetorical importance because of the difference in effect on my audience. But choosing "spring algae" or "scum" is a conceptual option entailing different ways of classifying the same physical phenomenon. Any serious analysis of rhetoric resorts to discussion of the abstractive process, as the work of Francis Christensen so well shows, although I wish he had kept it in the context of motive. The designs a speaker has on his audience and the operations he performs on his subject govern jointly every feature of a discourse—from word choice, punctuation, and sentence structure to paragraph development and overall organization. A subject is a *what* but *what for?* So my second assumption is that the rhetorical process occurs only in conjunction with the abstractive process, and neither can be separated from the other. A discourse is intent multiplied by content.

At this point let me connect this line of thought with another major concern of English teachers today—the search for a central structure in English that can serve to magnetize the whole curriculum. Plenty of structures exist—the lexicographer's word, the linguist's sentence, the logician's paragraph, and the litterateur's form—but none is large enough to accommodate the famous trivium of language, literature, and composition (a nonparallel series if I ever heard one, since composition ought to be an activity, not a corpus). The litterateur's form furnishes the largest context, but the genres and their subdivisions are not detachable from literary criticism and hence cannot apply to most kinds of spontaneous and utilitarian discourse. The word, the sentence, and the paragraph are all substructures lacking precisely that context of purpose and intent which is the heart of rhetoric. I do not see how a teacher can possibly be serious about rhetoric and continue to assign workbook exercises or the writing of isolated sentences and paragraphs. *What for?* This is not composition, it is decomposition.

Although I understand how tempting it is to apply directly some of the very successful codifications about language achieved by linguists, I can only deplore the basing of assignments on structure that does not rise above the level of syntax. How can you teach, not only rhetoric, but

style, diction, semantics, or logic within a structure stripped of everything that determines them? Style and diction with no reason for
choosing one word or sentence structure over another? Semantics with
a meaningless fragment out of context? Logic with one proposition?
Abstraction with no subordinates or superordinates except internal
words and phrases? What you can teach with the sentence alone are the
linguistic codifications themselves but not how to speak or write. To
the children who underscore the modifier clusters those exercises must
look exactly the same as the diagraming of sentences did to us. And
when they make up a sentence or paragraph demonstrating such and
such kind of structure, they are not learning what the teacher thinks
they are: they are learning that there is such a thing as writing
sentences and paragraphs for their own sake, that discourse need not be
motivated or directed at anyone, that it is good to write even if you have
nothing to say and no one to say it to just so long as what you put
down illustrates a linguistic codification. The student learns to dope
out the teacher's preference for subordinate clauses and give him what
he wants. This is a fine lesson in rhetoric indeed. He will throw in lots
of modifier clusters because the teacher will reward him and make him
feel good about himself, not because clusters are an appropriate rhetorical ploy in such and such kind of whole, authentic discourse, because
he isn't at the time writing any such discourse. He may at some other
time of course be asked to write a complete theme, but, so far as I know,
the assumption that exercises carry over to real speech and writing has
never been proved, even though it is the same old assumption that has
always underlain the old-fashioned grammar drills.

The reason I have criticized exercises is that they typify two errors
which I think are obstructing the kind of curriculum we would all like.
One error is basing assignments on *a* structure instead of on *the* structure. A word, sentence, or paragraph simply cannot do justice to the
truth of real discourse. Too small a context actually promotes mis-
learning that must be undone somewhere else in the curriculum. In
this way we constantly work against ourselves for lack of a global
rationale. The second error is to focus too much on the subject and not
enough on the student. Intent on discovering what language is about
we neglect to examine how children learn. To paraphrase Earl Kelley,
we build the right facilities, organize the best course of study, work out
the finest methods, create the appropriate materials, and then, come
September, the wrong students walk through the door. Just as the
rhetorical and abstractive processes must be multiplied together to
produce a real discourse, the teaching and learning processes must be
multiplied together to produce real education, which is a two-way

transaction, not a one-way transmission. We must mesh the structure of the subject with the structure of the student.

However much students may vary in genetic and environmental background, they all come equipped with nervous systems built on the same ground plan. Their emotional and cognitive apparatuses work in a *structurally* similar way, however idiosyncratic the results. One generalization that can be made about the way our apparatus works is one I invoked in disapproving the use of exercises: whenever a child learns a certain content he also learns the way of learning that surrounds the content; he gets the hidden message implied by the learning context and emerges with a general disposition that is of a higher level of complexity than the content itself. Thus in an a-rhetorical learning situation, the child learns to discourse a-rhetorically.

Another principle is that we pay attention to and retain what is presented to us only in the measure that we can immediately integrate it into previously built knowledge systems within us. Now of course anything can be *made* relevant, and the child's attention and memory thus trained, by creating a system of instrumental rewards and punishments, in which case he will not relate the things learned to each other, as the teacher intends, but will relate them directly to his status with the teacher.

Piaget has formulated one of the most useful and general laws of learning and one that bears profoundly on rhetoric: the cognitive perspective of the child expands gradually from himself outward so as to incorporate points of view foreign to his initially preferred egocentric outlook, to accommodate audiences remote from himself, and to encompass subjects broader and broader in time and space. A corollary of this law is that decentering, the correction of cognitive perspective, depends very much on feedback from the environment. (Ignoring the structure of the student is, precisely, a failure to decenter and hence a failure of our own rhetoric.) The thought and speech of the child, says Piaget, gradually socialize, adapt to a listener. Adapting to a listener is exactly what successful rhetoric entails; the speaker must embrace the other's world by incorporating his point of view and by speaking his language. Thus Piaget enables us to tie rhetoric to the cognitive processes and to the basic biological fact of adaptation in general.

Since one of the chief ways of influencing others through words is intellectual, by means of our logic, the categories and logical relations the child uses must gradually approximate universal ones. The problem is not that the child begins with no logic and has to acquire some, no more than that he starts life without a rhetoric; but his logic is subjective, unconscious, and unsystematic. The progress he makes in logical and cognitive development is his progress in forging higher abstractions from lower ones and in being able to tell the difference. But the problem here is in understanding what abstraction really is. Primitive thought tends toward very broad categories and propositions (wild generalizations, if you like), so that the use of words and sentences having a large extension or range of applicability may indicate undeveloped rather than sophisticated thought. I'm afraid we teachers are often taken in by pseudo-concepts and pseudo-abstractions, which, incidentally, the too early assigning of exposition naturally invites. Real advances in verbal growth should be measured not only by the extension of the concepts and propositions but by whether they are ranged in a hierarchy of subordinates and superordinates. In other words, discrimination and complexity make the difference. Also the consciousness of abstracting. Hence another principle of growth: the child becomes more and more able to create new classes, range the classes in relation to each other, reclassify, and move with awareness from one level of the hierarchy to another. Above all, abstracting is the processing of matter by mind in stages from the ground up. Each state subsumes the ones below, builds on them, and is in turn subsumed in the next stage. Therefore no stage can be skipped. It follows that students will learn to abstract properly only if they are asked to discourse about some raw material from their own life, for to the extent that assignment topics are preabstracted for them the students are prevented from working their way through the prerequisite stages.

Armed with this double model of the student decentering as he adapts to the outside and ascending as he integrates hierarchical systems, I return now to the meshing of the structure of English with that of the student. What makes it possible to do this is that they have a common substrate owing to the fact that discourse is, after all, a product of our own symbol-making organism and inevitably reflects it, in somewhat the same way that furniture mimics our body and architecture our psyche. My own point of departure several years ago was to classify actual kinds of discourse according to rhetorical distance and abstractive altitude. To make this analysis I had to invoke a concept that could adequately frame it. This concept is what I am going to propose as the master context or superstructure of English.

No doubt you have noticed that I construe English as simply all discourse in our native tongue. For teachers this seems to me to be the only realistic definition. The universe of discourse is staked out by a first person, a second person, and a third person; and their interrelations make up the dynamics of discourse. So the concept I am referring to is the venerable trinity—*I, you,* and *it;* informer, informed, and information; narrator, auditor, and story; transmitter, receiver, and message. Like all trinities, this one is a unity—somebody-talking-to-somebody-else-about-something. Indivisible as it is in reality, to talk about it we must divide it. The *I-you* relation is the existential, behavioral, rhetorical relation of speaker and spoken-to. It has primacy over the *I-it* relation, which is symbolic, referential, and abstractive. Cross these two relations and you have some whole, authentic discourse; omit one and you do not. Intent times content. In the new curriculum I am proposing, students would never be asked to create or contemplate anything less than a whole, authentic discourse. But if the units are to be kinds of discourse, what are they and how would they be ordered so as to devise a sequence?

Rhetorical distance and abstractive altitude furnish coordinates by which we can map the universe of discourse. To take rhetorical distance first, if speaker and listener are the same actual person, the activity of the discourse must be silent self-verbalization, better known as thinking. If speaker and listener are two separate people face to face, the activity is vocalizing or speech. If the audience is small and known but situated in another time or place than is the speaker, the discourse must be written. If the audience is large and anonymous, far flung in time and space, the discourse must be written for publication. Now, imagine a speaker discoursing on the same subject but successively to each of these four audiences. Consider the shifts all down the line in all the substructures of the language that must take place each time the audience becomes larger and more remote, or, to calibrate more finely, each time the identity of the audience and its relation to the speaker changes at all. Allusion, diction, punctuation, style, sentence structure, paragraphing, logic—all adjust to what that audience can understand, appreciate, and respond to. If, for example, I were to give this talk over a national television network, as a starter I would have to go through my text and change most of the key nouns.

As the second person recedes from the first, other things happen. Spontaneous discourse becomes deliberate. Feedback becomes slower, more long-range, and more diffuse. Vernacular language gives way to literary language. Private and parochial modes of thought universalize. Ongoing dialogue becomes composed monologue. Because they correspond to a growth schedule, these shifts entailed by increasing separation of speaker from audience would make a good curriculum sequence.

Taking now the abstactive relation of speaker to spoken-about—in order to delineate a similar continuum here, I am going to use verb tenses because they predicate subjects in a time relation to the speaker. But I may regard the Civil War as what happened once upon a time or as what happens whenever an agrarian aristocracy and an industrial democracy try to coexist or as what will happen again if we are not careful. I am exercising a conceptual option. So time difference is another name for level of abstraction. Thus we can create a continuum of shifts in speaker-subject relation according to which level of the hierarchy the speaker has chosen to abstract some raw material to. Compare a record of *what is happening* with a report of *what happened* with a generalization about *what happens* with a theory about *what will, may, or could happen.* Arrayed in this order, these four *what's* or speaker-subject relations form an abstractive hierarchy in at least two ways. First, if we imagine the same raw material as being originally the subject matter of them all, then it is clear that this matter is being progressively processed by mind in such a way that concrete qualitites are ceding to logical properties. Secondly, each stage depends on the preceding one because it subsumes it. A report is a summary of recordings, a generalization is a synthesis of reports, and a theory is a transformation of some generalizations. For example, imagine an on-the-spot recording of what is happening before the guillotine, then an eyewitness account of what happened one day during the French Revolution, then an historical generalization about the Reign of Terror, then a political scientist's theory about revolutions starting right and moving left. This is precisely how abstraction works, and we perform a similar operation all the time in building our own thought structures.

Put another way, if I record what is happening, I produce a drama. If I report what happened, I produce a narrative. If I generalize what happens, I produce an exposition. If I theorize what will, may, or could happen, I produce an argumentation. Redefined, these traditional divisions of discourse are seen as levels of abstraction at which some given raw material may be symbolized. Furthermore, these stages bring to the fore in succession the three essential kinds of logic—the chrono-logic of ordering things as they happen, the analogic of classifying by similarity and difference, and the tautologic of transforming by rela-tions of classes and propositions. Each kind of logic becomes in turn the organizing principle of the total discourse and further converts the random order of events into the man-made order of his own internal operations.

Returning now to the practical problem of deriving curriculum units—almost any intersection of these progressions identifies a kind of discourse familiar to either literature or everyday communication, usually both. Thus writing *what happens* to a mass audience is formal exposition. Writing to a friend *what happened* is a narrative letter. Vocalizing *what will, may, or could be true* is socratic dialogue.

Verbalizing *what is happenng* is a kind of sensory interior monologue. The units of the curriculum would be spontaneous monologues and dialogues; letters; diaries; various first person narratives such as autobiography, memoir, and eyewitness accounts; third person narratives such as biography, case histories, chronicle, and history; essays of generalization; and essays of argumentation. Notice that all the techniques of drama and fiction are easily accommodated. Literature and nonliterature would be read and practiced side by side within the same unit so that constant comparison could be made. Thus epistolary fiction would be studied along with actual correspondence and journal fiction along with actual diaries. Under the unit of face-to-face vocalization, plays could be studied along with transcripts of court trials and socratic dialogues.

A spiraled sequence would be created by crossing each of the four stages of the rhetorical progression with each of the four stages of the abstractive progression. Thus a student would tell what happened first in vocal dialogues, letters, and diaries, and then in journalistic reports, biography, and chronicle. Generalizing what happens would proceed from reflective interior dialogue to socratic dialogue to dialectical letters and diaries to formal exposition. Roughly, the sequence teaches how to record, report, generalize, and theorize, in that order. In effect, chronology, analogy, and tautology begin as subjective, shadowy logic buried in sentences and emerge as an explicit organizing principle of the whole discourse.

Professional writing and the students' own productions would be the only texts examined. The substructures of the language would be studied constantly and simultaneously within each kind of discourse. Word choice, punctuation, sentence structure, grammar, paragraphing, and organizational form would be issues every day and would remain in relation to the rhetorical distance and abstractive altitude of the particular discourse at hand. The appropriate teaching method would be a workshop discussion in which the student's efforts to act on a certain audience at a certain level—his theme—would be read and commented on by both the teacher and the other students. Since it is a natural communication model, the discussion itself would come under scrutiny in a modified kind of group dynamics. The very important understanding derived from the lexicographer, the linguist, the logician, and the litterateur would be behind the teacher helping him to exploit the twists and turns of the workshop method. The approach is based on trial and error but with the trials carefully keyed into the learning schedule and the errors benefiting from maximum feedback and correction. Since instruction occurs just when the student needs it, when he is discoursing himself, it is readily assimilated and retained.

Motivation should be high because the student is mostly writing about the raw material of his own experience and observations; the teacher never assigns a content, only an abstraction level and audience relation.

I have been through a lot of theorizing to arrive at what should have been the most natural thing in the first place—to let a student of English spend his time practicing the full range of actual discourse and examining the results in collaboration with his peers and a guiding adult. In Edward Albee's *The Zoo Story* Jerry says, "Sometimes you have to go a long distance out of your way to go a short distance correctly." This is why all education is reeducation.

14 Using Student Writing Response Groups in the Classroom

Mary K. Healy

Mary K. Healy uses response groups to give audience reactions to her student writers while they are engaged in the process of writing. The term *response group* emphasizes "the active involvement of group members—giving reactions, asking questions, making suggestions" (p. 1). She notes the following improvements in students' writing after working in such groups: more specificity of detail, more supporting evidence or examples, more transitional and introductory phrases for the reader, and more fluent and complete pieces of writing. Ed.

If students have had no previous work in response groups, I find it necessary to encourage them to become conscious of how they respond to language they hear and read. What do they like or dislike? Often, they have never been asked that question in school before, so at first they have no immediate answer. Unless they *can* respond, they cannot function effectively in a small group because they have nothing concrete to offer a writer.

One way of making students aware of effective writing is frequently to reproduce selections from student journals or other first draft writing, have students read these anonymous selections aloud, in turn, and then have each student underline any word, phrase, sentence, or passage which she particularly likes, for whatever reason. Each person in the class, including the teacher, selects something to read aloud. Repeating the same words someone else has read is encouraged because the purpose of the lesson is to call attention to effective use of language, and repetition emphasizes the most effective language in each piece. Below are some examples from eighth grade student journals. The underlinings were made by other students in the class and the adjacent

Source: Excerpt from "Preparing for Small Group Response Sessions," in *Using Student Writing Response Groups in the Classroom,* Curriculum Publication no. 12 (Berkeley: Bay Area Writing Project, University of California, 1980), pp. 5-7. Reprinted with permission of the Bay Area Writing Project.

numbers indicate how many students in the room read that particular line.

> My mind, as stupid as it is, is just right for me. If it wasn't it wouldn't be on my head. My mind seems to have a short memory, but is quite good at figuring things out. That is why I am the worlds worst speller and a semi-good mathematician. The only things that stay on my mind are girls, soccer and work, not that I like work, but just that I am so far behind in it I can't get it off my mind. (5) At night my mind is still at work keeping me awake.
>
> When I think of my mind I think of a room filled with little gears, motors, wires and tubes. The gears and motors make my body function and the wires and tubes absorb information and knowledge. When I hit my head a tube gets broken or a gear gets jammed and I get a headache, but it always repairs itself. When someone dies from a head injury, I think of it as if they broke all the motors and tubes in their head. I think of skin as a gooey substance that is poured on and dries and then provides a little protection for the insides. (4)
>
> On cold rainy mornings, I am so cold, I can't even get out of bed. I'm like a cold and stiff nail stuck in a block of ice. (4) Then I wait until someone turns on the heat, then my room gets warm I begin to defrost and slowly get out of bed.
>
> Today all I have done is rush. When I got up in the morning I had to rush. To get my work done in class I had to rush and immediately when I got home I started to rush and now I am rushing to do this original. When I was told to do an original on a rambling thought I tried and tried to ramble but I couldn't so I thought. I thought and thought but I couldn't ramble. (3) Then I had to rush so I never ended up rambling.

This activity, repeated once or twice a week, accustoms the students to listen for effective use of language and to individually choose their own preferences. They grow in confidence about their ability to recognize strong writing; they no longer feel they must wait for the teacher's final judgment. When they are at ease with this activity, I usually begin the first stages of small group work.

The Whole Class as a Response Group

Deciding just when to begin response groups is crucial. Beginning too early in the year or the semester is counter-productive because it takes time for students to become more fluent writers. I usually wait until after students have been writing original drafts for about one month and then introduce the idea of working in small response groups before they write their final drafts. Over the years, I have accumulated audio and video tapes of group work by my previous classes. I play several excerpts to introduce the process, asking students to comment afterwards on what they hear and see.

Via Overhead Projector Transparency

Next I plan a whole class writing assignment, usually a childhood memory piece. When the first drafts are completed, I choose several papers to reproduce on transparencies for class response. Before working with the transparencies, however, I emphasize to the students the difference between *evaluation* and *response:*

Evaluation: The final assessment of a finished piece of written work which has already gone through drafts. Final evaluation will be the teacher's responsibility.

Response: The initial reaction to a piece of first draft writing, usually in the form of questions to the writer about the content or form of the piece. Response will be the responsibility of the student and the teacher.

After reading the piece aloud, I have the students respond to the writing on the transparency by asking questions about the writing. Then I write the students' questions on the transparency next to the appropriate line, repeating the procedure with each of the transparencies. The session ends with students exchanging their own papers with a partner and writing questions which occur to them about each other's papers.

Via Ditto

Within several days of the overhead transparency response lesson, I plan another whole class writing assignment, again a personal narrative piece—perhaps based on the memory of a childhood fear or a frightening experience. Then I choose several of the original drafts and run off dittoed copies of them exactly as written, after asking the writers' permission. I ask the students to write responses, either questions or comments, directly on the dittoed sheets and hand them in to me so that I see how they are responding to each other's work. I comment on the type of response each student is offering and try to indicate whether it would be helpful to the writer. The written responses are a useful indication of the students' understanding of the process, and they alert me to students who will need further encouragement and direction.

The Model Small Group

After completing the overhead transparency and ditto response sessions, I find it helpful to have one or two "live" sessions with a group
of students or teachers responding to one another's writing in front of
the rest of the class. For example, my team teaching partner and I often
role play different types of response to our writing, attempting to
illustrate the spectrum of response possibilities:

1. Useless: "Oh, your story is O.K." (No specific help for the writer)
2. Marginally useful: "I thought the part about your brother throwing spinach was funny." (Encouragement for the writer)
3. Useful: "How old was your brother when that happened?" (The
   writer learns what information the reader needs.)
4. Very useful: "I was confused when you said your aunt came in. I
   thought you said earlier that you were alone in the house."
   (Again, the writer hears from someone who *wasn't* there when it
   happened, someone who needs more information.)

*Subsequent sections of the chapter contain transcripts of student
conversations and describe establishing response groups, monitoring
their progress, and the teacher's response and evaluation. Ed.*

15 The All-City High Project

Miles Myers

The following description of a community-based independent study program is based on Miles Myers's experience with the All-City High Project in Oakland, California. The assignments introduce students to their community and to the skills of note taking, interviewing, and composing for a variety of audiences. Ed.

The walls of the classroom can impose limits on the teacher's search for new subjects and new audiences for students' writing. After class observations and interviews with the school librarian, where can students find subjects which engage them in personal discovery? After writing to the school secretary and principal, who but the teacher is available as an adult audience?

The outside community can provide the needed resources. And schools can help students reach these resources. Independent study programs like the All-City Project allow students to discover and address the adult audiences of their own communities in situations that demand communication skills for real-life purposes.

At the outset, each student negotiates a contract with the instructor. The agreements describe the students' schedules for periods varying from one to ten weeks. They include dates of appointments with the instructor, and deadlines for completion of intermediate phases and of the final project. The contracts list the people to be interviewed in the community, as well as one or two adults in the community who will read and evaluate the students' reports before they are submitted to the instructor. In some cases, additional audiences are specified. For instance, a multi-media report could be presented before another class in the school.

Source: Adapted from "Independent Study in the High School," in Sarah Dandridge, John Harter, Rob Kessler, Miles Myers, and Susan Thomas, *Independent Study and Writing,* Curriculum Publication no. 2 (Berkeley: Bay Area Writing Project, University of California, 1979), pp. 5–8. Used with permission of the Bay Area Writing Project.

The classroom needs to be equipped with at least one outside phone, twenty phone books, two dozen city and neighborhood maps, bus schedules, diagrams of a model business and of a government agency, posters showing coming community events, and a library of materials from community groups. The library will grow as students collect material during their projects.

After negotiating a contract, each student is given a letter of introduction, on the school's official letterhead, describing the student's project briefly and giving the phone number and address of the instructor. (Some people do check up. Occasionally they wonder if they are being investigated by a mysterious agency.)

The writing projects that students can undertake are as varied as the community in which the students live. The following are a few examples of projects which have been undertaken in the Bay Area.

The Courthouse

Each courthouse has a secretary who knows which cases are coming up and which judges are willing to have students in their courts. A friendly judge may stop to explain points of law to a student and allow the student to examine exhibits. A jury trial lasting two weeks could have the following sections:

Jury Selection. Write a letter to one person who was considered for the jury and explain to that person his/her acceptance or rejection.

Diagram. Prepare a diagram of the crime, showing site and location of participants and witnesses, and describe the diagram to the jury.

Attorney Interview. Interview the defense attorney and the attorney from the district attorney's office to determine the arguments on both sides. Include both notes and summary of the interview. The best time to conduct the interview is toward the end of the trial. The audience will be the two attorneys.

Final Argument. Present for the jury (whom you have watched in the court and know from the jury selection) your final argument, taking the position of either the district attorney or the defense attorney.

Decision. Write a brief report on the final disposition of the case. Indicate what witness or witnesses most influenced the decision, at least in your opinion. Your audience is the judge.

Stock Broker

Stock brokers are very happy to meet with students, provide films on investing, whatever. The assignment usually has some variation of investment record and the brochure.

Investment Record. The student is given an old listing on the New York Stock Exchange and an example investment record sheet. The student is told that he/she has $100,000 which he/she must now invest in listing on the NYSE. The student makes two copies of the investment record, showing number of stocks of each type, purchase price (the price on the old listing), and so forth. Then the student is asked to keep a daily record for one week of what happens to the investments, turning in each day a record of sales, new purchases, and present status of the original $100,000 invested.

Brochure. At the end of the week, the student invents a name for the imaginary mutual fund and prepares a brochure for stockholders and new customers explaining the growth or decline in value of the original $100,000. Students are encouraged to use art work, are required to include the investment records from the week, and are given some example brochures to imitate.

Neighborhood Profile

The student is asked to select one block in the downtown area and prepare a profile of the block, including the following sections in the report:

Map. The map should show the location of each store or residence, the address, the names of the owners or operators, the name of the business or the name of the main family. In addition to the student's map of the block as it now is, the student could be asked to prepare copies of maps showing what the area was like in the past. The Oakland Museum, for example, has some old maps of the Oakland area. Another option is to require a topographical map of the area, available from the U.S. Geological Survey, and still another option is an aerial photograph of the block, available from Customer Relations, EROS Data Center, Sioux Falls, South Dakota 57198.

Interview. The student will interview at least one person at each address, submitting to the instructor both notes and a summary from the interview. The summary should describe the individual's recollection of the history of the area, his/her view of the present problems faced by the neighborhood, and his/her estimate of the neighborhood's special qualities. The student should send each person interviewed a follow-up letter thanking the individual for his/her time.

Property Values. The student prepares a property list showing the estimated value of each building on the block. The tax stamps in the county office will provide information on last purchase price and the records of the county assessor show recent tax estimates.

Profile. The student will write a profile of the neighborhood, using the maps, interviews, and property records as a resource. The profile should capture the "personality" of the area—its history, present problems, and commerical or residential function—and be written for out-of-town visitors.

What to Do Brochure

The student selects one situation or problem which commonly confronts citizens in the community and prepares for citizens an information brochure on what to do. For example, what should one do if someone in the family dies? This problem requires a visit to a hospital, an insurance company, possibly the coroner's office, the social security agency, a mortician, and possibly an office of one of the armed services. In an accident case, the student will need to visit the local police department. The student will submit to the instructor examples of forms that must be completed, notes taken during the interviews, and the completed brochure. Again the student will be asked to send follow-up letters thanking agencies for their help. The teachers should ask some students to tape-record their interviews because the tapes are very useful for classroom discussions to improve interviewing techniques. Other situations for which brochures could be prepared are a birth in the family, the arrest of a juvenile, a destructive earthquake or invasion from Mars, unemployment, running for public office, improving city services in your area, or a lost person report.

How It Works Brochure

This assignment is similar to the one above except in this instance the student is asked to explain to adults or peers how some private or public agency works. The brochure will be handed out by the public relations division of the agency (at least as an imaginary condition of the assignment). This assignment requires *diagrams* showing organizational structure, *maps* of the building, sample *forms* used by the agency, and *interviews* of personnel in the various divisions. For an assignment of this type, requiring two weeks or more in a single place, the student should have an introductory letter from an official of the firm.

Opinion Surveys

The student prepares an opinion survey on some topic of interest to him/her, and after piloting the survey with a sample population, prepares a final draft for distribution. The student should present the surveys personally and, in fact, may ask for oral responses. The polls may be conducted with a cross-section of people or in a particular area. One possibility is to conduct a survey on BART (Bay Area Rapid Transit) trains. The train riders accept the polls from the students as a social event, and BART in the past has been willing to provide a letter of introduction on official stationery.

Other assignments include the *Tour Guide,* planned tours of the city; the *Consumer Guide,* market-basket surveys around the city; *Job Surveys,* including descriptions of available working conditions and salary ranges; *Roots,* showing the family tree, profiles of individuals, and possible family values as expressed in the family's choice of outcasts; *Folk Tale Studies,* explaining the populace's various versions of the tooth fairy, Santa Claus, or the bogeyman.

Part Four: Modeling

Introduction to Modeling

Processing, distancing, and *modeling* have different functions in the classroom. First, *processing* assignments help students learn how language can be used to discover what one does know and does not know, and how breaking the writing task into parts—drawing, mapping, drafting—can help the writer concentrate first on fluency and then on organization and rhetorical stance. Second, *distancing* assignments help the students attend to relationships between the writer and the reader, and between the writer and the subject. These relationships can be varied, moving from close, personal audiences, for instance, to more distant ones. Third, *modeling* assignments help students attend to the relationships of the text—how sentences can be combined into one, how parts of a sentence or discourse can be moved to different positions, how the predicate of an idea sentence shapes the organization of an essay, how different authors connect material in different ways.

Even though *processing, distancing,* and *modeling* have a different primary focus, they have overlapping subsidiary concerns. As a result, in many of the *modeling* theories and lessons that follow, *distancing* and *processing* concerns are evident. The writing act, despite the necessity to analyze the parts to help our students, always remains, to some extent, an undivided enterprise in our classrooms.

Modeling as Sentence Adding and Combining

There are three ways to teach sentence combining, each with its own research tradition. The oldest tradition (and usually the hardest to teach) is the Mellon sentence (Mellon, 1969). This sentence results from the transformation of two or three simple sentences and then the combination of these sentences into one:

The two judges _____A_____ hoped _____B_____ .

    A. The judges bet money on the race. (Who-T)

    B. Bill will win the race. (Infinitive-T)

The two judges *who bet on the race* hoped *for Bill to win the race.*

The Mellon-type exercise introduces sentences that students will not usually write: *The fact that* the man lost the race meant *that he had to sell his house.* But if the writers are beginning writers, the cost in fluency is usually too great to make the exercise worthwhile. William Strong (1973) and Frank O'Hare (1975) helped solve the problem of fluency by simplifying Mellon's lessons, with Strong dropping the parenthesis altogether. In a second approach to sentence combining, many teachers simply give students a few simple sentences, ask groups of two or three students to combine the several sentences into one, and then each day "take away" the two or three most popular connectives. For instance, on Tuesday, students try the combination without the words *and, so, then;* on Wednesday, without *and, so, then, who, which, that;* and on Thursday, without *and, so, then, who, which, that, because, although,* and *if.* What is subtracted can be based on what the students do, and as connectives are withdrawn, the students are forced to search for other ways to combine material. If many sentences are read aloud, the students borrow from each other and develop a keener sense of the sentence's flexibility.

Francis Christensen introduced the third approach to sentence combining in the early 1960s after teaching freshman English for many years at the University of Southern California, Los Angeles. His approach is reproduced in "A Generative Rhetoric of the Sentence." By the summer of 1968, James Gray was trying Christensen's approach in the summer Upward Bound Program for high school students at the University of California, Berkeley. Gray added an overhead picture that the entire class could use for subject matter, created a workshop atmosphere, and, by focusing on one part of the sentence at a time, made it relatively easy for beginning writers to model the writing of professionals. His method is detailed in "Sentence Modeling."

Modeling as Imitating Voice

Walker Gibson reminds us in "Hearing Voices: Tough Talk, Sweet Talk, Stuffy Talk" that in the experience of reading, the reader both confronts a particular personality reflected in the style of the piece and allows a temporary transformation of self. The writer, therefore, must, as Henry James said, "make his reader very much as he makes his characters." Gibson describes three kinds of talkers who appear in writing—Sweet, Tough, and Stuffy. Each has a way of talking that creates a particular set of values and assumptions. Readers are expected to go along with these values and assumptions when they confront one of these personalities. Gibson's theories are obviously important for writers to understand, but how can such theories be translated into lessons that involve the students?

Phyllis Brooks's approach to paraphrase provides one avenue. She focuses on the persona paraphrase as a way of teaching a particular structure—parenthetical expression, apposition and modification, and statement and predication. But some of these structures, according to Gibson, are used to create a particular kind of voice. Therefore, style imitation, as outlined by Brooks in "Mimesis: Grammar and the Echoing Voice," can introduce students to how voices differ and what impact these voices have on readers.

Two suggestions are important to make imitation work at various grade levels. First, select pieces that have a distinctive voice and avoid pieces that are much too difficult for the students to read. Second, in some classes the introduction of the assignment must be very explicit to avoid any confusion about what to do. In such instances, underline all the connective words (prepositions, conjunctions, and so forth) in the selections and tell the students to substitute words from their own experiences for these connectives. After the students have heard a few samples written by other students in the class, they will know what to do and will begin to change some of the connective words. In class, the students are learning a sense of style by ear. They hear many examples written in the same style but with different content, and they hear many examples of contrasting styles.

Modeling as Predication

Josephine Miles argues in "Writing in Reason" that we do not receive raw materials through the senses and then try to make meaning of these materials. Rather, we begin with meaning and look for materials of experience that support or refute the meaning. The meaning or ideas of an essay, says Miles, is a sentence, and this sentence has a predicate that determines how an idea will be developed—either as conjunction (chronology, spatial description, comparison), disjunction, concession, or conditional.

Rebekah Caplan's lessons in "Showing, Not Telling" illustrate how some of Miles's notions translate into practice. For instance, Caplan begins with the daily sentence. The sentence is the idea, complete with predication, that the students must develop. In telling paragraphs, the students seem not to know that an idea sentence is, in fact, an idea that can be developed. In showing paragraphs, the students seem to have learned that a sentence can be an idea that requires development.

But the knowledge of structure that Caplan's students are learning is sometimes tacit. That is, the students' focal awareness (Polyani, 1958) is on what details are needed to develop an idea and on what order to use for the details. However, the daily reading of sentences and discussion of alternatives seems to develop some tacit awareness of conjunction, disjunction, and other methods of organization.

A number of researchers have presented information helpful in the area of predication and development. W. Ross Winterowd (1970) argues that there are seven relationships that prevail in coherent discourse: (1) coordination (*also, too, furthermore*), (2) obversativity (*yet, however, on the other hand*), (3) causativity (*for*), (4) conclusivity (*for this reason, therefore*), (5) alternativity (*or*), (6) inclusivity (*:, as follows*), and (7) sequential (*first, second, later on*). (Winterowd has since reduced the seven relationships to six, putting sequential in the same category as coordination.)

16 A Generative Rhetoric
of the Sentence

Francis Christensen

If the new grammar is to be brought to bear on composition, it must be brought to bear on the rhetoric of the sentence. We have a workable and teachable, if not a definitive, modern grammar; but we do not have, despite several titles, a modern rhetoric.

In composition courses we do not really teach our captive charges to write better—we merely *expect* them to. And we do not teach them how to write better because we do not know how to teach them to write better. And so we merely go through the motions. Our courses with their tear-out work books and four-pound anthologies are elaborate evasions of the real problem. They permit us to put in our time and do almost anything else we'd rather be doing instead of buckling down to the hard work of making a difference in the student's understanding and manipulation of language.

With hundreds of handbooks and rhetorics to draw from, I have never been able to work out a program for teaching the sentence as I find it in the work of contemporary writers. The chapters on the sentence all adduce the traditional rhetorical classification of sentences as loose, balanced, and periodic. But the term *loose* seems to be taken as a pejorative (it sounds immoral); our students, no Bacons or Johnsons, have little occasion for balanced sentences; and some of our worst perversions of style come from the attempt to teach them to write periodic sentences. The traditional grammatical classification of sentences is equally barren. Its use in teaching composition rests on a semantic confusion, equating complexity of structure with complexity of thought and vice versa. But very simple thoughts may call for very complex grammatical constructions. Any moron can say "I don't know who done it." And some of us might be puzzled to work out the

Source: College Composition and Communication 14 (1963): 155–61. Reprinted with permission of the National Council of Teachers of English. Some usages that appear in this article are not consistent with the present NCTE Guidelines for Nonsexist Use of Language; they have not been changed in this reprint.

grammar of "All I want is all there is," although any chit can think it and say it and act on it.

The chapters on the sentence all appear to assume that we think naturally in primer sentences, progress naturally to compound sentences, and must be taught to combine the primer sentences into complex sentences—and that complex sentences are the mark of maturity. We need a rhetoric of the sentence that will do more than combine the ideas of primer sentences. We need one that will *generate* ideas.

For the foundation of such a generative or productive rhetoric I take the statement from John Erskine, the originator of the Great Books courses, himself a novelist. In an essay "The Craft of Writing" (*Twentieth Century English,* Philosophical Library, 1946) he discusses a principle of the writer's craft, which though known he says to all practitioners, he has never seen discussed in print. The principle is this: "When you write, you make a point, not by subtracting as though you sharpened a pencil, but by adding." We have all been told that the formula for good writing is the concrete noun and the active verb. Yet Erskine says, "What you say is found not in the noun but in what you add to qualify the noun . . . The noun, the verb, and the main clause serve merely as the base on which meaning will rise . . . The modifier is the essential part of any sentence." The foundation, then, for a generative or productive rhetoric of the sentence is that composition is essentially a process of *addition*.

But speech is linear, moving in time, and writing moves in linear space, which is analogous to time. When you add a modifier, whether to the noun, the verb, or the main clause, you must add it either before the head or after it. If you add it before the head, the direction of modification can be indicated by an arrow pointing forward; if you add it after, by an arrow pointing backward. Thus we have the second principle of a generative rhetoric—the principle of *direction of modification* or *direction of movement*.

Within the clause there is not much scope for operating with this principle. The positions of the various sorts of close, or restrictive, modifiers are generally fixed and the modifiers are often obligatory— "The man who came to dinner remained till midnight." Often the only choice is whether to add modifiers. What I have seen of attempts to bring structural grammar to bear on composition usually boils down to the injunction to "load the patterns." Thus "pattern practice" sets students to accreting sentences like this: "The small boy on the red bicycle who lives with his happy parents on our shady street often coasts down the steep street until he comes to the city park." This will never do. It has no rhythm and hence no life; it is tone-deaf. It is the seed that will burgeon into gobbledygook. One of the hardest things in writing is to keep the noun clusters and verb clusters short.

It is with modifiers added to the clause—that is, with sentence modifiers—that the principle comes into full play. The typical sentence of modern English, the kind we can best spend our efforts trying to teach, is what we may call the *cumulative sentence*. The main clause, which may or may not have a sentence modifier before it, advances the discussion; but the additions move backward, as in this clause, to modify the statement of the main clause or more often to explicate or exemplify it, so that the sentence has a flowing and ebbing movement, advancing to a new position and then pausing to consolidate it, leaping and lingering as the popular ballad does. The first part of the preceding compound sentence has one addition, placed within it; the second part has four words in the main clause and forty-nine in the five additions placed after it.

The cumulative sentence is the opposite of the periodic sentence. It does not represent the idea as conceived, pondered over, reshaped, packaged, and delivered cold. It is dynamic rather than static, representing the mind thinking. The main clause ("the additons move backward" above) exhausts the mere fact of the idea; logically, there is nothing more to say. The additions stay with the same idea, probing its bearings and implications, exemplifying it or seeking an analogy or metaphor for it, or reducing it to details. Thus the mere form of the sentence generates ideas. It serves the needs of both the writer and the reader, the writer by compelling him to examine his thought, the reader by letting him into the writer's thought.

Addition and direction of movement are structural principles. They involve the grammatical character of the sentence. Before going on to other principles, I must say a word about the best grammar as the foundation for rhetoric. I cannot conceive any useful transactions between teacher and students unless they have in common a language for talking about sentences. The best grammar is the grammar that best displays the layers of structure of the English sentence. The best I have found in a textbook is the combination of immediate constituent and transformation grammar in Paul Roberts's *English Sentences*. Traditional grammar, whether over-simple as in the school tradition or over-complex as in the scholarly tradition, does not reveal the language as it operates; it leaves everything, to borrow a phrase from Wordsworth, "in disconnection dead and spiritless." *English Sentences* is over-simplified and it has gaps, but it displays admirably the structures that rhetoric must work with—primarily sentence modifiers, including relative and subordinate clauses, but, far more important, the array of

noun, verb, and adjective clusters. It is paradoxical that Professor
Roberts, who has done so much to make the teaching of composition
possible, should himself be one of those who think that it cannot be
taught. Unlike Ulysses, he doesn't see any work for Telemachus to
work.

Layers of structure, as I have said, is a grammatical concept. To
bring in the dimension of meaning, we need a third principle—that of
levels of generality or *levels of abstraction.* The main clause is likely to
be stated in general or abstract or plural terms. With the main clause
stated, the forward movement of the sentence stops, the writer shifts
down to a lower level of generality or abstraction or to singular terms,
and goes back over the same ground at this lower level.[1] "He has just
bought a new car, a 1963½ Ford, a Galaxie, a fastback hardtop with
four-on-the-floor shift." There is no theoretical limit to the number of
structural layers or levels, each at a lower level of generality, any or all
of them compounded, that a speaker or writer may use. For a speaker,
listen to Lowell Thomas; for a writer, study William Faulkner. To a
single independent clause he may append a page of additions, but
usually all clear, all grammatical, once we have learned how to read
him. Or, if you prefer, study Hemingway, the master of the simple
sentence: "George was coming down in the telemark position, kneeling, one leg forward and bent, the other trailing, his sticks hanging like
some insect's thin legs, kicking up puffs of snow, and finally the whole
kneeling, trailing figure coming around in a beautiful right curve,
crouching, the legs shot forward and back, the body leaning out
against the swing, the sticks accenting the curve like points of light, all
in a wild cloud of snow."

This brings me to the fourth, and last, principle, that of texture.
Texture provides a descriptive or evaluative term. If a writer adds to few
of his nouns or verbs or main clauses and adds little, the texture may be
said to be thin. The style will be plain or bare. The writing of most of
our students is thin—even threadbare. But if he adds frequently or
much or both, then the texture may be said to be dense or rich. One of
the marks of an effective style, especially in narrative, is variety in the
texture, the texture varying with the change in pace, the variation in
texture producing the change in pace. It is not true, as I have seen it
asserted, that fast action calls for short sentences; the action is fast in
the sentence by Hemingway above. In our classes, we have to work for
greater density and variety in texture and greater concreteness and
particularity in what is added.

I have been operating at a fairly high level of generality. Now I must
downshift and go over the same points with examples. The most
graphic way to exhibit the layers of structure is to indent the word

groups of a sentence and to number the levels. Since in the narrow columns of this journal indentation is possible only with short sentences whose additions are short, I have used it with only the first three sentences; the reader is urged to copy out the others for himself. I have added symbols to mark the grammatical character of the additions: SC, subordinate clause; RC, relative clause; NC, noun cluster; VC, verb cluster; AC, adjective cluster; Abs, absolute (i.e., a VC with a subject of its own); PP, prepositional phrase. With only a few exceptions (in some the punctuation may be questioned) the elements set off as on a lower level are marked by junctures or punctuation. The examples have been chosen to illustrate the range of constructions used in the lower levels; after the first few they are arranged by the number of levels. The examples could have been drawn from poetry as well as from prose. Those not attributed are by students.

1

1 He shook his hands,
  2 a quick shake, (NC)
    3 fingers down, (Abs)
      4 like a pianist. (PP)—Sinclair Lewis

2

  2 Calico-coated, (AC)
  2 small bodied, (AC)
  2 with delicate legs and pink faces (PP)
    3 in which their mismatched eyes rolled wild and subdued, (RC)
1 they huddled,
  2 gaudy motionless and alert, (AC)
  2 wild as deer, (AC)
  2 deadly as rattlesnakes, (AC)
  2 quiet as doves. (AC)—William Faulkner

3

1 The bird's eye, / , remained fixed upon him;
  2 bright and silly as a sequin (AC)
1 its little bones, / , seemed swooning in his hand.—Stella Benson
  2 wrapped . . . in a warm padding of feathers (VC)

4

(1) The jockeys sat bowed and relaxed, moving a little at the waist with the movement of their horses[2-VC].—Katherine Anne Porter

5

(1) The flame sidled up the match, driving a film of moisture and a thin strip of darker grey before it[2-VC].

6

(1) She came among them behind the man, gaunt in the gray shapeless garment and the sunbonnet[2-AC], wearing stained canvas gymnasium shoes[2-VC].—Faulkner

7

(1) The Texan turned to the nearest gatepost and climbed to the top of it, his alternate thighs thick and bulging in the tight jeans$^{\text{2-Abs}}$, the butt of his pistol catching and losing the sun in pearly gleams$^{\text{2-Abs}}$.—Faulkner

8

(1) He could sail for hours, searching the blanched grasses below him with his telescopic eyes$^{\text{2-VC}}$, gaining height against the wind$^{\text{2-VC}}$, descending in mile-long, gently declining swoops when he curved and rode back$^{\text{2-VC}}$, never beating a wing$^{\text{2-VC}}$.—Walter Van Tilburg Clark

9

(1) The gay-sweatered skaters are quicksilvering around the frosty rink, the girls gliding and spinning$^{\text{2-Abs}}$, the boys swooping and darting$^{\text{2-Abs}}$, their arms flailing like wings$^{\text{3-Abs}}$.

10

(1) He stood at the top of the stairs and watched me, I waiting for him to call me up$^{\text{2-Abs}}$, he hesitating to come down$^{\text{2-Abs}}$, his lips nervous with the suggestion of a smile$^{\text{3-Abs}}$, mine asking whether the smile meant come, or go away$^{\text{3-Abs}}$.

11

(1) Joad's lips stretched tight over his long teeth for a moment, and (1) he licked his lips, like a dog$^{\text{2-PP}}$, two licks$^{\text{3-NC}}$, one in each direction from the middle$^{\text{4-NC}}$.—Steinbeck

12

(1) We all live in two realities: one of seeming fixity$^{\text{2-NC}}$, with institutions, dogmas, rules of punctuation, and routines$^{\text{3-PP}}$, the calendared and clockwise world of all but futile round on round$^{\text{4-NC}}$; and one of whirling and flying electrons, dreams, and possibilities$^{\text{2-NC}}$, behind the clock$^{\text{3-PP}}$.—Sidney Cox

13

(1) It was as though someone, somewhere, had touched a lever and shifted gears, and (1) the hospital was set for night running, smooth and silent$^{\text{2-AC}}$, its normal clatter and hum muffled$^{\text{2-Abs}}$, the only sounds heard in the whitewalled room distant and unreal$^{\text{2-Abs}}$: a low hum of voices from the nurse's desk$^{\text{3-NC}}$, quickly stifled$^{\text{4-VC}}$, the soft squish of rubber-soled shoes on the tiled corridor$^{\text{3-NC}}$, starched white cloth rustling against itself$^{\text{3-NC}}$, and outside, the lonesome whine of wind in the country night$^{\text{3-NC}}$, and the Kansas dust beating against the windows$^{\text{3-NC}}$.

14

(1) The beach sounds are jazzy, percussion fixing the mode$^{\text{2-Abs}}$—the surf cracking and booming in the distance$^{\text{3-Abs}}$, a little nearer dropped bar-bells clanking$^{\text{3-Abs}}$, steel gym rings, flung together$^{\text{4-VC}}$, ringing$^{\text{3-Abs}}$, palm fronds rustling above me$^{\text{3-Abs}}$, like steel brushes washing over a snare drum$^{\text{4-PP}}$, troupes of sandals splatting and shuffling on the sandy cement$^{\text{3-Abs}}$, their beat varying$^{\text{4-Abs}}$, syncopation emerging and disappearing with changing paces$^{\text{5-Abs}}$.

15

(1) A small negro girl develops from the sheet of glare-frosted walk, walking barefooted$^{2\text{-VC}}$, her bare legs striking and coiling from the hot cement$^{3\text{-Abs}}$, her feet curling in$^{4\text{-Abs}}$, only the outer edges touching$^{5\text{-Abs}}$.

16

(1) The swells moved rhythmically toward us irregularly faceted$^{2\text{-VC}}$, sparkling$^{2\text{-VC}}$, growing taller and more powerful$^{2\text{-VC}}$, until the shining crest bursts$^{3\text{-SC}}$, a transparent sheet of pale green water spilling over the top$^{4\text{-Abs}}$, breaking into blue-white foam as it cascades down the front of the wave$^{5\text{-VC}}$, piling up in a frothy mound that the diminishing wave pushes up against the pilings$^{5\text{-VC}}$, with a swishmash$^{6\text{-PP}}$, the foam drifting back$^{5\text{-Abs}}$, like a lace fan opened over the shimmering water as the spent wave returns whispering to the sea$^{6\text{-PP}}$.

The best starting point for a composition unit based on these four principles is with two-level narrative sentences, first with one second-level addition (sentences 4,5), then with two or more parallel ones (6,7,8). Anyone sitting in his room with his eyes closed could write the main clause of most of the examples; the discipline comes with the additions, provided they are based at first on immediate observation, requiring the student to phrase an exact observation in exact language. This can hardly fail to be exciting to a class: it is life, with the variety and complexity of life; the workbook exercise is death. The situation is ideal also for teaching diction—abstract-concrete, general-specific, literal-metaphorical, denotative-connotative. When the sentences begin to come out right, it is time to examine the additions for their grammatical character. From then on the grammar comes to the aid of the writing and the writing reinforces the grammar. One can soon go on to multi-level narrative sentences (1,3,9-11,15,16) and then to brief narratives of three to six or seven sentences on actions that can be observed over and over again—beating eggs, making a cut with a power saw, or following a record changer's cycle or a waves's flow and ebb. Bring the record changer to class. Description, by contrast, is static, picturing appearance rather than behavior. The constructions to master are the noun and adjective clusters and the absolute (13,14). Then the descriptive noun cluster must be taught to ride piggy-back on the narrative sentence, so that description and narration are interleaved: "In the morning we went out into a new world, a glistening crystal and white world, each skeleton tree, each leafless bush, even the heavy, drooping power lines sheathed in icy crystal." The next step is to develop the sense for variety in texture and change in pace that all good narrative demands.

In the next unit, the same four principles can be applied to the expository paragraph. But this is a subject for another paper.

I want to anticipate two possible objections. One is that the sentences are long. By freshman English standards they are long, but I could have produced far longer ones from works freshmen are expected to read. Of the sentences by students, most were written as finger exercises in the first few weeks of the course. I try in narrative sentences to push to level after level, not just two or three, but four, five, or six, even more, as far as the students' powers of observation will take them. I want them to become sentence acrobats, to dazzle by their syntactic dexterity. I'd rather have to deal with hyperemia than anemia. I want to add my voice to that of James Coleman (*CCC*, December 1962) deploring our concentration on the plain style.

The other objection is that my examples are mainly descriptive and narrative—and today in freshman English we teach only exposition. I deplore this limitation as much as I deplore our limitation to the plain style. Both are a sign that we have sold our proper heritage for a pot of message. In permitting them, the English department undercuts its own discipline. Even if our goal is only utilitarian prose, we can teach diction and sentence structure far more effectively through a few controlled exercises in description and narration than we can by starting right off with exposition (Theme One, 500 words, precipitates *all* the problems of writing). The student has something to communicate—his immediate sense impressions, which can stand a bit of exercising. The material is not already verbalized—he has to match language to sense impressions. His acuteness in observation and in choice of words can be judged by fairly objective standards—is the sound of a bottle of milk being set down on a concrete step suggested better by *clink* or *clank?* In the examples, study the diction for its accuracy, rising at times to the truly imaginative. Study the use of metaphor, of comparison. This verbal virtuosity and syntactical ingenuity can be made to carry over into expository writing.

But this is still utilitarian. What I am proposing carries over of itself into the study of literature. It makes the student a better reader of literature. It helps him thread the syntactical mazes of much mature writing, and it gives him insight into that elusive thing we call style. Last year a student told of re-reading a book by her favorite author, Willa Cather, and of realizing for the first time *why* she liked reading her: she could understand and appreciate the style. For some students, moreover, such writing makes life more interesting as well as giving them a way to share their interest with others. When they learn how to put concrete details into a sentence, they begin to look at life with more alertness. If it is liberal education we are concerned with, it is just possible that these things are more important than anything we can achieve when we set our sights on the plain style in expository prose.

I want to conclude with a historical note. My thesis in this paragraph is that modern prose like modern poetry has more in common with the seventeenth than with the eighteenth century and that we fail largely because we are operating from an eighteenth-century base. The shift from the complex to the cumulative sentence is more profound than it seems. It goes deep in grammar, requiring a shift from the subordinate clause (the staple of our trade) to the cluster (so little understood as to go almost unnoticed in our textbooks). And I have only lately come to see that this shift has historical implications. The cumulative sentence is the modern form of the loose sentence that characterized the anti-Ciceronian movement in the seventeenth century. This movement, according to Morris W. Croll[2], began with Montaigne and Bacon and continued with such men as Donne, Brown, Taylor, Pascal. Croll calls their prose baroque. To Montaigne, its art was the art of being natural; to Pascal, its eloquence was the eloquence that mocks formal eloquence; to Bacon, it presented knowledge so that it could be examined, not so that it must be accepted.

But the Senecan amble was banished from England when "the direct sensuous apprehension of thought" (T. S. Eliot's words) gave way to Cartesian reason or intellect. The consequences of this shift in sensibility are well summarized by Croll:

> To this mode of thought we are to trace almost all the features of modern literary education and criticism, or at least of what we should have called modern a generation ago: the study of the precise meaning of words; the reference to dictionaries as literary authorities; the study of the sentence as a logical unit alone; the careful circumscription of its limits and the gradual reduction of its length; . . . [3] the attempt to reduce grammar to an exact science; the idea that forms of speech are always either correct or incorrect; the complete subjection of the laws of motion and expression in style to the laws of logic and standardization—in short, the triumph, during two centuries, of grammatical over rhetorical ideas. (p. 1077)

Here is a seven-point scale any teacher of composition can use to take stock. He can find whether he is based in the eighteenth century or in the twentieth and whether he is consistent—completely either an ancient or a modern—or is just a crazy mixed-up kid.

Notes

1. Cf. Leo Rockas, "Abstract and Concrete Sentences," *CCC*, May 1963. Rockas describes sentences as abstract or concrete, the abstract implying the concrete and vice versa. Readers and writers, he says, must have the knack of

apprehending the concrete in the abstract and the abstract in the concrete. This is true and valuable. I am saying that within a single sentence the writer may present more than one level of generality, translating the abstract into the more concrete in added levels.

2. "The Baroque Style in Prose," *Studies in English Philology: A Miscellany in Honor of Frederick Klaeber* (1929), reprinted in A. M. Witherspoon and F. J. Warnke, *Seventeenth-Century Prose and Poetry*, 2nd ed. (1963). I have used the latter, and I have borrowed from Croll in my description of the cumulative sentence.

3. The omitted item concerns punctuation and is not relevant here. In using this scale, note the phrase "what we should have called modern a generation ago" and remember that Croll was writing in 1929.

17 Sentence Modeling

James Gray

> Is it useful to be aware of one's own style, or does such awareness interfere with being natural? My belief is that, once having become conscious of the possible choices and once having made the choices, one can be secure in them and they can become natural. Knowledge and conscious choice, in other words, support rather than oppose intuition, and give it flexibility as well as ease, sympathy as well as surety, a sense of alternatives as well as a sense of preferences. (Josephine Miles, 1979, p. 35)

> In speaking and writing, as in daily life, we develop certain habits of combining materials, so that we do not have to think through each combination each time. Our habits make our style . . . (P. 44)

Francis Christensen's work on the English sentence has had a lasting effect upon my own teaching of writing. What caught my attention initially and has kept my interest ever since—and it has been almost twenty years since I heard "The Generative Rhetoric of the Sentence" delivered as a paper at the Asilomar Language Arts Conference—was the simple yet powerful idea that we could teach students to write by examining how real writers write, particularly by noticing the frequent use of certain phrasal modifiers in the work of so many modern writers, a pattern so common that Christensen identified it as the dominant style of twentieth-century prose and named it "cumulative." Christensen opened a window for me in that presentation in the early sixties, letting me "see" what I had never seen before. He pointed out a common, syntactic pattern that I had never consciously noticed, even though I had read widely in the works of so many of the writers he examined, even though I had long been interested in style and thought I knew something about it.

But working out a way to turn these new insights into teaching ideas took some time, and as is the case with most teachers of writing I have known who try to adapt someone else's idea and make it their own, it took a great deal of trial-and-error experience in the classroom before I discovered what I really wanted to present from the work of Francis Christensen and how I could present it effectively to students.

The approach that I finally fixed upon is the approach I've stayed with over the years. Although I keep refining it in small ways, adding new material, sharpening the focus, simplifying here and discarding there, the approach remains basically the same: students examine variations of the cumulative sentence in scores of sentences written by a number of professional writers and imitate these methods of modification in sentences of their own. In the most important step in the process, students apply these now-familiar structures by writing longer, extended sequences. After several repetitions of this pattern— sentence exercises to extended sequence—they have the confidence to use the cumulative sentence in the longer papers they write.

The Steps in the Process

As a first-day exercise, prior to any instruction, I project a transparency of a photograph onto the screen—possibly a close-up of Louis Armstrong's face, or a joyous young mother hugging her baby, or an old woman, dressed conservatively in black but sitting on a trash can reading a paperback—and ask my students to write about half a page, describing what they see. I ask volunteers to read papers aloud, and I begin to comment on the accuracy of certain observations and the implications of particular details. With this initial written exercise I have my own pretest sampling of student writing, written before I have taught what I have to teach, writing that can be put aside for a while and compared later with future work. With this exercise I have also introduced students to my use of transparencies and the overhead projector. A single photograph, blown up on the screen in a semi-darkened room, can bring a powerful moment of experience into the classroom, an experience—common to everyone in the room—that students can write about. Such writing demands close observation for writers to capture with words what they see. And so important is close observation with the sentence exercises that will follow, that with younger classes I have set aside days for observation exercises before the introduction of any writing task—that is, listing everything noticed in the photograph, listing the contributing details to dominant impressions, and so forth.

Following this first written exercise, I distribute a packet of prose passages, richly cumulative in style, that I have selected deliberately from both fiction and nonfiction: essay, short story, science, autobiography, history, novel. The passages are short, a paragraph to a page in length, short enough to be read aloud. I read the first two passages through without comment and ask if anyone noticed any similarities in the writing of these different passages, the first from *Cider with Rosie,* an autobiography by Laurie Lee, the second from *The Civil War,* a nonfiction work by Shelby Foote.

> The June grass, amongst which I stood, was taller than I was, and I wept. I had never been so close to grass before. It towered above me and all around me, each blade tattooed with tiger skins of sunlight. It was knife-edged, dark and a wicked green, thick as a forest and alive with grasshoppers that chirped and chattered and leapt through the air like monkeys. . . . Our Mother too was distracted from duty, seduced by the rich wilderness of the garden so long abandoned. All day she trotted to and fro, flushed and garrulous, pouring flowers into every pot and jug she could find on the kitchen floor. Flowers from the garden, daisies from the bank, cow parsley, grasses, ferns and leaves—they flowed in armfuls through the cottage door until its dim interior seemed entirely possessed by the world outside—a still green pool flooding with honeyed tides of summer.—Laurie Lee

> Polk meanwhile was completing his preparations to evacuate Columbus, working mainly at night to hide his intentions from prying enemy eyes. This was no easy task, involving as it did the repulse of a gunboat reconnaissance on the twenty-third and the removal of 140 emplaced guns and camp equipment for 17,000 men, but he accomplished it without loss or detection. By March 2, the heaviest guns and 7,000 of his soldiers having been sent downriver to New Madrid, he was on his way south with the remainder. Within the week he reached Humboldt, the crossing of the Mobile and Ohio and the Memphis and Louisville Railroads, where he stopped. From here, his 10,000 troops could be hurried to meet whatever developed in any direction, either up where they had just come from, or down at Corinth, or back in Memphis. Little as he approved of retreat in general, the militant churchman had shown a talent for it under necessity.—Shelby Foote

At this point the students have little idea of what I am after. I might get a response or two, but usually not much more than "They use a lot of description." This response is not bad, really, for most of the passages are representational rather than discursive. I focus students' attention on a sentence from each passage:

> All day she trotted to and fro, flushed and garrulous, pouring flowers into every pot and jug she could find on the kitchen floor.

> Polk meanwhile was completing his preparations to evacuate Columbus, working mainly at night to hide his intentions from prying enemy eyes.

I ask the question again. I might get more this time; I might not. In any case, I am beginning to lead them to "see" what they too have seen but not noticed before:

> that both sentences start with a statement that could have been a sentence by itself
>
> that both writers, with the simple use of the comma, have added more to this initial sentence
>
> that the sentences, in effect, have two parts, a base clause plus additions
>
> that the additions are not mere decoration, but add detail to the more general first statement
>
> that the additions frequently carry the weight of the meaning

We read more passages aloud, something from a story by Updike, an essay by Orwell, and I ask the students to identify patterns similar to those we examined earlier. The students begin to be conscious of the common pattern of base clause plus additions, and they begin to see—because I point it out—that descriptive/narrative sentences and passages are common not just to fiction but to a wide range of writing.

To focus even more on the power and use of additions, we examine two or three more passages at the beginning of the next class session, but this time they are presented in both original and altered versions. I often use a passage on bullfighting by Ernest Hemingway.

Altered Version (without additions)

Inside they all stood around in the bull ring. Out in the arena the picadors had galloped their decrepid horses around the ring. Then a bull came into the arena. He came out all in a rush. He stood as if he were frozen. Then he charged.

Original Version (with additions)

Inside they all stood around in the bull ring, talking and looking up in the grandstand at the girls in the boxes. Out in the arena the picadors had galloped their decrepid horses around the ring, sitting straight and stiff in their rocking chair saddles. Then, ducking his head as he came up out of the dark pen, a bull came into the arena. He came out all in a rush, big, black and white, weighing over a ton and moving with a soft gallop. He stood as if he were frozen, his great crest of muscle up, firmly planted, his eyes looking around, his horns pointed forward, black and white and sharp as porcupine quills. Then he charged.

I ask the obvious question: "What difference *do* the additions make?" There is much here for students to notice as we compare these different versions:

the power of particular but ordinary detail as the basis of good writing

the use of the addition as an effective way to state that detail, allowing the writing to say everything the writer wants to say

the possibility of using a single addition or a whole string of additions, one following the other

the placement of the additions, usually following the base clause but sometimes preceding it or interrupting it

the difference between thin texture (altered version) and dense texture (original version) and how a writer can vary the texture in his or her writing

But I am impatient to have the students write sentences of their own. I distribute examples of sentences by popular writers demonstrating the use of the base clause plus additions that students can examine and use as models for their own writing. First I identify the base clauses in some sample sentences:

He was snoring softly, with a little bubbling at the lips at every outbreath.—Walter Van Tilburg Clark

Varner looked at him sharply, the reddish eyebrows beetling a little above the hard little eyes.—William Faulkner

Standing for a moment on the edge of the pavement to adjust his cap—the cleanest thing about him—*he looked casually to left and right and,* when the flow of traffic had eased off, *crossed the road.*—Alan Sillitoe

He lay down for half an hour, pressed under the fallen tree where he had hidden, *to give time for the thing to go right away and for his own heart to cease thundering.*—T. H. White

Then the class examines a collection of sentences demonstrating various uses of the phrasal modifier as addition:

1. He lay for a quarter of an hour without thinking, lips parted, legs and arms extended, breathing quietly as he gazed at the figures in the wallpaper until they were hidden in darkness.— Saul Bellow

2. She draws a cigarette from the turquoise pack of Newports and hangs it between her orange lips and frowns at the sulphur tip as she strikes a match, with curious feminine clumsiness, away from her, holding the paper match sideways and thus bending it.—John Updike

3. A moment later she was swimming back to the side of the pool, her head of short-clipped auburn hair held up, straight ahead of her, as though it were a rose on a long stem.—Philip Roth

4. Working with an enormous team of 18 editorial staffers, field editor Stuart Baird—his perpetual pallor now accented by red-rimmed eyes—could almost always be found holed away in his darkened office at the back of the cutting room, poring over footage running through the Moviola.—David Michael Petrou

5. The road was littered with squashed grasshoppers; and, their wings crackling, a number of live grasshoppers sailed through the air back and forth across the road as if the summer sun, having thawed out their nearly frosted bodies, had set them abruptly to sizzling.—John Nichols

6. It seemed more sedate than I remembered it, more perpendicular and straight-laced, with narrower windows and shinier wood-work, as though a coat of varnish had been put over everything for better preservation.—John Knowles

7. His walk was belly-heavy, as if he had to remind himself not to step on his own feet.—Saul Bellow

8. An occasional involuntary sob shook her—like pre-ignition in an overheated engine which has already been switched off.—Lawrence Durrell

9. Croissants, coffee, chatter, screams of laughter, two women in the ease of no child to get off to school, no husband to be fed, no boy friend to be watched for signs of a morning mood, talking, charting the movements and marriages of former friends, calling out anecdotes to each other as Peg hurried to do her hair and put on her suit, the chat so good and the time so quick and easy until the moment came when they kissed each other, hugged, promised to keep in touch, and then, suddenly, Peg was gone.—Brian Moore

10. She placed it on the table in front of Mike who stood up and carved it, cutting the slices very thin, laying them gently on the plates for the maid to take around.—Roald Dahl

11. He looked at Ralph, his thin body tensed, his spear held as if he threatened him.—William Golding

12. Lying beside the dark wharf, all strung, all beaded with round golden light, the Picton boat looked as if she was more ready to sail among the stars than out into the cold sea.—Katherine Mansfield

13. She was dressed as on the day before, in a white frock, and her shiny white boots with their high heels, her fat legs bulging over the tops of them, were strange things on that exotic scene.—Somerset Maugham

14. He shook the sand through the screen, and left the sand-crabs wriggling and scuttling on the wire, heavy little creatures, shaped like scarabs, with gray-mottled shells and orange un-derparts.—John Steinbeck

15. Feld could trust him with anything and did, frequently going home after an hour or two at the store, leaving all the money in the till, knowing Sobel would guard every cent of it.—Bernard Malamud

16. The hamburgers came, the plates clattering down on the counter, and the cups of coffee, the coffee sloshing into the saucers.—Robert Penn Warren

17. Now both the Warden and the deputy looked at the emissary, the deputy's mouth open a little, the cigar poised in his hand to have its tip bitten off.—William Faulkner

18. Flat and unruffled it stretched across, like a filled blue cup, to the woods on the other side.—Irwin Shaw

19. It was almost, but not quite, dark when he emerged from between the two granite pillars of the cemetery entrance; a slight boyish figure, not tall, moving with an easy swiftness, an air of confidence, no urgency, head tilted to one side although he did not dart glances in either direction, wearing a black turtleneck sweater, slim tight slacks, also black, and dark tennis sneakers. He climbed over the stone wall near the edge of the pond and turned toward the parking area, making his way between the trees, wet branches snapping at his face and his boots sinking into the sodden earth, making squishing sounds as he lifted them.—Joseph Hayes

I take a good deal of time working through many of these sentences, asking "What is the base clause?" with one, "What are the additions?" with another, and pointing out a variety of details that I want my students to notice: that the base clause can be as brief as "He looked at Ralph" (11) or of some length (2), that there can be several additions (14) or only one (7). I lead students through a sentence like Philip Roth's (3) with some care and wonder aloud with them why this sentence was written as it was, suggesting that physical detail alone was not doing what Roth wanted done, that he had to resort to a comparison, a metaphor to capture what he wanted to say. We look at the sheer amount of detail provided by the additions (19) and the exotic use of the base clause plus addition in the sentence by Brian Moore (9).

When I sense that the students are seeing what I want them to see—and the fact that I'm working with so many models rather than just one or two makes all the difference—I project another photo transparency and ask the class to observe it and to put together a similar sentence out loud. I call for a base clause, and some student will come up with something like "He stood there." I ask what can be added. A student might say, "He's crying," and I ask if this second *He* is necessary. Wouldn't the single word *crying* be enough? Additions can, as we have seen, be single words. One student questions whether the man is really crying: "Isn't he holding it back? He's trying not to cry." The students are looking closely at a photo from World War II of a grief-stricken Frenchman, and I stay with this picture until we have put together a satisfactory sentence with two or three additions. I might have students try to compose another sentence orally; I might move them immediately into writing. It depends on the signals I get from the class. When I feel they're ready to write, I project another transparency and ask the students to describe what they see in a sentence exactly like the model sentences we've been examining together. They observe the photo closely. They write. They observe some more. They take their time trying to get it right. When they have finished, I ask them to read their sentences aloud. There's never a problem. The students have given this sentence some care. It is usually far better than what they normally would have written. They are pleased with—even proud of— what they have been able to do, and they are interested in hearing what the other students wrote, working with the same material. The following sentences were written by a group of tenth-graders in response to a photo from *Stop, Look and Write* by Hart Day Leavitt and David A. Sohn:

1. Vacant eyed, he slouched against the counter, like a mannequin without support, the splintery wood biting into his arm and back.
2. He leaned against the counter top, silent, motionless, with a cup of coffee in one hand, the short remains of a cigarette in the other, and a thoughtful, rather sly look on his face; he knew it now, the terrible, haunting feeling after a doctor's first un-successful operation.
3. The doctor gazed sadly at the floor, fiddling carelessly with his hands, the ashes from his cigarette falling into his coffee.
4. He leaned against the counter, silent and mournful, drinking coffee and smoking a cigarette, like a convict awaiting his execution.
5. He stood, defeated and ridiculed, a beaten old man, with eyes melting in his head.
6. He is deep in thought, with head down and mouth grimly set, slumped, tired and disraveled, a warm cup of coffee in his hand.

If I hear a problem—a run-on sentence, a sentence without additions, a questionable word—I deal with it on the spot. "Take out those last two *ands;* use commas instead. Now read it. Isn't that better?" Most of the sentences will be good first trys; some will be excellent. I let them know that I am pleased with what they have written, and this is no phony praise of encouragement, for some student sentences will be as good as the models. I continue, directing the class's attention to something particularly fine, such as "She comforted him, her arm around him like a bandage," written by a tenth-grade student in response to a photo of a young Vietnamese girl ministering to her wounded younger brother. At the close of this first session of controlled writing, there is almost always a sense of excitement, a sense of great expectations among the students. What several students have written— and no matter that it was just a sentence—was good, and they know it. I have given honest praise to many. The students know they have learned something; they will be eager to come back for more, and in the classroom there is no greater motivation for students than the elation that comes with having learned and accomplished something.

What happens next depends solely on the particular group of students I am teaching, and I have introduced this approach to students at all levels, seventh-graders to adults. Some students and classes will need more time, another day with the basic pattern, more initial sentence practice; others are ready to apply what they have learned in longer, extended sequences. I move as rapidly as I can, because I am impatient to have them apply what they have learned to something longer. But first there is more to introduce at the sentence level. I distribute selections of model sentences using verb phrases and clusters:

1. She walked slowly, *picking her way as though she were afraid she would fall.*—John Steinbeck
2. He was exhilarating to watch, *sweating and swearing and sucking bits of saliva back into his lips.*—John Updike
3. Manuel, *facing the bull, having turned with him each charge,* offered the cape with his two hands.—Ernest Hemingway
4. He stayed quite still, *listening as raptly as some wandering night-beast to the indiscriminate stir and echoings of the darkness.*—Walter de la Mare
5. Rosalind dropped the exercise-book on the floor, looked at it, hesitated, and, putting her hands over her mouth, went upstairs, *choking back her sobs.*—Elizabeth Bowen
6. *Standing for a moment on the edge of the pavement to adjust his cap*—the cleanest thing about him—he looked casually to the left and right and, when the flow of traffic had eased off, crossed the road.—Alan Sillitoe
7. He lay down for half an hour, *pressed under the fallen tree where he had hidden,* to give time for the thing to go right away and for his own heart to cease thundering.—T. H. White
8. The air was warm and tense, *stretched so taut that it quivered.*— Elizabeth Bowen
9. It flew in, with a battering of wings, from the outside, and waited there, *silhouetted against its pinched bit of sky, preening and cooing in a throbbing, thrilled, tentative way.* Neither did it fly. Instead it stuck in the round hole, *pirouetting rapidly and nodding its head as if in frantic agreement.* Then the pigeon fell like a handful of rags, *skimming down the barn wall into the layer of straw that coated the floor of the mow on this side.*— John Updike

10. Asa deliberately busied himself about the post, *filling the bin beneath the counter with navy beans and green coffee, leafing through the packet of letters in the drawer, making a long rite out of feeding the occupants of the picket corral.*—Conrad Richter

11. The trail moved up the dry shale hillside, *avoiding rocks, dropping under clefts, climbing in and out of the old water scars.*—John Steinbeck

12. And then the cub saw his mother, the she wolf, the fearless one, *crouching down till her belly touched the ground, whimpering, wagging her tail, making peace signs.*—Jack London

13. One remembers them from another time—*playing handball in the playground, going to church, wondering if they were going to be promoted at school.*—James Baldwin

14. The little girls heard him muttering on, *holding up one hand, patting the air as if he were calling for silence.*—Katherine Anne Porter

And I hand out examples of model sentences using absolute phrases:

1. Sometimes I lay, *the sharp bones of my hips meeting only the hardness of the sand, the sun puckering my skin.*—Nadine Gordimer

2. All along the road to Bestwood the miners tramped, wet and gray and dirty, but *their red mouths talking with animation.*—D. H. Lawrence

3. Mrs. Koch knitted without looking, *a fine sweat cooling her brow, her eyes absently retaining a look of gentle attention,* as if she had forgotten that she was not listening to someone.—Nadine Gordimer

4. I must have stood there then—fifteen minutes shivering in my nightshirt, *my heart pounding inside of me like a ramrod working on a plugged up bore,* and listening for the gun again, if it was going to shoot some more.—Erskine Caldwell

5. They saw him later, up on the platform; he was squeaking out his little patriotic poem, *his eyes,* shining like stars, *fixed on one broad, smiling face in the audience.*—Dorothy Canfield Fisher

6. *Eyes watching, horns straight forward,* the bull looked at him, watching.—Ernest Hemingway

7. After that we rode on in silence, *the traces creaking, the hoofs of the horses clumping steadily in the soft sand, the grasshoppers shrilling from the fields and the cicadas from the trees overhead.*—Edwin W. Teale

8. He turned away from the window, came over to the bed where she lay outstretched, *face half-buried in the pillow, hair loose and golden, a twist of sheet barely covering her hips.*—Helen MacInnes

9. Others were having trouble, too, and we pulled to the job again, and held it, *all the hoofs trampling squilch-squilch,* and *little clods popping gently out of the side and rolling toward the water.*—Walter Van Tilburg Clark

10. I had come at just the proper moment when it was fully to be seen, *the white bone gleaming there in a kind of ashen splendor,* water worn, and about to be ground away in the next long torrent.—Loren Eiseley

11. It was a bright, cold day, *the ground covered with a sleet that had frozen so that it seemed as if all the bare trees, the cut brush and all the grass and the bare ground had been varnished with ice.*—Ernest Hemingway

12. At my back the turntable shirred, *the needle making a dull scrape among the last grooves.*—Saul Bellow

Within the same structure of base clause plus addition, the students now examine the particular use of different phrasal modifiers. I highlight the differences, not only in construction but in purpose and effect. We examine model sentences, setting the verb phrase beside the absolute:

She walked slowly, picking her way as though she were afraid she would fall.—John Steinbeck

Sometimes I lay, the sharp bones of my hips meeting only the hardness of the sand, the sun puckering my skin.—Nadine Gordimer

Wanting the class to see the distinctions, I ask, "How are they alike? How do they differ?" I read aloud again the phrase beginning "picking her way" and compare it with the phrase "the sun puckering my skin." They notice the similarities of the *-ing* words and soon realize that the absolute phrase also contains a subject, that the absolute phrase is in effect a verb phrase with its own subject. I point out that the subject in the absolute phrase has a real purpose, that it allows the writer to focus and then expand on some detail, some part of the whole. The sentence by Dorothy Canfield Fisher (5) describes the speaker as looking not at the whole Fourth-of-July-like crowd but at one particular face in that crowd. The absolute phrase gives her the means to say just that. I want the students to see that these different patterns are not used willy-nilly by writers, that each phrasal modifier has its own unique use.

Again I ask the students to produce sentences aloud before I ask them to write, believing that if they can say it correctly they can write it correctly. I might pace up and down before the class, asking them to supply a base clause, an absolute phrase, a verb phrase, another absolute. I ask the students to look at a particular student and describe exactly what they observe: "nervously tapping his pen" (verb phrase), "his left arm resting on the corner of his desk" (absolute phrase). Then they write and, when ready, read aloud what they have written. I listen to their use of the verb phrase and the absolute and frequently ask them to reread a phrase. Once again, any problems that arise are worked out immediately. The verb form in the absolute causes some trouble: "her hand was raised in greeting" should read "her hand raised in greeting."

At this point, usually by the fourth day, I ask students to write an extended description, using the sentence patterns and the particular sentence modifiers we have been studying, in a short piece that runs a half to a full page in length. We examine more passages, and I project whole pages so that the students can see these sentences in context. We look closely at the powerful use of a short sentence by Updike, coming as it does after a very dense passage. We note the variation in texture used by different writers, and I comment again on thin and dense texture and how the density of modification can vary.

This extended sequence assignment is the most important step in my approach to teaching writing. To be able to use these previously unfamiliar modification patterns, students must apply what they have learned. I state this as strongly as I can to my students. I remind them that this is my goal; I suggest that these sentences can be used in the longer piece I have assigned, that they will not be penalized for using these sentence patterns in their own writing.

I send the students out of the room to observe whatever there is to be seen: another student, a group of students, a particular tree, something they have never noticed before. I make the point that their topic is unimportant, that any content well handled can become the stuff of good writing. The students also know that they will be reading aloud the next day in small groups and that this sharing will become common practice with all longer papers. With older groups I ask that they bring at least five copies of this first extended piece to class so that other group members can follow along during the reading.

Students return to class with paragraphs like the following, writing that demonstrates control, even mastery, of a structure they have consciously applied in a longer sequence:

> The dog moved along slowly, stopping first now to sniff the grass, then to scratch his ear or lick his side. He continued on, drawing closer to a child who, sitting on a bench, was holding an ice cream cone with both hands. The child seemed unaware of the dog's approach, his attention captured by the ice cream. Carefully, he raised the cone to his lips, and, turning it slowly around, he licked the cone from the bottom to top in a spiral motion. Then, thoughtfully, ponderously, he lowered the cone to his lap. The dog,

having continued his methodical approach to the child, now drew up beside him, and lowering his backside carefully to the ground, sat down. The child stared at the dog; the dog stared at the cone. Straining his neck slightly forward, the dog extended his tongue, and raising his eyes to the child's face he licked the tip of the cone.

L. Worthington

She sat there facing the foot traffic, one arm extended over the back of the bench, left leg crossed over the right, her left foot slowly moving back and forth as though it were a pendulum keeping time with her thoughts. Sitting perfectly erect with her head held high, as though long years of practice had taught her how to execute each of her movements with a high degree of grace and precision, she silently watched the passersby. She reached into the paper sack next to her and drew a potato chip from it. She held the chip between her index finger and thumb, daintily placed it on her partially extended tongue and pulled the chip into her mouth. She ate every chip this way, always letting it ride into her mouth on her tongue before she started to chew, never once biting into the chip, letting the crumbs fall where they might. When she finished eating the potato chips she smoothed the paper sack along the edges, folded it in half, then in fourths, and finally put it into her book bag. She stood up, turned around to face the bench and brushed the imaginary crumbs meticulously from her chest and skirt. Next she picked up her purse, which had been resting on the bench, and stationed the strap on her shoulder, carefully assuring herself that the strap rested under—not over—the lapel of her gray blazer. She tossed her head back, placed her hand at the nape of neck and drew it out along the underside of her long blond hair, lifting her head and letting it fall into place. With this done she picked up her book bag and joined the foot traffic.

Carmel Zimmerman

The grizzled old bum paces the corner, papers cradled in his left arm, waving a single copy with his right. Short and rumpled, he thrusts the headlines stiffly at passersby, with arthritic emphasis, droning in a grim, monotonous voice, "final, final-closing stocks, latest sports-final." A man walks past him, resolutely ignoring his pitch; the old man turns away, cursing under his breath.

He is grey: his greasy dark hair is shot with it, his filthy black overcoat is stained a lighter shade, his baggy pants with tight checks are slate-colored, as if from too many washings in hard water. But they have never been washed, these pants. His boots, though, are new, and barely marked. One catches a glimpse of a faded red shirt underneath the overcoat, the lone hint of color in this twilit panoply; but beneath it, a grey undershirt.

His face is disproportionately long, stretched vertically by the weight of his massive jaw. A few teeth sprout from this jaw, long grey kernels streaked with yellow. The whites of his sunken eyes are yellow too, and the man uses them to great effect, transfixing one and all with a jaundiced glare that is avoided only by a conscious act of will. His very skin is slightly grey, as the years of handling newsprint have leached into the man's gnarled hands, gradually diffusing throughout his body and affecting his soul.

David Mendelson

They wait at the bus stop, feet stamping out a restless rhythm, faces half-buried in newspapers or now and then looking up to mutter at passing cars, their eyes straining to glimpse the bus's approach. They have been waiting for over half an hour. Grim faced, a man steps into the street, bending sideways to look past parked cars. "It's coming," he announces. They now move together, clumping around the pole, jockeying for position, still silent except for occasional sighs. The bus, brakes squealing to a heavy stop, is jammed with commuter bodies which fill the aisle completely. The riders stare out with eyes made listless by the stifling air; the people on the corner groan. The doors slide open, whooshing-in much needed air with the motion. Anxious to get on, the people on the corner collide with the few who have wormed their way through the crowd in the aisles, stopping entrance or exit completely. Like a cowboy herding cattle onto a train, the bus driver bellows and beats his hands on the hand-rail, yelling at the crowd on the corner to wait their turn, yelling at those on the bus to let people get to the exits. Driving those in the aisle back with words like a snapping whip, he makes room for everyone waiting on the corner. The silence presses heavily against the riders as bodies move unnaturally close. Standing, forced to face sideways, one woman reads a French novel; another woman mutters that at least she's not being goosed. Lurching to stops at nearly every corner, sending feet shuffling as bodies bounce together, the bus finally empties at the BART station.

Sandy Begin

This is excellent writing by any standard, and it is writing that has resulted from a step-by-step process of instruction. The students are writing, in these short sequences, as well as the professional writers they have examined in similar short sequences, and they are writing like professionals because they are consciously employing structures commonly found in professional writing.

The students, reading their own work aloud and hearing what the other students have written, know that this is excellent writing. They know that they can do it, that they can write, that they can become writers. It is an important moment in the class, one that I have been aiming at. Everything that I will ask of them from this point on, in a sequence of more and more demanding assignments, will seem possible to the students. They know they can do it!

However, there is still more that I want to do with the sentence. By means of the same approach—examining model sentences, then writing their own sentences—the students are first introduced to the use of adjective phrases and clusters as free modifiers:

1. Eva, *shy and chinless,* straining her upper lip over two enormous teeth, would sit in corners watching her mother. —Katherine Anne Porter

2. As she came home, up the hill, looking away at the town, *dim and blue on the hill,* her heart relaxed and became yearning.— D. H. Lawrence

3. Now his son's face, *dappled, feminine in the lips and eyelashes narrow like a hatchet, anxious and snearing,* gnaws at Caldwell's heart like a piece of unfinished business.—John Updike

4. There was the paper bag she had been carrying, lying on a table by the door; macaroons, *all squashy from being carried the wrong way,* disgorging, through a tear in the paper, a little trickle of crumbs.—Elizabeth Bowen

5. Thus she passed from generation to generation—*dear, inescapable, impervious, tranquil, and perverse.*—William Faulkner

6. The head of the filing department, *neat, quiet, attentive,* stood in front of the old man's desk.—James Thurber

7. He saw her face, *lit, transfigured, distorted, stricken, appealing, horrified.*—Walter de la Mare

8. She had a smooth, long-suffering countenance, *slightly tearful even when she smiled, and most mournful when you met her by chance,* as Moses did on Broadway, and saw her face—she was above the average height—coming toward him, *large, smooth, kindly,* with permanent creases of suffering beside her mouth.— Saul Bellow

9. The square chimneys, *broken and uneven,* looked drunken.— A. J. Cronin

10. Wearing the hat, Cress felt just as she had known she would: *gentle, and frail and drooping.*—Jessamyn West

11. They loved to tell stories, *romantic and poetic, or comic with a romantic humor.*—Katherine Anne Porter

12. Gabriel, *unhappy in his lyric satin and wig,* stood about holding his ribboned crook as though it has sprouted thorns.— Katherine Anne Porter

13. Her grey eyes picked out the swaying palms, *precise and formal against a turquoise sky.*—Marjorie K. Rawlings

14. He awoke at two o'clock in the afternoon, *very thirsty and dizzy,* and rang for ice water, coffee and the Pittsburg papers.— Willa Cather

Students are surprised to learn that the adjective can be a phrase rather than a single word and that this phrase can be positioned *after* rather than *before* the word it modifies. They begin to experience some of that early excitement I felt when I was led to see things that I had not seen before. When students produce their own sentences using the idea of the adjective in this new way, the resulting sentences immediately seem more mature, more dramatically so with the use of this modifier than with any other.

Next I present examples of noun phrases and clusters, and students pattern their own sentences after these models:

1. On a sandy patch she saw her own footprint, *a little square toe and a horseshoe where the iron heel had sunk.*—Alison Uttley

2. The lighter's flame lighted up his features for an instant, *the packed rosy jowl, the graying temple under Tyrolean hat's brim, the bulging, blue, glazed eye.*—Kay Boyle

3. They will enjoy nothing but the bleakest of New England scenery—*a few hardbitten pastures, a rocky wall, a moth-eaten hill that is neither a bold mountain nor a stirring plain, and a stern and pointless old house.*—Donald C. Peattie

4. All the magic of Camusfearna was fixed in that morning: *the vivid lightening streak of an otter below water; the wheeling, silver-shouldered flight of the geese as they passed to alight ahead of us; the long, lifting, blue swell of the sea among the skerries and the sea tangle; the little back rivers of froth and crystal that spilled back from the rocks as each smooth wave sucked back and left them bare.*—Gavin Maxwell

5. For hours at a time, he sat on the backless kitchen chair before the shack, *a wide-shouldered man,* white bearded, motionless; *a seer despite his grotesquely baggy trousers, his collarless shirt.* —Sinclair Lewis

6. The chestnut stallion was coming into its strength, *gleaming, round quarters, bunched muscles at the juncture of the throat and chest, a ripple of high-light and shadow on the withers, arched neck, pricked small Arab ears, a bony head, eyes and nostrils of character and intelligence.*—Oliver La Farge

7. She sat thus, forever in the pose of being photographed, *a motionless image in her dark walnut frame with silver oak leaves in the corners,* her smiling gray eyes following one about the room.—Katherine Anne Porter

8. He was a fellow I disliked and feared; *a handsome, sulky, spoiled and sneering lout.*—Frank O'Connor

9. August got the license of the county clerk, *a little crippled man with one shoulder higher than the other.*—Ruth Suckow

10. I had found before a bank of crocuses, *pale, fragile, lilac-colored flowers with dark veins,* pricking up keenly like a myriad of little lilac-colored flames among the grass, under the olive trees—D. H. Lawrence

11. The world outside the deep-silled windows—*a rutted lawn, a whitewashed barn, a walnut tree with fresh green*—seemed a haven from which he was forever sealed off.—John Updike

12. Now and then she came in with a shallow box full of newly hatched chickens, *abject dabs of wet fluff,* and put them on a table in her bedroom where she might tend them carefully on their first day.—Katherine Anne Porter

13. What one could see of her face made a striking impression— *serious hard eyes, a long slender nose, a face waxen with thought.*—Joyce Carol Oates

14. The great passions of man, *his lust for power, his vanity, his search for truth, his passion for love and brotherliness, his destructiveness as well as his creativeness, every powerful desire which motivates man's actions,* is rooted in this specific human source.—Erich Fromm

15. This seemed an utterly enchanted sea, *this lake you could leave to its own devices for a few hours and come back to, and find that it had not stirred, this constant and trustworthy body of water.*—E. B. White

16. They sped down the road in a black car, *an expensive limousine designed for speed,* and soon after came another.—F. Scott Fitzgerald

17. He remembered how he had stood, *a small, thrilled boy,* prepared to follow the dingy lady upon the white horse, or the band in its faded chariot.—Stephen Crane

18. There was only the sound made by a man in the corner who drew noisily on a pipeful of rum-flavored tobacco, causing it to glow on and off, *a red disk in the dark.*—Ralph Ellison

19. About fifteen miles below Monterey, on the wild coast, the Torres family had their farm, *a few sloping acres above a cliff that dropped to the brown reefs and to the hissing white waters of the ocean.*—John Steinbeck

20. He tilted back in his chair, and leered at each gentleman, separately, *the leer of an animal that knows its power, the leer of a leopard loose in a bird-and-dog shop.*—James Thurber

After these two sentence modeling exercises with adjective and noun phrases, the students write another extended sequence. At this point in the class, usually the end of the second or third week, my intensive work with sentence modeling is over. It never altogether stops, however. I point out the use of other phrasal modifiers and clausal structures used as additions—such as prepositional phrases and constructions starting with "as if" and "as though"—and I continue to bring in new passages for the class to examine, their own best work as well as professional examples. But the emphasis for the remainder of the course will be on applying what students have learned to the writing of longer papers—autobiographical fragments, personal essays, profiles, saturation reports, essays—assignments that move, as a sequence, from the personal and the immediate to the more distant and general, assignments that place a premium on the use of representational prose in the exposition and development of ideas.

My collection of sample writings by students proves the continued success of my approach. I close with two short passages as a sampling of the excellent student writing that this approach to teaching writing has sparked:

Autobiographical Fragment

It is summer, hot and breezy, lazy and playful. Across the street, there is a park with children playing baseball and four-square, and an old, red bungalow with a ping-pong table, all kinds of balls, and more children. From here, through the curtains, one can see the baseball game, a disorganized affair, with no uniforms, few mitts, one ball, and one bat.

Here, inside a room, a small boy is sitting tensely at a piano, producing what might loosely be called music. On a long, gray sofa sits a thin, ancient woman, the music teacher, listening to the boy's sounds.

"No, no, no!" she cries. "That's wrong! Start again."

The boy says nothing. His jaws are clenched, fist-like and quite as threatening. His eyes are riveted straight ahead, though they don't seem to be focused on the music. He dashes a quick, angry glare at the old woman, much too quick for her perception. His fingers reach tentatively, stiffly for the keys, as if he were a spastic, trying desperately to control himself. The sound comes stumbling and jerking out of the piano, and anger and disappointment cover the old woman's face. She sits perfectly still and bolt-upright, poised like a jungle cat about to spring, but stiff like the starched curtains on the window. The anger covers her face, but her body rigidly holds it back. She only screeches at the boy and his unsatisfactory, forced performance, her screech hectic and atonal, like the music. They sit inside a room, caged like birds, the boy pecking away at the piano, the old woman pecking away at the boy.

Outside, summer continues to flow, formless and easy.

James Beasley

From a Saturation Report on Today's Haight-Ashbury District in San Francisco

Today the ghosts of this dream haunt the streets of the Haight. The faded, peeling paint of the storefronts, like ancient ruins on a long-dead civilization, barely reveals the once bright aliveness of the people who lived there. The streets are still filled with young people, but there is a deathlike air about them, wandering zombie-like along the sidewalks, trying to make a little bread by selling the BARB to passers-by, lurking in the dark doorways, pale and tired, rarely smiling, their eyes grown old. At the end of this sad street is Bob's Drive-In, open twenty-four hours a day, gathering place for those who find themselves cold and tired, in need of coffee and a juke box, in the darkest hours of the night.

Ann Kibling

What Josephine Miles suggests will happen, that "knowledge and conscious choice . . . support rather than oppose intuition," has indeed happened. The students are secure in the knowledge of what they can do. Their use of cumulative structures is now natural and intuitive, and they write with a mature and easy style.

18 Hearing Voices: Tough Talk, Sweet Talk, Stuffy Talk

Walker Gibson

Walker Gibson begins his analysis of modern prose by emphasizing the importance of nonverbal elements when people are
introduced—voice, physique, manner of dress, cut of hair, facial
expression, gesture, and so forth. The writer is not physically
present to the reader and must depend solely on the written word.
Therefore the particular words chosen by the writer to introduce
himself or herself have "an absolute kind of importance and
finality," for the reader "can shut the book at any moment, at the
slightest displeasure" (p. 8). Gibson first looks at the transformation the reader undergoes, then turns his attention to how writers
introduce themselves. Ed.

The experience of reading, then, is a confrontation with a voice, or
personality, clear or confused—a personality who by means of words
on paper gets himself *introduced* to us. But what about *us*, the reader?
It is not generally understood that the reader too, like the author,
undergoes a transformation, that he too becomes a kind of ideal or
second self as he exposes himself to the expectations of the language.
Early in his career Henry James argued that an author has to "make his
reader very much as he makes his characters," and this is quite literally
true. As readers, we are made over every time we take up a piece of
writing: we recognize that there are assumptions and expectations
implied there and that as sympathetic listeners to the voice speaking to
us, we must share these assumptions. Sophisticated readers are able to
move in this manner in several directions, and to keep separate their
true-life personalities from the roles that the language is temporarily
asking them to play. Thus, to mention obvious examples, it is possible
for nonbelievers to be successful readers of *Paradise Lost* or the poems
of Hopkins; it is possible, with one of one's selves, to suffer the

Source: Excerpt from *Tough, Sweet, and Stuffy* (Bloomington and London: Indiana
University Press, 1966), pp. 12-24. Reprinted with permission of the publisher. The
notes have been renumbered.

appropriate moral agonies posed by a Victorian novel, while at the same time recognizing that in one's true-life self, facing a similar situation in a true-life world, one would adopt another point of view. Much of the force of modern advertising comes from the writer's skill in defining a particular set of ideal characteristics with which the confused real reader may be expected to desire identification. Some of the rhetoric involved in "getting sold" will concern us in [chapter 6 of the Gibson book].

In all our reading, however, it is vital for us to maintain clearly a distinction between ourselves as real people acting in a real world, on the one hand, and ourselves as that particular bundle of assumed values that any piece of language implies. This, in the case of advertising, is the way we keep our money in our pockets. In the case of polemical writing, it is the way we keep from changing our party with every word we read. In the case of fiction, it is the way we keep from imposing the values of art too crudely on the problems of life.[1]

In what follows, I shall be asking how writers introduce themselves in those crucial opening paragraphs of prose works. How, that is to say, they present to us a *self*, the assumed author, not to be confused with that complex mass of chaotic experience making up the writer as human being. The procedure can be simple enough. Of the beginnings of assorted prose works, let us ask: (1) Who's talking? Who is being introduced? (2) To whom is he being introduced? Who are *we* expected to be as we read this prose sympathetically? (3) By what magic was all this done? How were words chosen and arranged in order to make these effects possible, without physical voice, or gesture, or facial expression?

By such a process, I hope to define three kinds of personality that seem to me recognizable in modern American prose. These personalities I call the Tough Talker, the Sweet Talker, and the Stuffy Talker. I will be examining some extreme forms of their three styles of talk, to make identification and definition possible. But my proposal is that all prose (including this sentence) can be looked at as an adjustment or compromise of some sort among these three possible ways of addressing the reader.

Suppose we begin to read—to expose ourselves to an introduction.

Suppose we pick up, for instance, a magazine, the *Saturday Review*. We riffle its pages. Already we are taking on some attributes of an assumed reader: we have some experience of this magazine and its general personality, and we know vaguely the sort of person we are expected to be as we read it. We are not, at any rate, at this moment, the assumed reader of *The Hudson Review*, or *The New Yorker*, or *House Beautiful*, or *Frisky Stories*. The eye lights on a title. Just our subject. Who's speaking here?

The Private World of a Man with a Book

The temptation of the educator is to explain and describe, to organize a body of knowledge for the student, leaving the student with nothing to do. I have never been able to understand why educators do this so often, especially where books are concerned. Much of this time they force their students to read the wrong books at the wrong time, and insist that they read them in the wrong way. That is, they lecture to the students about what is in the books, reduce the content to a series of points that can be remembered, and, if there are discussions, arrange them to deal with the points.

Schools and colleges thus empty books of their true meaning, and addict their students to habits of thought that often last for the rest of their lives. Everything must be reduced to a summary, ideas are topic sentences, to read is to prepare for a distant test. This is why so many people do not know how to read. They have been taught to turn books into abstractions.[2]

Everything depends on the *personality* to whom we have just been introduced. His message can never be divorced from that personality, that speaking voice—or at least not without becoming essentially another message. The question I am asking is not "What is he saying?" but "Who is he? What sort of person am I being asked to *be*, as I experience these words?" A difficulty immediately arises. We can hardly describe with justice the fellow talking except by quoting his own words. He is what he says, precisely. The minute we lift an assumed "I" out of the text and start to describe or reproduce his personality in *our* language, or in language that we infer might be his, we are admittedly altering him, mangling him, killing him perhaps. But it is the only way. The biologist studying cellular structure has to dye his specimen under the microscope so he can see its parts, but the dye kills the living tissue, and what he sees is dead and gone. It is a familiar intellectual dilemma, and there is nothing to do but be cheerful about it, applying one's dye as liberally as necessary while recognizing its poisonous possiblities.

With that proviso, then, who's talking in the first two paragraphs of "The Private World of a Man with a Book"? What assumptions is he sharing with his ideal reader? What follows is, as I hear it, a between-the-lines communication between the assumed author and the assumed reader:

You and I know all about the shoddy academic situation, where lazy and wrongheaded teachers do so much harm to the true meaning of books. You and I share a true knowledge of true meanings, and can recognize instantly when wrong books are taught at the wrong time in the wrong way. I am a rugged no-nonsense character, for all my academic connections, and you, thrusting out your jaw, couldn't agree more.

Now it is clear from this effort that I (the assumed author of this essay) do not very successfully engage myself as the ideal assumed reader of these two paragraphs. It is clear that when I have the speaker saying "You and I share a true knowledge of true meanings" I am not writing a paraphrase at all, but a parody. I am exaggerating what I take to be a sort of arrogance in the speaker, with a view to ridicule. How did I reach this curious position?

I reached it because, as I read the two paragraphs, I suffered a conflict. I was aware, on the one hand, of the person I was supposed to be (one who knows what "true meanings" are, for instance). But I was also aware, much too aware, that I was *not* that person, and, more important, didn't want to pretend to be. This is not a question of changing one's beliefs for the sake of a literary experience—that is easy enough. One can "become" a Hindu or a Hottentot if the speaker is suffficiently persuasive and attractive. But that's the rub: the speaker must be attractive to us. And in this case, because of qualities I have called "arrogance" and "rugged no-nonsense," I have become not the assumed reader at all, but a hostile reader.[3] Consider one moment where hostility, at least in this reader, was aroused. It is the second sentence—"I have never been able to understand why educators do this. . . ." The difficulty here is that we sense hypocrisy in that remark. Just how is the assumed reader being addressed? Is it this?

> I've tried and tried to understand why teachers go at books this way, but I just can't get it.

Or is it this?

> The trouble with teachers is that they're either too dim-witted or too lazy to teach books the right way. Oh I understand it all right!

Now which is it? Let's admit it could be either (a fault in itself?), but insofar as we may strongly suspect it's the second, then the actual phrasing ("I have never been able to understand") seems falsely prevaricating in its covert antagonism.

I have used such expressions as "rugged no-nonsense," "covert antagonism," and "thrusting out your jaw." In the next-to-last sentence of our passage we can illustrate one rhetorical technique by which impressions like these are conveyed. "This is why so many people do not know how to read." We have here, to anticipate, some rhetoric of Tough Talk. The phrasing does not allow the possibility that not so many people are so benighted after all. No doubts are permitted. By placing its "many people do not know how to read" in a subordinate clause, the voice assumes a *fact* from what is at best an extreme statement of an arguable position. The independent clause ("This is why") merely speculates on the cause of the "fact." The reader is pushed around by a tough-talking voice.

But insofar as we can divorce the utterance here from the utterer—and I have said that this is strictly impossible—then what is being said in this paragraph seems to me both true and important. Indeed, I would personally agree, books *are* too often taught as abstractions, and in any vote in any faculty meeting, the assumed author and this reader would vote together on this issue. But we do not take pleasure in reading for such reasons as that. In fact it may have been this very agreement, this sense that I personally did not need persuading, that led me to read no further in the article than the two paragraphs I have quoted. But surely it was not only that. I read no more because I felt that the assumed author was browbeating me, and changing me over in ways I did not like. I don't care how "right" he is: he's got to be *nice* to me!

But unfortunately, it is not enough to be nice. Life is very hard. Let us consider now another assumed author—same magazine, a few years earlier, same general subject—and listen to a voice that goes out of its way to be nice.

Unrequired Reading

The title of this essay may strike you as a typographical error. You may be saying to yourself that the writer really means required reading, and the phrase conjures up for you, I suspect, lists distributed on the first days of college courses: Volume one of this distinguished scholar's work on the Byzantine empire in the fourth century, that brochure on the economic interpretation of the Constitution, this pundit's principles of economics, that pedant's source book.

Or, perhaps, still under the apprehension that I mean required reading, you are reminded of what by now is one of the more maddening insolences of criticism, or at any rate of book reviewing. "This," says Mr. Notability, "is a *must* book." This in the atomic age is compulsory reading. In a world of anxiety this uneasy novel is not to be passed by.

I beg of you to forget such obligations and responsibilities. To this day you have to forget that you *had* to read "Macbeth" in order to begin to remember how perturbingly moving a play it is. Hardly anyone would reread Burke's "Speech on Conciliation" if he recalled how he had to make an abstract of it in high school.[4]

Once again let us try to assess the sort of person addressing us here, remembering that this person bears no necessary connection with its author. In listening to this voice, we become aware as always of an ideal listener, a "you," whose characteristics we are expected to adopt as we read.

> I am a sweet professorish sort of fellow, full of big words but
> simple at heart—you are younger than I, and though you have of
> course been through college, you are by no means an academic
> professional like me. My charm is based on an old-fashioned sort
> of formality ("I beg of you") combined with a direct conversational
> approach that I trust you find attractive. I wear my learning
> lightly, occasionally even offering you a tricky phrasing *(pundit's
> principles, pedant's source book)* or a modern cliché *(world of
> anxiety)* to show you I'm human. But we share, you and I, a
> knowledgeable experience of literature; we both recognize for
> example how "perturbingly moving" *Macbeth* really is.

It is easy to identify at least one rhetorical device by which the
professorial voice is often dramatized. It is the device of parallel
structure. A pattern of balanced phrasings suggests a world similarly
balanced, well ordered, academic. The first paragraph's list is an
example: *this distinguished scholar, that brochure, this pundit, that
pedant.* A somewhat similar effect occurs later: *this is a must book, this
is compulsory reading, this is not to be passed by.* Triplets like that are
characteristic of the fancier tones. In the last two sentences we have the
balanced device of chiasmus, a criss-cross relation of parallel ideas. The
clauses there are arranged in an order of time past, time present, time
present, time past.

> You have to forget that you *had* to read to remember how per-
> turbingly moving it *is.*
>
> Hardly anyone *would reread* Burke (now) if he recalled how he *had*
> to make an abstract.

Very neat, literary, elegant. Parallel structure alone, of course, could
not produce a sweet-professorish voice. But it can support the meanings of the words, as it does here.

The assumed reader, here as always, is a sympathetic yes man,
responding uncritically (yet of course intelligently) to the speaker's
invitations. When a reader responds critically, in the negative sense,
and begins to disagree, he forsakes his role as assumed reader and lets
his Real-Life Self take over. If this goes on very long, he will simply
stop reading, unless he has some strong motive for swallowing his
irritation and continuing.

We can imagine a sympathetic conversation going on between
speaker and assumed reader in our passage, something like this:

> The title of this essay may strike you as a typographical error.
> [Why, yes, as a matter of fact it did.] You may be saying to yourself
> that the writer really means required reading [I did rather think
> that, yes], and the phrase conjures up for you, I suspect, lists
> distributed on the first days of college courses [Oh yes, those

dreadful things]: Volume one of this etc. [You certainly have it down pat! And I do appreciate your gentle scorn of pundits and pedants.]

But suppose, once again, that one does not enjoy playing the part of this particular assumed reader. Suppose one is uncomfortably aware of an insupportable gap between one's Own True Self and the role one is here being asked to adopt. Again it is probably obvious that I (still the assumed author of this essay) suffer from just such an uncomfortable awareness. The mechanical and prissy straight man that I have constructed out of the assumed reader reveals my own antagonism, both to him and to the sweet talk of the speaker. Suppose we were to play it my way, and invent a conversation between the speaking voice and a hostile reader who refused to take on the required qualities:

> The title of this essay may strike you as a typographical error. [Why, no, as a matter fact that never occurred to me.] You may be saying to yourself that the writer really means required reading [Don't be silly. I would be more surprised to see a title so trite. In fact your title embodies just the sort of cute phrase I have learned to expect from this middlebrow magazine.] and the phrase conjures up for you, I suspect, lists distributed on the first days of college courses [That's a dim memory at best. How old do you think I am?]: Volume one of this distinguished etc. etc. [You bore me with this lengthy list and your affected effects of soundplay.]
>
> Or, perhaps, still under the apprehension that I mean required reading ["Perhaps" is good. How *could* I be "still" under such an apprehension?], you are reminded of what by now is one of the more maddening insolences of criticism [You're maddened, not I. Calm down.], or at any rate of book reviewing. "This," says Mr. Notability, "is a *must* book." [Do even book reviewers use such language?] This in the atomic age is compulsory reading. In a world of anxiety this uneasy novel is not to be passed by. [I appreciate you are ironically repeating these tired phrases, but they're still tired.]

Now of course this mean trick can be worked by anybody against almost anything. The assumed reader of this essay, for example, may so far forget himself as to try it on *me*, though I deeply hope he doesn't. Again it is important to emphasize that the argument here is not between two people disagreeing about an issue. I agree with the educational stand taken here about reading, just as I did with the similar stand taken in our first passage. *The argument is between two people disagreeing about one another.* And this time it is not a case of the Tough Talker pushing the reader around, but a case of the Sweet Talker who condescends and irritates in a totally different way.

The general subject our two writers have been discussing comes down to something we could call The Teaching of Reading. It is a subject that can easily be confronted in some other voice, of course; in fact it seems to me doubtful that there can be *any* subject which by definition *requires* any particular voice. To illustrate the third of my triumvirate of styles, and to exhibit The Teaching of Reading as attacked with a very different voice, I offer the passage that follows. Again it presents a thesis with which I am quite in agreement—as who is not?

Teaching Literature

Rapid and coherent development of programs in modern litera-ture has led to the production of excellent materials for study from the earliest years of secondary education through the last of under-graduate study. The sole danger—if it be one, in the opinion of others—lies in easy acceptance of what is well done. The mechanics of mass production can overpower and drive out native creative-ness in reflecting on literature and so stop individual interpretation in teaching. We hear a good deal of the dangers to imaginative experience in youth from excesses of visual exposure, and we know that they therefore read much less, in quantity, from longer works of prose and poetry. It may prove to be true, therefore, that in the study of literature the critical authority of the printed page will seem an easy substitute for individual analysis of original texts, first for the teacher and next inevitably for students who have never learned to read, with conscious effort in thinking, through verbal symbols.[5]

After making necessary allowances for a passage ripped from context (for I have had to choose this time a paragraph from inside a work rather than an introduction), the fact remains that this is a Stuffy voice. It is by no means an extreme example of Stuffy Talk, but it is Stuffy enough to be marked off as distinct from the Toughness of "Private World" and the Sweetness of "Unrequired Reading." We become, as we read, solemn; the brow furrows; perhaps we are a little Stuffy ourselves. This transformation is the direct result of certain habits of vocabulary and sentence structure by which the Stuffiness is conveyed. I put off identification of these habits until we have examined the Tough Talker and Sweet Talker more thoroughly. Meanwhile, my point is that a *style* is not simply a response to a particular kind of subject-matter, nor is it entirely a matter of the writer's situation and his presumed audience. It is partly a matter of sheer individual will, a desire for a particular kind of self-definition no matter what the circumstances.

Gibson reinforces the importance of individual will and self-definition by concluding the chapter with an example of an introduction that falls into none of his classifications. This is the example of the "speaker as famous man," a voice impossible in fiction writing and an option open only to the very famous, who are aided by their stature and reputation. Ed.

Notes

1. An earlier statement of this argument, with various examples, appears in my "Authors, Speakers, Readers, and Mock Readers," *College English,* XI (February, 1950), 265–69. The term "mock reader" for the reader's second self now seems to me misleading. Would ideal reader be better? Expected reader? Assumed reader? The assumed reader of this essay, that sympathetic fellow, has grasped the general idea with his usual acumen. Yes, he says, yes yes, go on.

2. *Saturday Review,* XLIV (January 7, 1961). The author is Mr. Harold Taylor.

3. This has of course absolutely nothing to do—or almost nothing to do—with the writer as an actual person. See Chapter 1 [of the Gibson book] and the distinction between real-life author and assumed author.

4. *Saturday Review,* XXXIII (November 4, 1950). By Irwin Edman.

5. David H. Stevens, *The Changing Humanities* (New York, 1953), p. 173. Title added.

19 Mimesis: Grammar and the Echoing Voice

Phyllis Brooks

If English teachers at the university level are supposed to be adding some new element, some sophistication, some elegance to the prose of their students, and not just making up for real or imagined deficiencies in teaching in high schools, they must continually seek new methods and resurrect into a more glorious life some old ones. Teachers at the "remedial" level are all too frequently inclined to regard such an effort as icing on the cake, as a luxury that can be indulged in only at the lofty level of "regular" freshman composition courses, or even in advanced courses in creative writing or stylistics. The remedial course, tacked onto the bottom of the English department or otherwise shunted into some sub-academic campus position, is the place for tire-patching and bringing the truth about the dangling modifier to an unbelieving mass of ignoramuses. The idea that the student in a "remedial" course may be there through no fault of his own and that he may be as intelligent, or even more intelligent than his brother who has escaped the indignity of such a course has only recently been challenged, by Sabina Thorne Johnson in her article "Remedial English: The Anglocentric Albatross" (*College English*, 33 [1972], 670-685). Once we accept this premise we must necessarily go on to the further idea that he may not only be able to write as correctly as any other student but may even be able to write as stylishly.

Style is a vague concept, but some writers do have an individual style, or an effective style, or a curious style that sets them apart from all other writers. It is an indefinable quality that everyone can recognize. I do not want to get into a deep discussion of the nature of style, but would rather concentrate on a few technical details that can contribute to something recognizable as "good" style, and how these can be encouraged and nurtured in a course that has as its first purpose the

Source: College English 35 (1973): 161-68. Reprinted with permission of the National Council of Teachers of English. Some usages that appear in this article are not consistent with the present NCTE Guidelines for Nonsexist Use of Language; they have not been changed in this reprint.

correcting of grammatical and organizational errors. In fact, I should like to claim that the conscious encouragement of variety, elegance, and individual voice in writing may prove to be a useful tool in impressing students with the value of precision and accuracy in syntax and word choice—major aims of the remedial course as well as of the regular freshman composition course.

One way to encourage the variety and elegance lacking in the prose of freshman students is the archaic technique of paraphrase, but a form of paraphrase revived and reconsidered with specific purposes in mind. During the past few years the members of the Subject A Department at the University of California at Berkeley have been teaching droves of students ranging from the children of Chinese-American households where English is a shallowly acquired *lingua franca* to the Chicano from the pachuco-speaking barrio of Los Angeles to the dialect-wielding black from the East Oakland ghetto to the middle-class white who has conned his way through his high school English classes but really has no notion of how to make a statement, or how important it is to be able to make that statement. We have adopted the somewhat unorthodox techniques described by Mrs. Johnson in her article: give the student something to say, make him aware of an audience that he must try to reach, and demand that it be his voice that comes through the writing, not some depersonalized characterless spirit. It is true that the urgent desire to get his opinion across and to make his point of view on a question very clear will drive the student to refine his grammar and vocabulary, especially with a certain amount of peer criticism to egg him on. But the student seeking to express his own personal voice needs further help beyond the correction of his errors and the encouragement to speak for himself.

Successful writers, whether sincerely or not, often make the statement that they learned to write by copying other writers. I still have to wrestle mightily with the effects of an early infatuation with Carlyle combined with translation, sentence by sentence, of large chunks of Cicero. All influence from writers of the past is not necessarily good. But how are we to get our students to imitate desirable models? Are we simply to hand them a piece of prose by a famous writer with the instruction that they are to prepare a paraphrase? If students have heard of paraphrasing at all, they are likely to have seen it only in the form of what we prefer to call the "translation" paraphrase: "Take this sonnet by Shakespeare and rewrite it, showing what he really meant." Shakespeare knew very well what he meant, and the average high school or university student is well aware of the presumption and futility involved in trying to turn the sonnet into modern English

prose. Sometimes, more profitably, the material presented for paraphrase is in prose and so more amenable to translation into an idiom
readily understandable to the common reader. The translation paraphrase tests the student's ability to read, and to write an acceptable
form of standard English, but it does not *add* anything to his repertoire
of skills.

On the other hand, carefully selected *persona* paraphrases can help
the student towards an awareness of the variety of expression possible
in the language and can add to his stock of usable sentence structures.
In fact, I firmly believe that the *persona* paraphrase can be used to good
effect in teaching everything from the use of the verb "to be" to the
selection of the apposite structure to suit a particular pattern of
thought. I hope that the following selections may bolster my argument
and encourage others to try more daring and possibly more fruitful
paraphrase exercises.

In planning and assigning a *persona* paraphrase the instructor
hopes to get from his students a valuable imitation of the voice and
sentence patterns of a particular writer. The novice writer is unsure of
himself. He doubts his own abilities, especially in dealing with a
sentence including such complications as apposition, parallel structure, or parenthetical expressions. If we give a certain number of
workbook exercises in detecting errors in parallel structures and correcting them, we still have no assurance that the student will actually
go out and try to use the structure he has been laboring over. In fact, he
may come away from his workbook more overawed than ever by the
complexities that lurk in the depths of such sentences. If, however, he is
handed a passage from a writer whose name he may recognize, and is
then told to imitate her sentence structures, there is a chance that by
building up his own sentences on this model he will gain the confidence to experiment further with the arcane skill he has proved he can
handle.

We have found that students are easily discouraged by this kind of
assignment; they have to be led into it. Rather than demand that the
students "write a paragraph in Norman Mailer's style" after having
read a passage by Mailer, we present them with a more carefully
composed exercise. We select a specific passage, illustrating a particular
kind of structure, and require that the student copy its structure, phrase
by phrase, sentence by sentence, but substitute a completely different
subject matter. Each instructor who has used this particular tool
approaches it in a slightly different way, but in general we proceed as
follows: The students are given a paragraph—rarely more than twenty
typewritten lines—double spaced on a sheet of paper. The instructor

reads the passage, emphasizing the pattern of the passage, the natural breaks in sentences, the switches in tone. The class is then guided into some discussion of how the passage works. What are the main features of the prose and where does the writer reach his point? Are there any confusing syntactical structures? Any particular little tricks that make the passage effective? From there on the student is on his own. We tell him to try out several possible topics, writing in pencil above the actual words on the page, until he finds one that is amenable to expression within the structure there on the page in front of him. But an example can show the method much more clearly than can further discussion.

Parenthetical Expression

When a student starts to modify his statements, he is inclined first of all to adopt a Christensenian style and tack all modification onto the end of his sentences. The next step is to put some of the modification at the beginning of the sentence. It is the rare brave soul who tries to add a parenthetical modification in some position other than those two. James Baldwin is a writer who, on almost every page, provides beautifully articulated examples of parenthetical modification. Here is a complex model for parenthetical style, from Baldwin's *Notes of a Native Son:*

> When I was around nine or ten I wrote a play which was directed by a young, white schoolteacher, *a woman,* who then took an interest in me, and gave me books to read, and, *in order to corroborate my theatrical bent,* decided to take me to see what she somewhat tactlessly referred to as "real" plays. Theatergoing was forbidden in our house, but, *with the really cruel intuitiveness of a child,* I suspected that the color of this woman's skin would carry the day for me. When, *at school,* she suggested taking me to the theater, I did not, *as I might have done if she had been a Negro,* find a way of discouraging her, but agreed that she could pick me up at my house one evening. I then, *very cleverly,* left all the rest to my mother, who suggested to my father, *as I knew she would,* that it would not be very nice to let such a kind woman make the trip for nothing. Also, since it was a schoolteacher, I imagine that my mother countered the idea of sin with the idea of "education" which word, *even with my father,* carried a kind of bitter weight.

Instructions to the student included the following specific pointers, good for all *persona* paraphrases:

> Start by substituting words and building a new atmosphere in the passage; you may find that you have to move to whole phrases, replacing, for instance, "with cruel intuitiveness" by "in a scarlet

rage," in order to make your new version of the paragraph understandable. Play around with the words and phrases, but try to keep
them in the same order, and the paragraph in the same shape.

But not only does the student have the structural model of Baldwin's
sentences before him; he also has to select a subject matter that fits the
structure, another set of "emotions recalled in tranquillity," as one of
our colleagues described the content of this passage. He has to try, and
reject, several possibilities before he reaches one that will not be
distorted by the structure he is bound by. Any old thought pattern
cannot be imposed on a paragraph. The student comes to realize very
rapidly that the *shape* of an idea is necessary, not whimsical, that there
is some purpose to our criticisms of the way he expresses himself.

What kind of thoughts can a freshman student pour into the
Baldwin mold? The variety is amazing. Here is an amusing example:

> When I was approaching the age of forty I got married to a young
> girl who was still in her teens and although I was twenty years her
> elder, she was quite infatuated with me, thinking that I made a
> great substitute for her father. The marriage would not have met
> with my father's approval, but, with an astuteness that had come
> with age, I suspected that my wife's small fortune of three million
> dollars would meet with everyone's approval. When, during our
> first week together, she suggested that we move out of my parents'
> house, I did not, as I might have done if she had been my mistress,
> find a way of discouraging her, but agreed that we should talk to
> Mother and Father about it. I then, very cleverly, left the details to
> my Grandpa Joe, who suggested to his children, my father and
> mother, that I was a grown boy with a wife and that the only fair
> thing to do would be to let me move out. Also, since I was about to
> turn forty, it would be a nice idea to celebrate at my new residence
> my birthday, which word, even with my father, hit a soft spot in
> his heart.
>
> Kevin Axelrad

The structure of the paraphrase, rather than limiting student imagination, provides the crutch that makes it possible for him to give his
imagination free rein, without the worry about how to finish a sentence
he has once started. The paraphrase, since it is such a close copy
structurally of a polished original, rarely shows any mechanical errors.
The student used to getting back an essay covered with markings often
looks at his first *persona* paraphrase with an expression of complete
disbelief. He has produced a piece of writing he can be proud of. And it
is his. Although he had a skeleton to build on, the flesh is all his own.
Almost inevitably the next formal essay he writes will contain some
turn of phrase, some sentence structure that he has "learned" from his
model. An unsolicited student criticism of one teacher's course as a

whole provided this comment on paraphrasing: "The topics which allowed for the most creativity and imagination produced the best results. The paraphrases were exceptionally good because they let us write on a variety of ideas. I honestly liked writing the paraphrases for they allowed me to express ideas of mine in styles which were pleasing to read."

Apposition and Modification

There need be no consistency of style among the models chosen. To give students a notion of the possible complexities of apposition, the restatement or amplification of an idea without the use of subordination or coordination, I have used with great success a highly mannered passage by Rose Macaulay, a richly textured description of the city of Istanbul that ends:

> Once the capital of imperial Rome; later the greatest city in Christendom, the richest city in the world, the spiritual head of the eastern Church, the treasure house of culture and art; then the opulent capital of Islam; this sprawl of mosques, domes, minarets, ruined palaces, and crumbling walls, rising so superbly above three seas, looking towards Europe, Asia, and ocean, oriental, occidental, brooding on past magnificence, ancient rivalries and feuds, modern cultures and the spoils of the modern world, Constantinople has ruin in her soul, the ruin of a deep division; to look on her shining domes and teeming streets is to see a glittering, ruinous, façade, girdled by great, broken, expungable walls.
>
> *The Pleasure of Ruins*

Instead of wondering that anyone would have the temerity to offer such a sentence to a freshman for imitation, look at some of the results. The students were told to replace Istanbul with any city they were familiar with that had a layering of different historical periods. Particular stress was placed on the care with which Rose Macaulay selected her words— all the adjectives work hard in her description. There is no vagueness, despite the final generalization, because of the concrete quality of the images—streets, façade and walls.

> [Bodie, California] First an assemblage of mining claims; later the largest gold camp in the north, the social hub of all the miners, the place where that shining vein of gold rose up to the earth's surface, the gathering of men in search of fortunes; next the prosperous community, the spread of general stores, town halls, homes that are vacant and drooping fences, sitting so quietly among tall mountains, gazing upon wilderness, nature, and undisturbed lands; silent, solemn, holding past memories within its decayed

walls, gold discoveries and finds, the absence of new inventions
and the industry of a modern world, Bodie has death in her future,
the death of a useless land; to view her boarded windows and dusty
streets is to visualize her glowing past, broken by long, uninter-
rupted, deplorable solitude.

                                                    Leslie Froisland

Obviously the appositions work, despite the complexity of the model.

Parallelism plus Reference

Parallel structure is one of the trickiest ideas to explain and to teach.
Errors in coordination, errors in apposition often have their roots in
some misunderstanding of the *balance* of a sentence. Students can
laugh at sentences like "He went to the White House in trepidation
and a tuxedo" (semantic parallelism abused) and can see dimly that
something is wrong with "He likes swimming and to row small boats"
(structural parallelism abused), but go on producing comparable
bastards in their own prose. As a result, any kind of balanced period of
the John Henry Newman type—"The true gentleman is never mean or
little in his disputes, never takes unfair advantage, never mistakes
personalities or sharp sayings for arguments, or insinuates evil which
he dare not say out"—is a very rare bird in a freshman paper. Yet with a
little conscious effort the student can prove to himself that complex
parallelisms are possible and usable.

A paraphrase that has proved useful in demonstrating balanced sentences governed by careful parallelism of structure and ideas is the
following passage from Mark Twain, a description of the Sphinx. At
the same time it is a valuable exercise in controlling the reference of
pronouns (thus the surprising bracketing of these two items in the
subhead). The passage is generously sprinkled with *its*. As the student
begins to construct his picture within the Twain frame, he has to
consider the reference of each pronoun in turn. There are no structural
its in the paragraph; each *it* functions as a true pronoun:

> After years of waiting, it was before me at last. The great face was
> so sad, so earnest, so longing, so patient. There was a dignity not of
> earth in its mien, and in its countenance a benignity such as never
> anything human wore. It was stone, but it seemed sentient. If ever
> image of stone thought, it was thinking. It was looking toward the
> verge of the landscape, yet looking at nothing—nothing but dis-
> tance and vacancy. It was looking over and beyond everything of
> the present, and far into the past. It was gazing out over the ocean
> of Time—over lines of century-waves which, further and further
> receding, closed nearer and nearer together, and blended at last

into one unbroken tide, away toward the horizon of remote antiquity. It was thinking of the wars of departed ages; of the empires it had seen created and destroyed; of the nations whose birth it had witnessed, whose progress it had watched, whose annihilation it had noted; of the joy and sorrow, the life and death, the grandeur and decay, of five thousand slow revolving years. It was the type of an attribute of man—of a faculty of his heart and brain. It was *memory—retrospection*—wrought into visible, tangible form. All who knew what pathos there is in memories of days that are accomplished and faces that have vanished—albeit only a trifling score of years gone by—will have some appreciation of the pathos that dwells in these grave eyes that look so steadfastly back upon the things they knew before History was born.

The Innocents Abroad

In this paraphrase, as in most others, students found themselves earnestly considering the structure of the passage and the progression of thought. From a concrete image Twain moves farther and farther into realms of abstraction—the thoughts suggested by the material object and its meaning for the observer. Only by trying to construct a new paragraph on Twain's model can the beginning student of language become completely aware of and involved in this process. Here is a student's effort:

[A College Dorm] After a lifetime of anticipation, it loomed before me. The tall structure was so cold, so bleak, so lonesome, so much without any personality or character of its own. There was nothing unique in it at all, and inside on the tile floor were heel marks of all the students who had been there before. The building wasn't human, but it wanted to speak. If the appearance of a building was ever trying to give a warning, then it was this building that was philosophizing. It was talking to me, yet also to others—others who would soon enter its halls. It was thinking of all that it had seen from the present to the past. It was fascinated by the movie of its memories—of all the single frames and incidents which, one by one, quickly add up till they produce a moving image. It was thinking of all the people who had come in wanting to make the world better; of all the idealism and romanticism that had once flourished; of the individuals with such questioning minds, whose regression it had watched, whose decay was observed; of the beginning and the end, hope and death, the illusions and reality, of all the people who had ended up as they did not originally want to. It was a lesson to Man—of the meaning of hypocrisy. It was *memory—knowledge*—brought into reality. All those who have a conception of life—who can easily realize what message is being conveyed—will realize what the warning is—for experience has told this college dorm that people who enter with young and optimistic ideas leave with old and rational realizations.

Craig Weintraub

Statement and Predication

Any teacher must be prepared to tackle both semantic (conceptual) and structural (grammatical) errors in statement and predication as well as in parallel structure. This double analysis of errors in the building of a sentence (semantic and structural) is useful when trying to convince a student that he needs to overcome sloppiness or inaccuracy in expression as well as outright grammatical errors. Students do not revolt at being reminded that the structure of English is such that plural nouns are followed by the word "are" while singular nouns are followed by "is." Grammar has rules. But conceptual errors are harder to pinpoint and explain; the reader sometimes has to patiently extricate the fundamental core of the sentence from a mass of distracting verbiage in order to point out semantic errors in predication and statement. Statement errors, errors in which there is a serious dislocation of meaning between subject and verb, or verb and object, are rife in student papers, especially those treating abstract subjects. At its most obvious, the fault is the familiar mixed metaphor: we have all seen "spirals of inflation" that two lines further on manage somehow "to slam the door in the face of prosperity." More subtle are misstatements like "Expressions were said differently by different classes." It is hard to convince a student that one says a word but uses an expression.

Any written exercise must be marked with a constant watch for the fitting together of subject and verb, verb and object. When the verb involved is the verb "to be," or any of the verbs that pattern like "to be," the dislocation (an error in a predication) can be examined closely through *persona* paraphrase exercises devoted to that structure specifically. Here poetry can be used as a rich source for materials.

Since poetry is metaphor, the most radical violation of the rules of predication, students can learn from looking at it why the logic of prose, if it is to explain rather than transform, must conform to a rather rigid system of etiquette. The poems of Emily Dickinson, in their blunt wrenching of the conventions normally governing the union of subject and object, are splendid places to confront students with outrageous comparison, and to instruct them in the absolute equality, the identifying nature of the verb "to be." For example, the lyric "Hope is the Thing with Feathers" says exactly that—Hope *is* the thing. We all know that hope, while it may be an emotion, an abstraction, a commendable virtue, is certainly *not* a thing, especially a thing with feathers. But then, of course, it is after all, for the thing "that perches in the soul" is the bird that traditionally symbolizes the longing for God. So, by yoking with a stark *is* that which both is and is not at the same time, the poet has pushed us to the point of contradiction which is the illumination of poetry.

Students can be invited to imitate her audacity by being asked to write four or eight lines of "Despair is the thing that . . ." and encouraged to shock the reader by breaking the rule as hard as they can. The instructor can at the same time cite examples of such misbehavior from their own essays, with the comment that while such violations may be the beginnings of fine poems, they cannot function as conveyers of logical thought since they negate the process of reason. Here is one of the results that delighted the students:

> Despair is the iron window,
> The lock slung closed,
> Receding footsteps hollow, slow,
> The chilly absence of repose.

Conclusion

These exercises are only a few of the paraphrases that we have used with great success over the past two or three years. Admittedly I have selected some of those that worked best—a paraphrase is a deceptive creature: those that you have high hopes for sometimes misfire, while others that you present with great misgivings (like the Rose Macaulay extract) catch the students' imagination and lead to glittering results. But I must stress that this is only a small sampling of the paraphrases we have found useful.

The same process of selection went on in the choosing of student samples to accompany each paraphrase. I did choose those that caught my eye for some particular spark of ingenuity or originality, but even after setting high standards I was forced to put aside with regret many that were equally as good. Even the least successful student paraphrases almost inevitably have good sentences; I have never had to hand back a paraphrase without at least one positive comment.

We intend to continue to use *persona* paraphrasing as a crucial tool in the developing of variety in student style, and we hope to refine further its use in the teaching of specific grammatical points. All we need now is the patience to comb piles of writing for suitable texts, and the luck to find what we need.[1]

Note

1. The members of the Subject A Department have contributed greatly to the writing of this article. Ruth Nybakken tried out specific paraphrases in her class, while Frank Cebulski and Nell Altizer made large and invaluable contributions to the final form of some of the ideas expressed here.

20 Writing in Reason

Josephine Miles

Prose-essay like prose-narrative or prose-drama is an art of prose, and as an art it works in basic patterns. Rather than a sequence of events, it is a sequence of ideas, and it shapes the sequence in certain ways, depending upon its main idea, its attempt or "essay."

It makes a leading statement, that is, predicates its subject, and then unfolds, develops, substantiates both subject and predicate in the specific relation it has proposed for them, with the specific connections of that relation: the conjunctive *and,* disjunctive *or,* conditional *if,* concessive *though.*

Students in California have usually read widely and well in books of essays in ideas. The first week of the Fall term of 1961, thirty freshmen, my teaching assistant, and I talked about ideas we had met with during the past year. We were able to range from Thoreau to Jung and Freud, from Milton to Edith Hamilton, from Plato to Riesman. There were enough ideas for months of talking and writing.

Then I asked the students each to make a statement of one idea which particularly interested him, and to suggest two or three different ways in which it might be developed into an essay. Blockade. Few associated the concept of an *idea* with the concept of a *statement* or a *sentence.* For many, ideas were at best abstract words or phrases; at worst, as one student suggested, "opinions or untrue facts." Inasmuch as a fact or topic assumes no responsibility for predication, no pattern of organization is obvious for it, and the student is at a loss to know what development may mean for it. Therefore the most typical response to the assignment is something like: "The importance of music: (a) development by examples, (b) general development." Or "The necessity

Source: Working Out Ideas: Predication and Other Uses of Language, Curriculum Publication no. 5 (Berkeley: Bay Area Writing Project, University of California, 1979), pp. 14–17. Originally published as "Essay in Reason" in *Educational Leadership.* Reprinted with permission of the Association for Supervision and Curriculum Development. Copyright © 1962 by the Association for Supervision and Curriculum Development. All rights reserved.

for world government: (a) subjective, (b) objective." Not many aids to reason here!

Idea as Structure

First need then is to talk about ideas as sentences, as saying something about something, as establishing relations, as predicating subjects. The student hopefully proposes, "Music is important" or "World government is necessary," and then goes on: "First I'll write a paragraph saying what I mean by *music* or *world government.* Then I'll develop my point in the predicate about important or necessary." But can importance or necessity be shown without showing possible alternatives? Says the student, "Here's where I switch from objective to subjective!" He becomes vague because his purposes are vague. Important? Necessary? For whom? In relation to what?

After some time discussing these terms as well as *general* and *specific,* demonstrating the need for both pairs and for the clarity of their relations, we come back to develop the useful structural implications of a good leading sentence. Here is one of the few really organizable ones achieved in the first week. Please ignore the horrors of its wordiness, and refrain from *Dic* or *WW* or *P* in the margin. These problems are secondary to sheer understanding of the point, and will mostly clear up when the student's thought clears up. And he is on the right track:

> A prevalent disease, mental retardation has received a minimum of public attention and this neglect has hampered any progress toward alleviating the problems of the disease.

What is the main point here? "Well, that lack of public interest in the disease has hampered progress in understanding it." Cheers. The subject is *lack;* the predicate, *has hampered;* so what will the basic organization be? "Chronological—stages of hampering, development of the verb. But now I see I don't want that kind of organization. I want to talk about ways of studying retardation and how they need public support." So? So: "Most ways of studying and improving mental retardation depend on public understanding and support." Then you'll have to demonstrate the predicate *depend,* and talk about *how* and *why.*"That's what I want to talk about—three *hows* and one *why.*" Now we are beginning to work out the development of an idea.

Chronology, spatial description, comparison, work mainly conjunctively: *and-and-and; then-then-then; also; moreover*—"Here are the main stages in the study of retardation." Disjunction strives to separate, to insist on mutually exclusive alternatives: *either-or; on the one hand-on the other; not this, but that*—"Either we get public interest, or we give up." Concession assumes but denies: *though-yet; nevertheless; however*—"Though we need public interest, yet we can take the following steps without it." Conditional shows interdependent causal relations, conjunctive but subordinative: *if-then; because-therefore*—"If public interest improves, our study of retardation will be aided in the following ways." This is the structure which, it turned out, our student intended to establish.

Elements of Support

The first help we can give the student then is to help him see whether the predication he has chosen to make, the verb he has chosen to apply to the subject, is really supportable by what he knows or can discover; and then, second, to see whether he has arranged the elements of support in the order and connection best for his purposes. A syllogism, the classic unit of reasoning, is in itself a small paragraph of substantiation. "I want to say something about Socrates, and what I want to say about him is that despite his great wisdom he is still mortal. Why is he mortal? Because all men are mortal, and Socrates is a man, as I can show in a paragraph of characteristics." Most of our thought concerns *some*, rather than the *all* referred to in this syllogism; the pattern may be adapted to *some* by taking explicit cognizance of negative as well as positive evidence: "Though two specific authorities deny it, public interest does help, and by public interest I mean not press-publicity, but active individual concern."

Reasoning means giving reasons: that is, it deals with the relations between statements, and these relations are of a few basic kinds; of cause or purpose—*if* this, *therefore* this, or this is so *because;* or of choice—this *or* this—both are impossible at once; or of association—this *and* this go along with this. These are the kinds of possible simultaneity or sequence of statements. Once a student recognizes that his own thought moves in these basic relations, he will be apt to enjoy both the art and the social force of the simple reasoning process of the paragraph. His planning or outlining will show first what main point or predication he is planning to make about his subject, then the main blocks of material he will use to support it, with *pro* connections *(and, or, if)* or negative *con* connections *(but, nor, though)* and finally a new main point, revised from the first hypothesis in the light of the evidence as it has developed. It is the predicate, not the subject, which is planned to be thus supported and modified. There is no such thing as too large or unwieldy a subject; what the student wants to say about the subject is what needs estimation. A student who tries to outline his material rather than his idea is trying, as one student has put it, to eat sardines without opening the can.

Man does not receive raw materials through the senses and then try to make meanings of them through the mind. Rather, the meanings that he makes, tentative and provisional as they may be at every stage, lead him to look for materials of experience which will test his meanings. So the student does not need to stuff his mind with so-called "facts" before he can be responsible for a tentative statement and so, on the other hand, for *any* statement he makes he can be held responsible. If we do not teach the student how to make responsible statements, we give in to the myths of "raw fact" or of individual autonomy, and let him be the victim of the extremes of either the outer world or the inner. Thus we see the dangers on the one hand of the so-called "report" in composition-writing, which leads to an inert sort of copying, and on the other hand the dangers of so-called "creative" writing in which anything goes because there seems to be no valid outer check.

A recent study of suggestions for teaching high school and college composition presented in journals and handbooks over the past few years found that either the so-called "creative" assignment or the so-called formal practical assignment like report-writing bulked large.[1] Hopefully we may soon change some of this emphasis—moving away from extremes of "raw material" or "self-expression" toward the center where they can meet in thoughtful argument, the making of statements based on interest and speculation and the supporting of them by evidence pro and con. To build community between personal and impersonal we need reason to compose our thoughts.

Note

1. Study by E. Kaupp and J. Wirth, College of San Mateo, San Mateo, Calif.

21 Showing, Not Telling

Rebekah Caplan

Year after year we make student writers cringe with the reminder to "be specific." We write in margins next to bracketed passages "explain," "describe." We extend arrows over words, under words, circling around and through words, accompanying them with the captions "What do you mean? Needs more detail; unclear." When we compose essay questions for exams, we underline the "why or why not" at the end of the question *twice* so that our students might feel the importance of that part of the response. Recently I talked with one teacher who had designed a rubber stamp which bore the words "Give an example," so that he would not have to scribble the phrase again and again.

The assumption behind this writing program is that most students have not been trained to *show what they mean.* By training, I do not mean the occasional exercises taken from composition texts, nor do I mean the experience gained by writing perhaps eight major essays over the course of a semester. What I mean by training is the performing of a daily mental warm-up, short and rigorous, not unlike the training routines of musicians, dancers, athletes. Six years ago, while teaching reading and composition in a suburban middle school, I realized the important connection between disciplined practice in the "arts" and the need for it in a writing program. My first students were eighth graders, and not knowing precisely what the junior high school student needed to learn about writing, I experimented for a while.

For approximately three weeks I assigned a potpourri of writing exercises, examining the papers carefully for common problems or strengths. I wanted to determine what the eighth grader already knew about good writing and how far I might expect to take him. It was not

Source: Excerpt from "The Training Program" in *Showing-Writing: A Training Program to Help Students Be Specific* by Rebekah Caplan and Catharine Keech, Classroom Research Study no. 2 (Berkeley: Bay Area Writing Project, University of California, 1980), pp. 1–13, 15. Reprinted with permission of the Bay Area Writing Project.

difficult to discover in those first few weeks of my teaching career that although students *did* write with enthusiasm and energy, not many of them wrote with color or sound or texture. In a description of a student's favorite movie I would read: "It was fantastic because it was so real!" For a strange person: "He is so weird." For a favorite friend: "She has the most fantastic personality."

The underlinings proved their earnestness, their sincerity. I attacked these "empty" descriptions, however, inscribing in the margins those same suggestions that teachers have "stamped out" for years. In class, I passed out models of rich description—character sketches by Steinbeck, settings by Twain, abstract ideas by Bradbury. I advised the students, as they scanned the model and glanced back at their own papers, that they needed to be *that* explicit, *that* good. *That* was what writing was all about. I said, "I know that you know what makes a thunderstorm so frightening. I know that you know the same things Mark Twain knows about a thunderstorm. Now what details did he use?" And we would list "the trees swaying" and the sky turning "blue-black" until we had every last descriptive word classified on the board. "And now," I continued, "you describe a beautiful sunset in the same way that Twain describes the storm."

The writings from such follow-up assignments were admittedly better, but without the prepping, without fussing and reminding, I could not get students to remember to use specifics naturally, on their own. With growing frustration I tried to examine my history as a student writer. I wanted to track down what it had been like for me to write in the eighth grade, and what it was like now. I wanted to uncover when it was that I had reached a turning point or gained a sense of discovery about language and expression. When I tried to recall my own junior high experience, however, I could not remember one assignment, let alone any instruction in writing. What I did remember was signing autograph books and passing notes in class, recording memories in diaries and signing slam books. These sorts of writings mattered the most. We cared deeply about who was one's friend and who was one's enemy, who was loved, who was hated, who was worthy of secrets, who was not. And as these issues came under judgment we based our verdict on the degree of someone's *good personality*. In fact, the supreme compliment one paid a friend in an autograph book amounted to "fantastic personality." And it is still so today.

This memory struck me as being significant. The notion that each person has a personality that is *separate* from his looks, his dress, or his wealth is a new thought to the junior high school student. I remember using that same phrase, "a great personality," with fresh, original intentions in diaries and school papers. My friends and I were intrigued by the idea of personality more than any other. We were fascinated by people's differences, yet we could not say exactly what made us like one person and dislike another. Could it be, then, that I was demanding writing that my students weren't ready to produce? It seemed crucial to respect their excitement over many of these clichéd discoveries. I had to allow room for naive, exploratory generalizations, but at the same time, challenge them to move beyond simple abstractions and discover what concepts like "personality" were based on—how they derived their meanings from concrete perceptions.

Next I looked at myself as an adult writer. What kinds of things did I strive for? What had I been successfully taught along the way? I surely strove for specificity. I had kept a journal for years, commenting on cycles of personal change. I usually began in a stream-of-consciousness style, listing sensations, noting the details that would explain my perceptions to myself. I wrote often, even if I had nothing to say, in the hope I would discover something to write about. I believe this ritual of writing regularly developed from my training as a dancer and a pianist. As a young piano student, I practiced daily finger exercises to strengthen manual agility at the keyboard, to prepare myself for a Bach concerto. As a young ballerina, I was forced to do leg-lifts at the bar for thirty minutes each lesson; the remaining fifteen minutes were devoted to dancing. (How we longed for it to be the other way around!) I notice that beginning artists practice drawing the human body again and again, from varying angles, using different materials—charcoals, oils, ink—to capture reality. In drama classes I attended in college, we began acting lessons with short improvisations that allowed us to experiment with emotions *before* we rehearsed major scenes for performance. In all these cases, the learning, the mastering, came more from the practice than from the final presentation.

After drawing these several conclusions about the training of artists, I decided to build into my curriculum a training program for student writers: a program that attempts to engrain craft, to make the use of specific detail automatic, habitual, through regular and rigorous practice. I created a writing program with these coordinating features:

1. Daily practice expanding a general statement into a paragraph.
2. Applying the difference between *telling* and *showing* in the editing process.
3. Practicing specific ways to select and arrange concrete details in developing an idea or structuring an essay.

Daily Practice Expanding a General Sentence

Since students need the discipline of a regular routine to reinforce use of concrete details in place of, or in support of, their generalities, I assign a daily homework challenge: I give them what I call a *telling sentence*. They must expand the thought in that sentence into an entire paragraph which *shows* rather than *tells*. They take home sentences like:

The room is vacant.

The jigsaw puzzle was difficult to assemble.

Lunch period is too short.

They bring back descriptive paragraphs—short or long, but always detailed, and focused on demonstrating the thought expressed in the assigned *telling* sentence. I challenge students not to use the original statement in the paragraph at all. I ask them to convince me that a room is empty or a puzzle is hard to assemble without once making that claim directly. The challenge is much like charades: they have to get an idea across without giving the whole thing away.

In order to establish the difference between telling and showing, I distribute the following two paragraphs to my students. The first is written by a seventh grader, the second by novelist E. L. Doctorow. Both passages concern a scene at a bus stop.

Telling:
Each morning I ride the bus to school. I wait along with the other people who ride my bus. Sometimes the bus is late and we get angry. Some guys start fights and stuff just to have something to do. I'm always glad when the bus finally comes.

Showing:
A bus arrived. It discharged its passengers, closed its doors with a hiss and disappeared over the crest of a hill. Not one of the people waiting at the bus stop had attempted to board. One woman wore a sweater that was too small, a long skirt, white sweater socks, and house slippers. One man was in his undershirt. Another man wore shoes with the toes cut out, a soiled blue serge jacket and brown pants. There was something wrong with these people. They made faces. A mouth smiled at nothing and unsmiled, smiled and unsmiled. A head shook in vehement denial. Most of them carried brown paper bags rolled tight against their stomachs.
The Book of Daniel (p. 15)

When asked to distinguish the differences between the two paragraphs, most students respond by saying the second paragraph is better because they can *picture* the scene more easily. They think the people in paragraph two are "weird, poor, and lonely," (all *telling* ideas). But this interpretation comes from the *pictures* (their word), pictures of people wearing torn clothing, carrying brown paper bags instead of lunch boxes, wearing unhappy expressions on their faces. Student writers can easily discern good description. Getting them to write with close detail is not managed as smoothly.

I remind students that the storybooks they read as very young children are filled with colorful illustrations that *show* the events described on accompanying pages; the writer does not have to describe the lovely red barn with the carved wooden trim, for the picture next to the caption "The barn was beautiful" reveals that idea. However, in more mature literature, drawings disappear from the pages, and the writer assumes the role of illustrator. Language must be his brush and palette. Following such a discussion, I initiate the daily training exercise, explaining to students that they will expand one sentene each night from telling to showing during the entire course of the semester.

Below are sample daily sentences. These sentences are given in no particular order and are not necessarily linked by recurring themes. Sometimes students themselves suggest sentences for successive assignments. By choosing generalizations familiar to students, I increase the likelihood of effective elaboration.

> She has a good personality.
>
> The concert was fantastic.
>
> The party was fun.
>
> The jocks think they're cool.
>
> The pizza tasted good.
>
> I was embarrassed.
>
> My parents seemed angry.
>
> My room was a mess.
>
> The movie was frightening.
>
> Foothill students have good school spirit.

The idea of daily writing is, of course, nothing new in itself. I know many teachers who have their students "write for ten minutes" the moment they come to class. My daily writing approach, however, is different in a number of ways. First, many teacher assign "topics" for elaboration like "School" or "Family" or "Sports." Although a topic is open-ended and allows more room for creativity, students often spend more time trying to find something to say than actually writing the composition. The type of statement I use is similar to the thesis sentence, the controlling sentence of an essay. The generalization supplies the point; the student is given the idea to support. Students are free then to concentrate on experimenting with expressions of that idea. Further, since they are all working on the same idea, they are in a position to compare results—to learn from one another's crafting.

Another departure from other daily-writing "warm-ups" is that this daily writing is done at home. Students must come to class with pieces finished and ready to be evaluated. We don't wait ten minutes while they hastily scribble some sort of solution. I want to give them time—if they will take it—to play with and think about what they are trying to do.

Finally, unlike private journals or some free-writing assignments, these exercises are written to be shared. I use the writings in much the same way a drama instructor uses improvisation as an instructional technique. The daily sentence expansion becomes a framework for practicing and discovering ways of showing ideas. Just as drama students search for ways of expressing "ambition" or "despair" by imagining themselves in real-life situations that would evoke these feelings and discovering ranges of bodily and facial expression, my students arrive at ways of showing "empty rooms" or "difficult puzzles" by experimenting with different kinds of language expression. I instruct them very little, preferring that students find their own solutions. But finally, although the experimenting at home is free—not judged—the practice includes an important element that parallels acting instruction: the daily "public" performance. The students know in advance that some papers will be read to the class for analysis and evaluation. However, they do not know which ones. As theirs might very well be among those I choose (my selections do not fall into a predictable pattern), the students are likely to be prepared.

The "performance" or sharing of improvisational or experimental efforts is an important learning experience for the selected performers *and* their audience. The first ten minutes of every class session, then, is devoted to oral readings, not writing. I choose between five and seven writing samples which I read aloud to the class, and as a group we evaluate the density of detail. Where did this writer have success with interesting description? Where were her details thin? This is the only time I will not comb the papers for grammar, spelling, and usage errors, for there is no time. Since we respond exclusively to content, students can give full attention to being specific without the pressure of grammatical perfection.

I grade each paper immediately as the discussion of that paper concludes. Besides assigning an A, B, or C grade, I quickly write a general comment made by the group: "great showing; too telling at the end," "great imagination, but write more." This process takes about ten seconds and then I move on to the next reading. I record a check in my gradebook for those papers not selected for reading. If students do not turn in writings they receive no credit. All papers are recorded and handed back before the end of the period, giving the students immediate response and recognition for their work. At the end of the semester I average the number of grades a student has earned in the series of assignments.

There are five major advantages to using such a daily training exercise with its follow-up sharing and discussion:

1. *Students write every day.* I do not assign sentences on the eve of exams, major assignment due dates, or holidays.

2. *I am freed from having to grade an entire set of papers each night, yet I provide a daily evaluation.* If a student is disappointed because a particular writing was not selected, I invite him to share it with me after class. This tends to happen when the student has written a good paragraph and wants me to enter a grade for this particular one, which I am glad to do. It may also happen when a student is unsure of his solution and wants help.

3. *Students selected to perform hear useful comments immediately.* They do not have to wait a week to receive response and criticism. The other students learn from the process of specifying weaknesses as well as strengths of the work and from hearing suggestions given to the "performing" students by peers and teachers.

4. *Students learn new developmental techniques and linguistic patterns from each other.* Students assimilate new ideas for specificity by regularly hearing other students' writing. In addition, they often internalize the linguistic patterns of other students either consciously or unconsciously. This process is similar to assimilating the speech patterns of a person with a different accent. After close association with this person, we may tune our speech to the inflections of an attractive or entertaining accent. I believe it is often easier for students to learn from other students who write well than from professional writers whose solutions may be out of the students' range.

5. *Students write for a specific audience.* They write with the expectation that classmates may hear their composition the following day. So they usually put more effort into their pieces than if they were intended for their private journals or for teacher-as-evaluator.

A selection of daily writing samples follows. Two students, a remedial freshman and a college-bound sophomore, show growth and change over a two-week time span. Their writings illustrate two important results of the daily practice:

1. Students write more—either because they are finding it easier to generate more writing or because they are working harder on the assignments (or both).
2. Students gain control over a wider range of techniques.

[Here is the first writing sample:]

Daily Sentence: *The new students were lonely.*

It was the first day of school and there were two new students, Dick and Dan, who had moved over the summer. They were brothers and this was a new city and school which they had come to, and in this school they would have to make friends because neither of them knew anybody or anyone.

Freshman Student

This piece of writing is composed entirely of generalities (telling sentences). The writer explains the cause of the loneliness—a new city, new school, necessity for making new friends—but unless he shows us some foreign streets, strange faces, and unusual customs to support these reasons, he will do little to convince us. Perhaps if he could contrast "playing pool with the gang at Old Mike's Pizza Parlor" to the "eyes avoiding his unfamiliar face in the study hall," the reader might appreciate the realities of "new city, new school, new friends."

Here is the same student's writing two weeks later.

Daily Sentence: *The crossword puzzle was difficult to solve.*

The sixth row down got me stuck. It was plain to tell that this crossword puzzle was rough. The puzzle as it was, was made for a 12th grade level, and it made me feel as if I was in the 6th grade level. Intellectual words such as "the square root" of 1,091,056 in four digits and others. The next one was a five-letter word for phyladendron, which was "plant" to my surprise. I, as a normal person, had a very hard time trying to figure out what an Australian green citrus fruit was with four spaces. Instinctively I gave up the whole game, as it was too frustrating to cope with.

This selection illustrates an improvement in generating examples. The writer introduces his subject by *telling* that the puzzle was tough, but immediately proves his claim with a series of illustrations—twelfth grade level versus sixth grade ability, intellectual words like square root, exotic plants and fruits that call for specialized knowledge. His writing is more enjoyable to read because of the examples he added.

Notice also that his paragraph is longer but never rambles or leaves the point.

Next, the sophomore:

Daily Sentence: *The room was vacant.*

The next show didn't start for another hour. As I repositioned the spotlight in the upper balcony, the squeaks of the rusty screws seemed to echo throughout the desolate building. I walked down the aluminum stairs that resounded with the sound of rain beating on a tin roof throughout the auditorium. I then opened the curtains to the large, lonely stage which looked dark and forbidding. As I put up the sets and decorated the stage, I guess it would seem to anyone walking in, that the room was very much alive with color and objects. But to me, even the set and decorated auditorium looked bare.

In the first half of the paragraph, this student carefuly constructs detail. Like many students trying to master a skill, he concentrates intensely at first, very mindful of his task. However, there comes a point when, losing his fervor, he reverts to *telling*. With the sentence "I then opened the curtains . . ." he abandons his use of specifics, relying instead on vague adjectives like "dark and forbidding," or general nouns such as "color and objects."

Within two weeks, this student increased his observational skills considerably. In addition, he was able to sustain his use of vivid details throughout a much longer piece of writing.

Daily Sentence: *The rollercoaster was the scariest ride at the fair.*

As I stood in line, I gazed up at the gigantic steel tracks that looped around three times. The thunderous roar of the rollercoaster sounded like a thunder cloud that has sunk into my ears and suddenly exploded. The wild screams of terror shot through me like a bolt of lightning and made my fingers tingle with fear. Soon I heard the roar of the rollercoaster cease. As the line started to move forward, I heard the clicking of the turnstyle move closer and closer. Finally I got onto the loading-deck and with a shaking hand gave the attendant my ticket.

It seemed like I barely got seated when I felt a jolt which signified the beginning of the ride. While the rollercoaster edged up the large track, I kept pulling my seatbelt tighter and tighter until it felt like I was cutting off all circulation from the waist down. At the crest of the hill, I caught a glimpse of the quiet town which lay before me and gave me a feeling of peace and serenity. Suddenly my eyes felt like they were pushed all the way back into my head, and the town had become a blur. All I could see was a mass of steel curving this way and that as the rollercoaster turned upside down. I was squeezing the safety bar so tight that my fingers seemed to be embedded in the metal. I could see the landing-deck, and I let out a deep breath that had been held inside ever since the first drop. As the roller coaster came to a halt, I felt weak and emotionally drained. When I stepped off onto the deck, I teetered a bit to the left, but caught my balance quickly when I saw my friends waiting for me at the exit gate. I tried to look "normal," while trying to convince them in a weak voice that, "Oh, it was nothing."

Even though he makes general claims—"I felt weak and emotionally drained"—he remembers to support his feeling with specific evidence: "When I stepped off onto the deck, I teetered a bit to the left. . . ." Or, as he tries to look "normal," he proves this with dialogue: "Oh, it was nothing." This student puts himself in the experience every step of the narration. Two weeks earlier, he could not sustain such a practice.

To summarize, the daily sentence expansions provide a framework in which students can experiment and discover ways of showing ideas. It is a time for self-exploration in the attempt to attach meaning to experience; it is also a time for increasing fluency and creating a style and voice.

Applying "Showing Not Telling" to Revision

The second feature of this training program consists of using this technique of sentence specificity and elaboration to help students revise first drafts of major compositions. Whenever students work on major writing assignments—an essay related to the reading of a novel, a character sketch for a short story, a narration of a personal experience—I have them work with rough drafts in small editing groups. In addition to helping another writer correct spelling and usage errors, a student editor is instructed to search for thinly developed ideas. If a student writer fails to develop adequately an important section of her composition, the editor underlines the sentence or sentences that generalize rather than specify and writes *show* in the margin. The writer must then take the *telling* sentence and expand it for homework. Instead of the usual daily routine in which everyone has the same sentence to develop, here students use sentences from their *own* materials. As the drama instructor stops the rehearsal of a scene midway and asks the actor to approach the scene from a different perspective through exercises in improvisation, so I halt my writers midstream in their discourse, urging them to consider important elements that need focusing and elaboration. With practice, students become more effective editors, for they train themselves to spot under-developed ideas and non-specific language.

When a writer has elaborated her own generalization, she may decide to insert the new version into the composition. The editors in her group work along with me to help her decide whether or not the change is effective. The revisions below illustrate the process.

Seventh Grade Assignment: Re-creation of a Favorite Childhood Experience

This writer describes the fun of playing hide-and-seek with her brother. As she attempts to create excitement and suspense around being found, she writes:

> Leonardo was approaching her. He was getting closer and closer.
> She thought for sure she was going to be caught.

Editors in her group suggested she *show* "He was getting closer and closer" because this sentence signals an approaching climax.
Her revision:

> She could hear him near the barn, his footsteps crunching the gravel. Next he was on the lawn, and the sounds of the wet grass scraping against his boots made a loud, squeaky noise. Next she could hear him breathing.

This writer is now *re-creating* her experience. By carefully remembering each sensation as her brother drew nearer—footsteps crunching gravel, sounds of boots in wet grass, breathing noises—she leads the reader through the experience. The showing sentences could be inserted smoothly into the original version in place of the telling sentence.

Senior Assignment: Description of a Photograph of Janis Joplin, 60's Blues Singer

One senior began:

> Sitting on the sofa she looked exhausted. . .

Having said so much for appearances, this student went on to suggest *why* Janis was so fatigued. A student editor thought it important for her to *show* the exhaustion, so she underlined that sentence.
The revision:

> Her eyes told of her pain—deep, set-back, reaching inside of herself. Dark caves formed where her cheeks were. Her mouth was a hardened straight line, down at the corners.

As if this writer were the camera lens itself, she zooms in for a close-up, examining in detail the elements that make Janis appear weary.
By applying the difference between *telling* and *showing* to editing, students are more likely to be better editors and evaluators of writing. Daily oral teacher evaluation of writing has served as a model. And because changing *telling* to *showing* has become a habit, they are better able to expand their ideas into rich, vivid prose.

Using Daily Writings to Learn Specific Techniques

After spending six weeks allowing students to experiment with showing, I begin deliberate instruction in developing ideas. I begin exposing my students to methods of generating details which they may not have discovered or practiced. This is the time for them to study literary devices for revealing ideas, a time to try different stylistic techniques. By altering the procedure in this way, I make two specific changes in the daily sentence practice:

1. I assign *telling* sentences derived from what the class is studying (e.g., persuasive argument, autobiography, short story writing).

2. I require students to expand these sentences in what may be unfamiliar ways. This requirement might be called *directed elaboration* as opposed to the undirected responses of earlier daily writings.

For instance, if we're currently doing a unit on persuasive argument, I structure all the *telling* sentences as opinions: *Lunch period is too short. Teenagers should have their own telephones. P.E. should not be required.* Each day we practice different strategies for developing arguments—dealing with the opposition first, saving the best argument until last—while at the same time examining published essays of persuasion. Students then have the opportunity to apply the new strategy in the assigned daily sentence.

Or, if we're practicing different sentence styles, such as the types of sentences described by Francis Christensen (1967) I require students to use certain modification structures—verb clusters, adjective clusters—in their assigned sentences.

In any case, a final composition assignment—an essay of persuasion, a character sketch—culminates the unit of study. Students write better compositions because the directed elaboration of the daily practices has given them a variety of techniques to draw on. Like the drama instructor advising the student who exaggerates Hamlet's lament, "Instead of delivering Hamlet's soliloquy to the balcony, looking up to the center spotlight, I'd like you to try that speech with your back turned, sitting in the wheelchair," I want my students to experiment with challenging and unfamiliar ways of expressing ideas. Probably the drama teacher does not expect her student to perform Hamlet in a wheelchair in the final presentation; she simply wants the student to experience a new way of delivering despair, an experience he can apply to his final performance. In the same way, I do not expect my students to follow some exact pattern or structure when designing arguments or creating characters, just to stretch their limits and discover options.

When my students write their final compositions, when they sit down to deliver their finest performances, I want them to feel that their hours of training have paid off. I want them to gain a notion of what writers are about. And if they freeze-up midway in the process, if they encounter the blank that all writers face, I hope they will learn to use the "art" itself as a tool of release.

Caplan's article concludes with two sample units of study: a study in characterization and a study in comparison and contrast. Ed.

Part Five: Afterword

22 The Relationship between the Teacher and the Researcher

Miles Myers

Theoretical and Methodological Decisions Facing Researchers

The researcher in the social sciences makes two kinds of initial decisions, one theoretical and the other methodological (M. Myers, 1980). In research on writing, the theoretical choice is among a *modeling* theory that describes types of texts (sentences, paragraphs, essays, and so forth), a *processing* theory that defines writing as cognitive stages or strategies, and a *distancing* theory that defines writing as interrelationships in social situations.

The methodological choices in research on writing are *rationalism*, *positivism*, and *contextualism*. In rationalism, the researcher examines contrasting pieces of data and uses the logic of reason and the insight of intuition to develop a hypothesis. For example, Noam Chomsky examined two contrasting sentences ("John is easy to please" and "John is eager to please") and hypothesized the existence of a deep structure in which the two sentences had different subjects ("Somebody pleases John" and "John pleases somebody"). Chomsky attempted to describe a speaker's innate competence by describing the contrasting surface data of performance.

In another example, Cicero (*De Oratore*) contrasted the parts of written texts and hypothesized the existence of such forms as *exordium* (introduction) and *perporatio* (summing up). Likewise, Francis Christensen (1976) analyzed contrasting paragraphs from professional writers and hypothesized three forms of organization (coordinate, subordinate, and mixed) and three sentence additions in what he identified as the cumulative sentence (nouns, adjectives, and *-ing* verbs). In these cases, the test of an idea's validity is the logical consistency of the argument and the reader's recognition of the examples as representative of personal experience.

In positivism, however, the test of an idea's reliability is the numerical weight of the descriptive statistics and the level of significance of the inference statistics. Descriptive statistics are the *mean* (the average), the *mode* (the high point), and the *median* (the midpoint). The inference statistics, such as the *T-test* and the *chi-square,* can tell us to what degree the numerical results are a matter of chance. Most writing researchers are willing to accept a 5 percent risk of error. That is, if the probability of chance can be reduced to one in twenty, then the writing researcher will accept the result as significant.

The probability of chance can, of course, be reduced by increasing the number of pieces of data. If the number is large enough, the result may have statistical significance but not educational or experimental significance. Experimental significance (or reliability) requires that the subjects in a writing experiment be randomly assigned to different experimental treatments, matching the subjects and the situation on all the variables except the key one for the experiment. Educational significance seems to come in two forms, one a matter of validity and the other a matter of practicality. While experimental significance or reliability refers to the accuracy with which something can be measured, validity refers to the evidence that one is measuring what one claims to be measuring. For instance, in research on writing, some researchers believe that the only valid way to measure a student's writing ability is to examine several samples of the student's writing. These researchers believe that multiple-choice grammar tests that claim to measure writing ability are not valid because these tests measure something other than writing.

Finally, even though an experiment might have validity, reliability, and statistical significance, it might still lack the second form of educational significance—that is, the finding may have no use. For instance, even though an experiment might "prove" that living in Paris for six months is the best way to learn French, the finding has no practical educational significance in most school systems because sending a French class to Paris is rarely possible.

In research on writing, the studies of Donald Bateman and Frank Zidonis (1966) and of John Mellon (1969) are examples of positivism, both using control and experimental groups to test the hypothesis that instruction in grammar or sentence combining increases what Mellon calls "syntactic maturity" and what Bateman and Zidonis call "structural complexity." Frank O'Hare (1973), also using control and experimental groups, examined whether sentence combining of the O'Hare variety would increase syntactic maturity and whether teachers would give higher ratings to those papers with syntactic maturity.

Although positivism has been the dominant method of research in writing, an increasing number of researchers have started to criticize the positivist assumption that in the pursuit of general laws in the social sciences one must strip away context and put subjects in an experimental or laboratory setting. Contextualism differs from positivism in that it examines subjects in their natural settings without imposing any experimental constraints from the outside. For example, Donald Graves (1975) began his study by examining the writing folders of ninety-four students in four classrooms and arrived at a tentative three-phase structure for the writing process (prewriting, composing, and postwriting). Next he observed fifty-three writing episodes in four classrooms and gathered detailed data on one student, including interviews with the parents.

Unlike rationalism, which focuses on the products of the writing act, contextualism examines the act of writing over time. Contextual studies can be *clinical* or *episodic*. The clinical approach, used by Piaget in his study of a child's concept of conservation, requires the researcher to give the student the writing problem. Wallace Chafe's studies of the pear tree stories (1980) exemplify a *contextual-clinical* study. Chafe showed the subjects a six-minute film about a boy who steals a basket of pears from a man and asked the subjects to tell "what happened in the film." Chafe was interested in what linguistic devices were used by the subjects to process and organize the information in the film.

An example of the episodic study is Claudia Mitchell-Kernan's study (1972) of the forms of Black discourse in Oakland, California. She recorded the conversations heard in her neighborhood and selected particular episodes for study. One episode was the situation in which a speaker "puts down" another person. William Labov and David Fanshell's studies of oral narratives in Harlem (1972) and the forms of therapeutic discourse (1971) are other examples. Another is Kellogg Hunt's study (1965) of how many clauses children at different ages could consolidate into a single sentence. Hunt collected one thousand words from each student. Each writing episode was part of the normal course work and free of any control from Hunt. His findings show that the average eighth grader could consolidate five clauses, the average fourth grader only three.

Not all studies are clearly marked as one type or another. For example, Linda Flower and Jack Hayes (1978) had their subjects talk aloud about what they were thinking as they were writing about a given subject. Some researchers feel that this method interferes with the context of the writing and creates an experimental setting closer to the positivist tradition. Other researchers feel the Flower-Hayes method does capture the writing context. Despite some uncertainties the general distinctions are valid and offer a useful way to understand how a methodology shapes the different kinds of data used to describe writing.

Theoretical and Methodological Decisions Facing Teachers

Teachers of writing also have two kinds of decisions in their planning of classes, one theoretical and the other methodological. The theoretical decision involves whether to plan steps and stages in a series of writing strategies (*processing*), to plan which texts or parts of texts to use and what order (*modeling*), or to plan a set of interrelationships in the classroom, assigning different roles to different students in group or individual activities (*distancing*).

The methodological decision is what one uses as a framework to find the best approach to teaching and to test the validity and reliability of the approach one is using. Three kinds of frameworks for testing teaching lessons have been proposed by Gary Fenstermacher (1980): (1) rules from research and institutions, (2) the image of a prototypical class or the prototypical day of a given class, and (3) theories about human learning and knowledge. As a way of ranking these frameworks, Fenstermacher reports that "I would condemn bridges built with rules, certify bridges built with evidence [images], and commend bridges built with schemata [theories]" (p. 128).

In the rule framework, the teacher simply follows rules identified by research or the institution. These rules are usually based on the assumption that teacher-proof materials are possible and desirable and that research findings can be converted into rules for teachers to follow. John Dewey (1929) argues that "no conclusion of scientific research can be converted into an immediate rule of educational art" (p. 19). Even if such a conversion were possible, one might argue that turning teachers into rule-following automatons would seriously damage the educational enterprise in areas not covered by the rules.

Eleanor Duckworth (1972) describes how a set of rules from a research study can have negative effects on teachers who have no sense of professional authority:

> It is just as necessary for teachers as for children to feel confidence in their own ideas. It is important for them as people, and also important if they are really going to feel free to acknowledge the children's ideas. If teachers feel that their class must do things just as the book says, and that their excellence as a teacher depends upon that, they cannot possibly accept children's divergence and children's creations. A teacher's guide must give enough indications, enough suggestions, so the teacher has ideas to start with and to pursue in some depth. But it must also enable the teacher to feel free to move in directions of her own when other ideas arise.
>
> For instance, the teachers' guides for his program include many examples of things children are likely to do. The risk is that teachers may see these as things that the children in their classes

must do—whether or not the children do them becomes a measure of successful or unsuccessful teaching. (P. 225)

In the framework of evidence and class images, the teacher has some image of how a class seems to work, based on the actual evidence from research ("three out of five children wrote longer stories after drawing pictures of the stories") or descriptions from other teachers (Herbert Kohl's *Thirty-Six Children*, 1968). These class images provide a useful guide for estimating how a class is proceeding. Unlike rules, these images require a thinking teacher who must exercise personal judgment in planning. Rebekah Caplan developed her approach to teaching writing from her experience in a drama class. The drama students, asked to act out particular scenes, had to think very carefully about details of speech, movement, gesture, appearance, and so forth. Caplan applied the image of the drama class to her English class and began making estimates about how to proceed. The result was the development of her showing-not-telling approach (1980).

In the framework of theoretical structure, the teacher plans with structures of learning and writing behavior. The notion of the idea as a sentence and the predicate as the organizer of development (Josephine Miles, 1979) provides a structure for understanding Caplan's work. The notion of participant and spectator writing (James Britton et al., 1975) is another structure that can help teachers plan and illuminate class behavior. For example, James Pierce's composition course can be viewed as organized around poetic-transactional structures.

Interaction between Researchers and Teachers

The direction of influence is not always from the researcher to the teacher. Courtney Cazden (1976), for one, argues that the direction can also be from the teacher to the researcher:

. . . the teachers all have to take courses at local colleges for salary increments and advanced degrees and rightfully resent being told what to do by professors who've never been in a classroom. (P. 76)

Of course, research knowledge about language isn't the only basis for improved action. I think it's fair to say that there is a general trans-Atlantic contrast at this point. Whereas Americans like me have worked "down," trying to derive implications for education from theories about language and its development, colleagues in England have worked "up" from instances of the best classroom practice. (P. 81)

In order to have descriptions of the best practice on which to base some research inquiry, teachers must write or tell about what they do that works. In the writing and telling, the teachers themselves will begin to suggest possible images and structures for understanding how a particular approach functions in the classroom. This is the beginning of classroom research by teachers. When teachers have established their own community of scholars and their own methods of inquiry, then they will have the professional authority to work with researchers as partners in understanding the educational enterprise.

The National Writing Project is an example of an attempt to create a community of teacher-scholars. In a classroom setting, teachers demonstrate various approaches to teaching writing, and other teachers become encouraged to try these teaching approaches and to research them further in their classrooms.

Teachers and researchers share the common theoretical framework of *modeling, processing,* and *distancing,* but this framework is used for different purposes. For researchers, the choice among the three theoretical approaches is a decision about which question to ask. For teachers, the choice is a decision about which way to plan lessons.

Where teachers and researchers have great difficulty communicating with one another is in the area of methodology. Of the three methods used by teachers to gather data on what works—rules and procedures, evidence and class images, and theoretical structures—the most frequently used method is the class image because the other two methods eliminate too many details of the context and appear too abstract, too far removed from classroom realities. The teacher's method of class image is very similar to the researcher's method of contextualism. Both methods emphasize the importance of context, and both are classroom centered. It is encouraging that researchers' increasing interest in contextual studies shows promise of diminishing some of the methodological difficulties that have plagued communication between teachers and researchers.

Bibliography

Ammon, Paul. 1977. "Cognitive Development and Early Childhood Education: Piagetian and Neo-Piagetian Theories." In *Psychological Processes in Early Education*, edited by H. L. Hom and P. A. Robinson. New York: Academic Press.

Appel, L. F., R. G. Cooper, N. McCarrell, J. Sims-Knight, S. R. Yussen, and J. H. Flavell. 1972. "Development of the Distinction between Perceiving and Memorizing." *Child Development* 43: 1365-81.

Applebee, Arthur. 1977. "The Elaborative Choice." In *Language as a Way of Knowing*, edited by Martin Nystrand. Toronto: Ontario Institute for Studies in Education.

Applebee, Arthur. 1978. *The Child's Concept of Story: Ages Two to Seventeen.* Chicago: University of Chicago Press.

Arnheim, Rudolph. 1969. *Visual Thinking.* Berkeley: University of California Press.

Asso, D., and M. Wyke. 1971. "Discrimination of Spatially Confusable Letters by Young Children." *Journal of Experimental Child Psychology* 9: 11-20.

Ausubel, D. P. 1965. Introduction to *Readings in the Psychology of Cognition,* edited by R. C. Anderson and D. P. Ausubel, 3-11. New York: Holt, Rinehart and Winston.

Bartlett, F. C. 1932. *Remembering: An Experimental and Social Study.* Cambridge: Cambridge University Press.

Bateman, Donald, and Frank Zidonis. 1966. *The Effect of a Study of Transformational Grammar on the Writing of Ninth and Tenth Graders.* Champaign, Ill.: National Council of Teachers of English.

Berch, D. B., and R. C. Evans. 1973. "Decision Processes in Children's Recognition Memory." *Journal of Experimental Child Psychology* 16: 148-64.

Bereiter, Carol. 1979. "Development in Writing." In *Cognitive Processes in Writing*, edited by Lee W. Gregg and Erwin R. Steinberg. Hillsdale, N.J.: Lawrence Erlbaum Associates.

Blodgett, H. C. 1929. "The Effect of the Introduction of Reward upon the Maze Performance of Rats." *University of California Publication on Psychology* 4: 113-34.

Bobrow, D. G., and Donald A. Norman. 1975. "Some Principles of Memory Schemata." In *Representation in Understanding: Studies in Cognitive Science,* edited by Daniel G. Bobrow and Allan M. Collins. New York: Academic Press.

Britton, James, Tony Burgess, Nancy Martin, Alex McLeod, and Harold Rosen. 1975. *Development of Writing Abilities (11-18)*. London: Macmillan Education.

Brogden, W. J. 1939. "The Effect of Frequency Reinforcement upon the Level of Conditioning." *Journal of Experimental Psychology* 24: 419-31.

Brooks, Phyllis. 1973. "Mimesis: Grammar and the Echoing Voice." *College English* 35 (November): 161-68.

Brown, Roger, and Ursula Bellugi. 1964. "Three Processes in the Child's Acquisition of Syntax." *Harvard Educational Review* 34: 133-51.

Brown, Roger, C. Cazden, and U. Bellugi. 1969. "The Child's Grammar from I-III." In *Minnesota Symposium on Child Psychology*, vol. 2, edited by J. P. Hill, 28-73. Minneapolis: University of Minnesota Press.

Brown, Roger, and D. McNeill. 1966. "The 'Tip of the Tongue Phenomenon.'" *Journal of Verbal Learning and Verbal Behavior* 5: 325-37.

Brown, Rollo. 1915. *How the French Boy Learns to Write*. Cambridge, Mass.: Harvard University Press. Reprint. Champaign, Ill.: National Council of Teachers of English, 1963.

Bruner, J. S., Jacqueline Goodnow, and G. A. Austin. 1956. *A Study of Thinking*. New York: John Wiley and Sons.

Bruner, Jerome. 1978. "Learning the Mother Tongue." *Human Nature* 1 (September): 42-49.

Buckley, Marilyn Hanf, and Owen Boyle. 1981. "Mapping and Composing." In *Mapping the Writing Journey*. Bay Area Writing Project, Curriculum Publication no. 15. Berkeley: University of California.

Burgess, Jackson. 1963. "Sentence by Sentence." *College Composition and Communication* 14 (December): 257-62.

Caplan, Rebekah, and Catharine Keech. *Showing-Writing: A Training Program to Help Students Be Specific*. Bay Area Writing Project, Classroom Research Study no. 2. Berkeley: University of California.

Cazden, Courtney. 1976. "How Knowledge about Language Helps the Classroom Teacher—or Does It: A Personal Account." *The Urban Review* 9 (Summer): 74-90.

Chafe, W. L. 1979. "The Recall and Verbalization of Past Experience." In *Current Issues in Linguistic Theory*, edited by R. W. Cole, 215-46. Bloomington: Indiana University Press.

Chafe, W. L., ed. 1980. *The Pear Tree Stories: Cognitive, Cultural, and Linguistic Aspects of Narrative Production*, vol. 3. Norwood, N.J.: Ablex Publishing Corp.

Chomsky, Carol. 1972. "Write Now, Read Later." In *Language in Early Childhood Education*, edited by Courtney Cazden, 119-26. Washington, D.C.: National Education Association.

Chomsky, Carol. 1974. "Invented Spelling in First Grade." Unpublished paper.

Chomsky, Noam. 1957. *Syntactic Structures*. The Hague: Mouton and Co.

Chomsky, Noam. 1959. "Review of Skinner's *Verbal Behavior*." *Language* 35: 26-58.

Chomsky, Noam. 1965. *Aspects of the Theory of Syntax*. The Hague: Mouton and Co.

Chomsky, Noam. 1968. *Language and the Mind.* New York: Harcourt, Brace and World.

Christensen, Francis. 1967. *Notes toward a New Rhetoric: Six Essays for Teachers.* New York: Harper and Row.

Clark, Herbert, and Eve Clark. 1977. *Psychology and Language: An Introduction to Psycholinguistics.* New York: Harcourt Brace Jovanovich.

Cooley, W. W., and R. Glasser. 1969. "The Computer and Individualized Instruction." *Science* 166: 574-82.

Dandridge, Sarah, John Harter, Rob Kessler, Miles Myers, and Susan Thomas. 1979. *Independent Study and Writing.* Bay Area Writing Project, Curriculum Publication no. 2. Berkeley: University of California.

Dewey, John. 1929. *The Sources of a Science of Education.* New York: Liveright Publishing Corp.

Duckworth, Eleanor. 1972. "The Having of Wonderful Ideas." *Harvard Educational Review* 42 (May): 217-31.

Elbow, Peter. 1973. *Writing without Teachers.* New York: Oxford University Press.

Elley, W. B., I. H. Barham, H. Lamb, and M. Wylie. 1976. "The Role of Grammar in a Secondary School English Curriculum." *Research in the Teaching of English* 10 (Spring): 5-21.

Emig, Janet. 1971. *The Composing Process of Twelfth Graders.* Urbana, Ill.: National Council of Teachers of English.

Ervin-Tripp, Susan. 1964. "Imitation and Structural Change in Children's Language." In *New Directions in the Study of Language,* edited by E. H. Lenneberg, 163-89. Cambridge, Mass.: MIT Press.

Fader, Daniel. 1966. *Hooked on Books.* New York: Berkley Publishing Corp.

Fader, Daniel. 1976. "The University of Michigan Writing Program." Lecture given at the 1976 Summer Institute of the Bay Area Writing Project. University of California, Berkeley.

Fenstermacher, Gary D. 1980. "On Learning to Teach Effectively from Research on Teacher Effectiveness." In *Time to Learn,* edited by Ann Lieberman and Carolyn Denham, 127-37. Sacramento: California Commission for Teacher Preparation and Licensing.

Fillmore, Charles. 1968. "The Case for Case." In *Universals of Linguistic Theory,* edited by E. Bach and R. T. Harms. New York: Holt, Rinehart and Winston.

Flavell, J. H. 1963. *The Developmental Psychology of Jean Piaget.* New York: D. Van Nostrand.

Flavell, J. H. 1970. "Developmental Studies of Mediated Memory." In *Advances in Child Development and Behavior,* vol. 5, edited by L. P. Lipsitt and H. W. Reese. New York: Academic Press.

Flavell, J. H. 1977. *Cognitive Development.* Englewood Cliffs, N.J.: Prentice-Hall.

Flower, Linda. 1979. "Writer-Based Prose: A Cognitive Basis for Problems in Writing." *College English* 41 (September): 19-37.

Flower, Linda, and John Hayes. 1978. "The Dynamics of Composing: Making Plans and Juggling Constraints." In *Cognitive Processes in Writing,* edited by Lee W. Gregg and Erwin R. Steinberg. Hillsdale, N.J.: Lawrence Erlbaum Associates.

Franklin, Benjamin. 1961. *Autobiography and Other Writings*. Edited by L. J. Lemisch. New York: Signet Books.

Frye, Northrop. 1957. *Anatomy of Criticism*. Princeton, N.J.: Princeton University Press.

Gagne, R. M., et al. 1962. "Factors in Acquiring Knowledge of a Mathematical Task." *Psychological Monographs*, vol. 76, no. 526. Washington, D.C.: American Psychological Association.

Gagne, Robert M. 1970. *The Conditions of Learning*, 2d ed. New York: Holt, Rinehart and Winston.

Gibson, Walker. 1966. *Tough, Sweet, and Stuffy*. Bloomington and London: Indiana University Press.

Graves, Donald. 1975. "An Examination of the Writing Processes of Seven Year Old Children." *Research in the Teaching of English* 9 (Winter): 227-41.

Gray, James. 1969. "Teaching the New Rhetoric." Article available from the Bay Area Writing Project, University of California, Berkeley.

Guthrie, E. R. 1942. "Conditioning: A Theory of Learning in Terms of Stimulus, Response, and Association." In *National Society for the Study of Education: The Forty First Yearbook*. Bloomington, Ill.: Public School Publishing Co.

Hagen, J. W. 1971. "Some Thoughts on How Children Learn to Remember." *Human Development* 14: 262-71.

Healy, Mary K. 1980. *Using Student Writing Response Groups in the Classroom*. Bay Area Writing Project, Curriculum Publication no. 12. Berkeley: University of California.

Hebb, D. O., W. E. Lambert, and G. R. Tucker. 1973. "A DMZ in the Language War." *Psychology Today* (April): 55-62.

Herriot, Peter. 1970. *Introduction to the Psychology of Language*. London: Methuen and Co.

Holstein, Barbara I. 1970. "Use of Metaphor to Induce Innovative Thinking in Fourth Grade Children." Ph.D. diss., Boston University.

Hood, Richard. 1967. *Précis Writing Practice*. New York: Educators Press Service.

Huey, Edmond B. [1908] 1968. *The Psychology and Pedagogy of Reading*. Reprint. Cambridge, Mass.: MIT Press.

Hunt, Kellogg. 1965a. *Grammatical Structures Written at Three Grade Levels*. Champaign, Ill.: National Council of Teachers of English.

Hunt, Kellogg. 1965b. *An Instrument to Measure Syntactic Maturity*. Tallahassee: Florida State University.

Hunt, Kellogg. 1966. "Recent Measures in Syntactic Development." *Elementary Education* 43 (November): 732-39.

Hunt, Kellogg. 1977. "Early Blooming and Late Blooming Syntactic Structures." In *Evaluating Writing: Describing, Measuring, Judging*, edited by Charles R. Cooper and Lee Odell, 91-104. Champaign, Ill.: National Council of Teachers of English.

Jaynes, W. E. 1956. "Imprinting: Interaction of Learned and Innate Behavior." *Journal of Comparative Physiological Psychology* 49: 201-206.

Kellogg, Rhoda. 1969. "Understanding Children's Art." In *Readings in Psychology Today*, 170-79. Del Mar, Calif.: CRM Books.

Kelly, George. 1963. *A Theory of Personality: The Psychology of Personal Constructs.* New York: W. W. Norton and Co.

Kinneavy, James. 1971. *A Theory of Discourse.* Englewood Cliffs, N.J.: Prentice-Hall.

Kohl, Herbert. 1968. *Thirty-Six Children.* New York: Signet Books.

Krashen, Stephen. N.d. "On the Acquisition of Planned Discourse: Written English as a Second Dialect." Distributed by author at a lecture at the University of California, Berkeley, May 1979.

Labov, William. 1972. "The Transformation of Experience in Narrative Syntax." *Language in the Inner City: Studies in the Black English Vernacular.* Philadelphia: University of Pennsylvania Press.

Labov, William, and David Fanshell. 1971. *Therapeutic Discourse: Psychotherapy as Conversation.* New York: Academic Press.

Larson, Richard L. 1968. "Discovery through Questioning: A Plan for Teaching Rhetorical Invention." *College English* 30 (November): 126-34.

Laurendeau, Monique, and Adrien Pinard. 1970. *The Development of the Concept of Space in the Child.* New York: International University Press.

Lauer, Sr. Janice. 1970. "Heuristics and Composition." *College Composition and Communication* 21 (December): 396-404.

Loban, Walter. 1976. *Language Development: Kindergarten through Grade Twelve.* Urbana, Ill.: National Council of Teachers of English.

Lorenz, Konrad. 1966. *On Aggression.* Translated by Marjorie K. Wilson. New York: Harcourt, Brace and World.

Macrorie, Ken. 1970. *Uptaught.* New York: Hayden Book Co.

Macrorie, Ken. 1973. *Telling Writing.* New York: Hayden Book Co.

Mellon, John. 1969. *Transformational Sentence Combining.* Champaign, Ill.: National Council of Teachers of English.

Menzel, E. W. 1973. "Chimpanzee Spatial Memory Organization." *Science* 182: 942-45.

Miles, Josephine. 1979. "Writing in Reason." In *Working Out Ideas: Predication and Other Uses of Language.* Bay Area Writing Project, Curriculum Publication no. 5. Berkeley: University of California.

Miller, George. 1951. *Language and Communication.* New York: McGraw-Hill.

Miller, George. 1967. "The Magical Number Seven Plus or Minus Two." In *The Psychology of Communication,* 14-44. New York: Basic Books.

Miller, George, Eugene Galanter, and Karl Pribram. 1960. *Plans and the Structure of Behavior.* New York: Holt, Rinehart and Winston.

Miller, N. E., and J. Dollard. 1941. *Social Learning and Imitation.* New Haven, Conn.: Yale University Press.

Minsky, M. A. 1975. "A Framework for Representing Knowledge." In *The Psychology of Computer Vision,* edited by P. H. Winston, 211-77. New York: McGraw-Hill.

Mitchell-Kernan, Claudia. 1972. "Signifying and Marking: Two Afro-American Speech Acts." In *Directions in Sociolinguistics: The Ethnography Communication,* edited by John J. Gumperz and Dell Hymes. New York: Holt, Rinehart and Winston.

Moffett, James. 1967. "Rationale for a New Curriculum in English." In *Rhetoric: Theories for Application*, edited by Robert M. Gorrell. Champaign, Ill.: National Council of Teachers of English.

Moffett, James. 1968a. *A Student-Centered Language Arts Curriculum, Grades K–13: A Handbook for Teachers*. Boston: Houghton Mifflin.

Moffett, James. 1968b. *Teaching the Universe of Discourse*. Boston: Houghton Mifflin.

Moffett, James. 1981. *Active Voice: A Program of Writing Assignments*. Montclair, N.J.: Boynton/Cook.

Moskowitz, Breyne Arlene. 1978. "The Acquisition of Language." *Scientific American*, November, 92–108.

Myers, Celeste, ed. 1976. *The Live Oak Curriculum: A Guide to Pre-School Planning in the Heterogeneous Classroom*. Oakland, Calif.: Alpha Plus Corp.

Myers, Miles. 1978. "Five Approaches to the Teaching of Writing." *Learning* 6 (April): 38–41.

Myers, Miles. 1980. *A Model for the Composing Process*. National Writing Project, Occasional Paper no. 3. Berkeley: University of California.

Myers, Miles. 1981. "What Kind of People Talk That Way?" *English Journal* 70 (November): 24–29.

Myers, Miles. 1982. "The Speech Events Underlying Written Composition." Ph.D. diss., University of California, Berkeley.

Neisser, Ulric. 1976. *Cognition and Reality: Principles and Implications of Cognitive Psychology*. San Francisco: W. H. Freeman.

Nystrand, Martin. 1977. "Language as Discovery and Exploration." In *Language as a Way of Knowing*, edited by Martin Nystrand. Toronto: Ontario Institute for Studies in Education.

Odell, Lee. 1977. "Measuring Changes in Intellectual Processes as One Dimension of Growth in Writing." In *Evaluating Writing: Describing, Measuring, Judging*, edited by Charles R. Cooper and Lee Odell. Urbana, Ill.: National Council of Teachers of English.

O'Donnell, R. C., W. J. Griffin, and R. C. Norris. 1967. *Syntax of Kindergarten and Elementary School Children: A Transformational Analysis*. Champaign, Ill.: National Council of Teachers of English.

O'Hare, Frank. 1973. *Sentence Combining: Improving Student Writing without Formal Grammar Instruction*. Urbana, Ill.: National Council of Teachers of English.

O'Hare, Frank. 1975. *Sentencecraft*. Lexington, Mass.: Ginn and Co.

Olson, David R. 1977. "From Utterance to Text: The Bias of Language in Speech and Writing." *Harvard Educational Review* 47 (August): 257–81.

Olson, David R. N.d. "The Language of Instruction." In *Schooling and the Acquisition of Knowledge*, edited by R. Spiro. Hillsdale, N.J.: Lawrence Erlbaum Associates. In press.

Pascual-Leone, Juan, Doba Goodman, Paul Ammon, and Irene Subelman. 1978. "Piagetian Theory and Neo-Piagetian Analysis as Psychological Guides in Education." In *Piaget and Education*, Knowledge and Development Series, vol. 2, edited by Jeannette Gallagher and J. A. Easley. New York: Plenum Publishing Co.

Permuter, M., and N. A. Myers. 1974. "Recognition Memory Development in Two-to-Four-Year-Olds." *Developmental Psychology* 10: 447–50.

Piaget, Jean. 1959. *Judgment and Reasoning in the Child*. New York: Little-field, Adams and Co.

Polanyi, Michael. 1958. *Personal Knowledge: Towards a Post-Critical Philosophy*. Chicago: University of Chicago Press.

Polanyi, Michael, and Harry Prosch. 1975. *Meaning*. Chicago: University of Chicago Press.

Pollack, I. 1953. "The Assimilation of Sequentially Encoded Information." *American Journal of Psychology* 66: 421–35.

Polya, G. 1957. *How to Solve It*. New York: Doubleday Anchor.

Postal, P. M. 1964. "Limitations of Phrase Structure Grammar." In *The Structure of Language: Readings in the Philosophy of Language*, edited by J. A. Fodor and J. J. Katz. Englewood Cliffs, N.J.: Prentice-Hall.

Richards, I. A. 1938. *Interpretation in Teaching*. New York: Harcourt, Brace and World.

Richards, I. A. 1943. *How to Read a Page: A Course in Efficient Reading with an Introduction to 100 Great Words*. London: K. Paul, Trench, Trubner and Co.

Rock, Irvin. 1979. "The Perception of Disoriented Figures." In *Image, Object and Illusion: Readings from Scientific American*. San Francisco: W. H. Freeman and Co.

Rosch, Eleanor. 1977. "Human Categorization." In *Studies in Cross-Cultural Psychology*, vol. 1, edited by Neil Warren. New York: Academic Press.

Rohman, D. Gordon. 1965. "Pre-Writing: The Stage of Discovery in the Writing Process." *College Composition and Communication* 16 (May): 106–22.

Rumelhart, D. E. 1975. "Notes on a Schema for Stories." In *Representation in Understanding: Studies in Cognitive Science*, edited by Daniel G. Bobrow and Allan M. Collins. New York: Academic Press.

Sapir, Ernest. 1961. *Culture, Language, and Personality: Selected Essays*. Edited by David G. Mandelbaum. Berkeley: University of California Press.

Scardamalia, Marlene. 1981. "How Children Cope with the Cognitive Demands of Writing." In *Writing: The Nature, Development, and Teaching of Written Composition*, vol. 1, *Writing: Process, Development, and Communication*, edited by J. F. Dominic, C. H. Frederiksen, and M. Whiteman, 81–103. Hillsdale, N.J.: Lawrence Erlbaum Associates.

Schank, R. C., and R. P. Abelson. 1975. "Scripts, Plans, and Knowledge." Paper presented at the Fourth International Conference on Artificial Intelligence, Tbilisi, USSR, August 1975.

Schlesinger, I. M. 1971. "Production of Utterances and Language Acquisition." In *The Ontogenesis of Grammar: A Theoretical Symposium*, edited by Dan Slobin. New York: Academic Press.

Schorer, Mark. 1952. "Technique as Discovery." In *Essays in Modern Literary Criticism*, edited by Ray B. West, 189–205. New York: Rinehart.

Searle, John. 1972. "Chomsky's Revolution in Linguistics." *The New York Review of Books*, 29 June, 16.

Shaughnessy, Mina. 1977. *Errors and Expectations: A Guide for the Teacher of Basic Writing.* New York: Oxford University Press.

Simon, Herbert A. 1981. *The Sciences of the Artificial,* 2d ed. Cambridge, Mass.: MIT Press.

Simon, Herbert A., and William G. Chase. 1977. "Skill in Chess." In *Current Trends in Psychology: Readings from American Scientist,* edited by Irving L. Janis. Los Altos, Calif.: William Kaufmann.

Skinner, B. F. 1938. *The Behavior of Organisms.* New York: Appleton-Century-Crofts.

Skinner, B. F. 1953. *Science and Human Behavior.* New York: Macmillan.

Skinner, B. F. 1957. *Verbal Behavior.* New York: Appleton.

Skinner, B. F. 1967. "A Functional Analysis of Verbal Behavior." In *The Psychology of Language, Thought, and Instruction,* edited by John P. De Cecco, 318-25. New York: Holt, Rinehart and Winston.

Skinner, B. F., and Sue Ann Krakower. 1968. *Handwriting with Write and See.* Chicago: Lyons and Carnahan.

Strong, William. 1973. *Sentence Combining: A Composing Book.* New York; Random House.

Strong, William. 1976. "Sentence Combining: Back to the Basics—and Beyond." *English Journal* 65 (February): 56, 60-64.

Tolman, E. C. 1932. *Purposive Behavior in Animals and Men.* New York: Appleton.

Tolman, E. C. 1948. "Cognitive Maps in Rats and Men." *Psychological Review* 55: 189-208.

Tulving, Endel. 1972. "Episodic and Semantic Memory." In *Organization of Memory,* edited by Endel Tulving and Wayne Donaldson. New York: Academic Press.

Vygotsky, L. S. 1962. *Thought and Language.* Cambridge, Mass.: MIT Press.

Winterowd, W. Ross. 1970. "The Grammar of Coherence." *College English* 31 (May): 828-35.

Wixon, Vincent, and Pat Stone [Wixon]. "Getting It Out, Getting It Down: Adapting Zoellner's Talk-Write." *English Journal* 66 (1977): 70-73.

Young, Richard. 1976. "Invention: A Topographical Survey." In *Teaching Composition: Ten Bibliographical Essays,* edited by Gary Tate. Fort Worth: Texas Christian University Press.

Young, Richard, and Alton Becker. 1975. "Toward a Modern Theory of Rhetoric: A Tagmemic Contribution." In *Contemporary Rhetoric,* edited by W. Ross Winterowd. New York: Harcourt Brace Jovanovich.

Zoellner, Robert. 1969. "Talk-Write: A Behavioral Pedagogy for Composition." *College English* 30 (January): 267-320.

Contributors

Owen Boyle, formerly English Department Chair of Pittsburg High School, Pittsburg, California, is currently a staff member of the Bay Area Writing Project, University of California, Berkeley.

James Britton is Emeritus Professor of Education at the University of London.

Phyllis Brooks is Lecturer in the Subject A Department, University of California, Berkeley.

Marilyn Hanf Buckley is Director of the Advanced Reading and Language Leadership Program at the University of California, Berkeley.

Tony Burgess is a member of the English Department, University of London Institute of Education.

Rebekah Caplan is Teacher Consultant to the Bay Area Writing Project, University of California, Berkeley, and English Instructor at Foothill High School, Pleasanton, California.

The late **Francis Christensen** was a member of the English Department at the University of Southern California at the time he wrote his article.

Walker Gibson is Professor of English at the University of Massachusetts at Amherst.

Lester S. Golub is Professor of English at The Pennsylvania State University.

James Gray is Director of the Bay Area Writing Project, University of California, Berkeley.

Mary K. Healy is Co-Director of the Bay Area Writing Project, University of California, Berkeley.

Rhoda Kellogg was Director of Golden Gate Nursery Schools in San Francisco at the time she wrote her article.

Nancy Martin formerly was head of the English Department, University of London Institute of Education.

Alex McLeod is a member of the English Department, University of London Institute of Education.

Josephine Miles is a poet and is retired from the Department of English, University of California, Berkeley.

James Moffett is an author and consultant in education.

Celeste Myers was a teacher at Circle Pre-School, Oakland, California, at the time she wrote her article.

Miles Myers is Administrative Director of the Bay Area Writing Project, University of California, Berkeley.

James Pierce is Chair of the English Department, Redwood High School, Larkspur, California, and Consultant to the Bay Area Writing Project, University of California, Berkeley.

D. Gordon Rohman is Professor of English and Lifelong Education, Michigan State University.

Harold Rosen is Professor of Education, University of London Institute of Education.

Gail Siegel is a teacher at Ross School, Ross, California, and Teacher Consultant to the Bay Area Writing Project, University of California, Berkeley.

Herbert A. Simon is Richard King Mellon Professor of Computer Sciences and Psychology at Carnegie-Mellon University.

Patricia Wixon is an English teacher at Ashland Junior High School, Ashland, Oregon, and directs the Oregon Writing Project.

Vincent Wixon is an English instructor at Crater High School, Central Point, Oregon, and directs the Oregon Writing Project.

Robert Zoellner is Professor of English at Colorado State University.